Praise for *Concurrency in C# Cookbook*, Second Edition

"The next big thing in computing is making massive parallelism accessible to mere mortals. Developers have more power available to us than ever before, but expressing concurrency is still a challenge for many. Stephen turns his attention to this problem, helping us all better understand concurrency, threading, reactive programming models, parallelism, and much more in an easy-to-read but complete reference."

—*Scott Hanselman, Principal Program
Manager, ASP.NET and Azure Web
Tools, Microsoft*

"The breadth of techniques covered and the cookbook format make this the ideal reference book for modern .NET concurrency."

—*Jon Skeet, Senior Software Engineer at
Google*

"Stephen Cleary has established himself as a key expert on asynchrony and parallelism in C#. This book clearly and concisely conveys the most important points and principles developers need to understand to get started and be successful with these technologies."

—*Stephen Toub, Principal Architect,
Microsoft*

SECOND EDITION

Concurrency in C# Cookbook

*Asynchronous, Parallel, and
Multithreaded Programming*

Stephen Cleary

Beijing · Boston · Farnham · Sebastopol · Tokyo

Concurrency in C# Cookbook, Second Edition

By Stephen Cleary

Published by O'Reilly Media, Inc., 1005 Gravenstein Highway North, Sebastopol, CA 95472.

O'Reilly books may be purchased for educational, business, or sales promotional use. Online editions are also available for most titles (*http://oreilly.com*). For more information, contact our corporate/institutional sales department: 800-998-9938 or *corporate@oreilly.com*.

Acquisitions Editor: Chris Guzikowski	**Indexer:** Angela Howard
Development Editor: Corbin Collins	**Interior Designer:** David Futato
Production Editor: Deb Baker	**Cover Designer:** Randy Comer
Copyeditor: Amanda Kersey	**Illustrator:** Rebecca Demarest
Proofreader: Sonia Saruba	

June 2014:	First Edition
August 2019:	Second Edition

Revision History for the Second Edition
2019-08-20:   First release

See *http://oreilly.com/catalog/errata.csp?isbn=9781492054504* for release details.

978-1-492-05450-4

[LSI]

Table of Contents

Preface

I think the animal on this cover, a common palm civet, is applicable to the subject of this book. I knew nothing about this animal until I saw the cover, so I looked it up. Common palm civets are considered pests because they defecate all over attics and make loud noises fighting with each other at the most inopportune times. Their anal scent glands emit a nauseating secretion. They have an endangered species rating of "Least Concern," which is apparently the politically correct way of saying, "Kill as many of these as you want; no one will miss them." Common palm civets enjoy eating coffee cherries, and they pass the coffee beans through. Kopi luwak, one of the most expensive coffees in the world, is made from the coffee beans extracted from civet excretions. According to the Specialty Coffee Association of America, "It just tastes bad."

This makes the common palm civet a perfect mascot for concurrent and multithreaded development. To the uninitiated, concurrency and multithreading are undesirable. They make well-behaved code act up in the most horrendous ways. Race conditions and whatnot cause loud crashes (always, it seems, either in production or during a demo). Some have gone so far as to declare "threads are evil" and avoid concurrency completely. There are a handful of developers who have developed a taste for concurrency and use it without fear; but most developers have been burned in the past by concurrency, and that experience has left a bad taste in their mouth.

However, for modern applications, concurrency is quickly becoming a requirement. Users these days expect fully responsive interfaces, and server applications are having to scale to unprecedented levels. Concurrency addresses both of these trends.

Fortunately, there are many modern libraries that make concurrency *much* easier! Parallel processing and asynchronous programming are no longer exclusively the domains of wizards. By raising the level of abstraction, these libraries make responsive and scalable application development a realistic goal for every developer. If you have been burned in the past, when concurrency was extremely difficult, then I encourage you to give it another try with modern tools. We can probably never call concurrency easy, but it sure isn't as hard as it used to be!

Who Should Read This Book

This book is written for developers who want to learn modern approaches to concurrency. I do assume that you've got a fair amount of .NET experience, including an understanding of generic collections, enumerables, and LINQ. I do *not* expect that you have any multithreading or asynchronous programming knowledge. If you do have some experience in those areas, you may still find this book helpful because it introduces newer libraries that are safer and easier to use.

Concurrency is useful for any kind of application. It doesn't matter whether you work on desktop, mobile, or server applications; these days concurrency is practically a requirement across the board. You can use the recipes in this book to make user interfaces more responsive and servers more scalable. We are already at the point where concurrency is ubiquitous, and understanding these techniques and their uses is essential knowledge for the professional developer.

Why I Wrote This Book

Early in my career, I learned multithreading the hard way. After a couple of years, I learned asynchronous programming the hard way. While those were both valuable experiences, I do wish that back then I had some of the tools and resources that are available today. In particular, the `async` and `await` support in modern .NET languages is pure gold.

However, if you look around today at books and other resources for learning concurrency, they almost all start by introducing the most low-level concepts. There's excellent coverage of threads and serialization primitives, and the higher-level techniques are put off until later, if they're covered at all. I believe this is for two reasons. First, many developers of concurrency, such as myself, did learn the low-level concepts first, slogging through the old-school techniques. Second, many books are years old and cover now-outdated techniques; as the newer techniques have become available, these books have been updated to include them, but have unfortunately placed them at the end.

I think that's backward. In fact, this book *only* covers modern approaches to concurrency. That's not to say there's no value in understanding all the low-level concepts. When I went to college for programming, I had one class where I had to build a virtual CPU from a handful of gates, and another class that covered assembly programming. In my professional career, I've never designed a CPU, and I've only written a couple dozen lines of assembly, but my understanding of the fundamentals still helps me every day. Still, it's best to start with the higher-level abstractions; my first programming class wasn't in assembly language.

This book fills a niche: it is an introduction to (and reference for) concurrency using modern approaches. It covers several different kinds of concurrency, including parallel, asynchronous, and reactive programming. It does not, however, cover any of the old-school techniques, which are adequately covered in many other books and online resources.

Navigating This Book

Here's how the book is broken down:

- Chapter 1 is an introduction to the various kinds of concurrency covered by this book: parallel, asynchronous, reactive, and dataflow.
- Chapters 2–6 are a more thorough introduction to these kinds of concurrency.
- The remaining chapters each deal with a particular aspect of concurrency, and they act as a reference for solutions to common problems.

I recommend reading (or at least skimming) the first chapter, even if you're already familiar with some kinds of concurrency.

 As this book goes to press, .NET Core 3.0 is still in beta, so some details around asynchronous streams may change.

Online Resources

This book acts like a broad-spectrum introduction to several different kinds of concurrency. I've done my best to include techniques that I and others have found the most helpful, but this book isn't exhaustive by any means. The following resources are the best ones I've found for a more thorough exploration of these technologies:

- For parallel programming, the best resource I know of is *Parallel Programming with Microsoft .NET* by Microsoft Press, the text of which is available online (*http://bit.ly/parallel-prog*). Unfortunately, it's already a bit out of date. The section on futures should use asynchronous code instead, and the section on pipelines should use Channels or TPL Dataflow.
- For asynchronous programming, MSDN is quite good, particularly the "Asynchronous Programming" (*http://bit.ly/async-prog*) overview.

- Microsoft has also made available documentation for TPL Dataflow. (*http://bit.ly/dataflow-tpl*)
- System.Reactive (Rx) is a library that is gaining a lot of traction online and continues evolving. In my opinion, the best resource today for Rx is *Introduction to Rx* (*http://www.introtorx.com/*), an ebook by Lee Campbell.

Conventions Used in This Book

The following typographical conventions are used in this book:

Italic
: Indicates new terms, URLs, email addresses, filenames, and file extensions.

`Constant width`
: Used for program listings, as well as within paragraphs to refer to program elements such as variable or function names, databases, data types, environment variables, statements, and keywords.

`Constant width bold`
: Shows commands or other text that should be typed literally by the user.

`Constant width italic`
: Shows text that should be replaced with user-supplied values or by values determined by context.

This element signifies a tip or suggestion.

This element signifies a general note.

This element indicates a warning or caution.

Using Code Examples

Supplemental material (code examples, exercises, etc.) is available for download at *https://oreil.ly/concur-c-ckbk2*.

This book is here to help you get your job done. In general, if example code is offered with this book, you may use it in your programs and documentation. You do not need to contact us for permission unless you're reproducing a significant portion of the code. For example, writing a program that uses several chunks of code from this book does not require permission. Selling or distributing a CD-ROM of examples from O'Reilly books does require permission. Answering a question by citing this book and quoting example code does not require permission. Incorporating a significant amount of example code from this book into your product's documentation does require permission.

We appreciate, but do not require, attribution. An attribution usually includes the title, author, publisher, and ISBN. For example: "*Concurrency in C# Cookbook*, Second Edition, by Stephen Cleary (O'Reilly). Copyright 2019 Stephen Cleary, 978-1-492-05450-4."

If you feel your use of code examples falls outside fair use or the permission given above, feel free to contact us at *permissions@oreilly.com*.

O'Reilly Online Learning

 For almost 40 years, *O'Reilly Media* has provided technology and business training, knowledge, and insight to help companies succeed.

Our unique network of experts and innovators share their knowledge and expertise through books, articles, conferences, and our online learning platform. O'Reilly's online learning platform gives you on-demand access to live training courses, in-depth learning paths, interactive coding environments, and a vast collection of text and video from O'Reilly and 200+ other publishers. For more information, please visit *http://oreilly.com*.

How to Contact Us

Please address comments and questions concerning this book to the publisher:

O'Reilly Media, Inc.
1005 Gravenstein Highway North
Sebastopol, CA 95472
800-998-9938 (in the United States or Canada)
707-829-0515 (international or local)
707-829-0104 (fax)

We have a web page for this book, where we list errata, examples, and any additional information. You can access this page at *https://oreil.ly/concur-c-ckbk2*.

To comment or ask technical questions about this book, send email to *bookquestions@oreilly.com*.

For more information about our books, courses, conferences, and news, see our website at *http://www.oreilly.com*.

Find us on Facebook: *http://facebook.com/oreilly*

Follow us on Twitter: *http://twitter.com/oreillymedia*

Watch us on YouTube: *http://www.youtube.com/oreillymedia*

Acknowledgments

This book simply would not exist without the help of so many people!

First and foremost, I'd like to acknowledge my Lord and Savior, Jesus Christ. Becoming a Christian was the most important decision of my life! If you want more information on this subject, feel free to contact me via my personal web page (*http://stephencleary.com/*).

Second, I thank my family for allowing me to give up so much time with them. When I started writing, I had some author friends of mine tell me, "Say goodbye to your family for the next year!" and I thought they were joking. My wife, Mandy, and our children, SD and Emma, have been very understanding while I put in long days at work followed by writing on evenings and weekends. Thank you so much. I love you!

Of course, this book wouldn't be nearly as good as it is without my editors and our technical reviewers: Stephen Toub, Petr Onderka ("svick"), Nick Paldino ("casper-One"), Lee Campbell, and Pedro Felix. So if any mistakes get through, it's totally their fault. Just kidding! Their input has been invaluable in shaping (and fixing) the content, and any remaining mistakes are of course my own. Particular thanks go to Stephen Toub, who taught me the Boolean Argument Hack (Recipe 14.5), as well as countless other `async` topics; and Lee Campbell, who has helped me learn System.Reactive and make my observable code more idiomatic.

Finally, I'd like to thank some of the people I've learned these techniques from: Stephen Toub, Lucian Wischik, Thomas Levesque, Lee Campbell, the members of Stack Overflow and the MSDN forums, and the attendees of the software conferences in and around my home state of Michigan. I appreciate being a part of the software development community, and if this book adds any value, it's because so many have already shown the way. Thank you all!

Concurrency: An Overview

Concurrency is a key aspect of beautiful software. For decades, concurrency was possible but difficult to achieve. Concurrent software was difficult to write, difficult to debug, and difficult to maintain. As a result, many developers chose the easier path and avoided concurrency. With the libraries and language features available for modern .NET programs, concurrency is now much easier. Microsoft has led the way in significantly lowering the bar for concurrency. Previously, concurrent programming was the domain of experts; these days, every developer can (and should) embrace concurrency.

Introduction to Concurrency

Before continuing, I'd like to clear up some terminology that I'll be using throughout this book. These are my own definitions that I use consistently to disambiguate different programming techniques. Let's start with *concurrency*.

Concurrency
    Doing more than one thing at a time.

I hope it's obvious how concurrency is helpful. End-user applications use concurrency to respond to user input *while* writing to a database. Server applications use concurrency to respond to a second request *while* finishing the first request. You need concurrency any time you need an application to do one thing *while* it's working on something else. Almost every software application in the world can benefit from concurrency.

Most developers hearing the term "concurrency" immediately think of "multithreading." I'd like to draw a distinction between these two.

Multithreading
A form of concurrency that uses multiple threads of execution.

Multithreading refers to literally using multiple threads. As demonstrated in many recipes in this book, multithreading is *one* form of concurrency, but certainly not the only one. In fact, direct use of low-level threading types has almost no purpose in a modern application; higher-level abstractions are more powerful and more efficient than old-school multithreading. For that reason, I'll minimize my coverage of outdated techniques. None of the multithreading recipes in this book use the `Thread` or `BackgroundWorker` types; they have been replaced with superior alternatives.

As soon as you type `new Thread()`, it's over; your project already has legacy code.

But don't get the idea that multithreading is dead! Multithreading lives on in the *thread pool*, a useful place to queue work that automatically adjusts itself according to demand. In turn, the thread pool enables another important form of concurrency: *parallel processing*.

Parallel processing
Doing lots of work by dividing it up among multiple threads that run concurrently.

Parallel processing (or parallel programming) uses multithreading to maximize the use of multiple processor cores. Modern CPUs have multiple cores, and if there's a lot of work to do, then it makes no sense to make one core do all the work while the others sit idle. Parallel processing splits the work among multiple threads, which can each run independently on a different core.

Parallel processing is one type of multithreading, and multithreading is one type of concurrency. There's another type of concurrency that is important in modern applications but isn't as familiar to many developers: *asynchronous programming*.

Asynchronous programming
A form of concurrency that uses futures or callbacks to avoid unnecessary threads.

A *future* (or *promise*) is a type that represents some operation that will complete in the future. Some modern future types in .NET are `Task` and `Task<TResult>`. Older asynchronous APIs use callbacks or events instead of futures. Asynchronous programming is centered around the idea of an *asynchronous operation*: some operation that is started that will complete some time later. While the operation is in progress, it doesn't block the original thread; the thread that starts the operation is free to do other work. When the operation completes, it notifies its future or invokes its callback or event to let the application know the operation is finished.

Asynchronous programming is a powerful form of concurrency, but until recently, it required extremely complex code. The `async` and `await` support in modern languages make asynchronous programming almost as easy as synchronous (nonconcurrent) programming.

Another form of concurrency is *reactive programming*. Asynchronous programming implies that the application will start an operation that will complete once at a later time. Reactive programming is closely related to asynchronous programming but is built on *asynchronous events* instead of *asynchronous operations*. Asynchronous events may not have an actual "start," may happen at any time, and may be raised multiple times. One example is user input.

Reactive programming
  A declarative style of programming where the application reacts to events.

If you consider an application to be a massive state machine, the application's behavior can be described as reacting to a series of events by updating its state at each event. This isn't as abstract or theoretical as it sounds; modern frameworks make this approach quite useful in real-world applications. Reactive programming isn't necessarily concurrent, but it is closely related to concurrency, so this book covers the basics.

Usually, a mixture of techniques is used when writing a concurrent program. Most applications at least use multithreading (via the thread pool) and asynchronous programming. Feel free to mix and match all the various forms of concurrency, using the appropriate tool for each part of the application.

Introduction to Asynchronous Programming

Asynchronous programming has two primary benefits. The first benefit is for end-user GUI programs: asynchronous programming enables responsiveness. Everyone has used a program that temporarily locks up while it's working; an asynchronous program can remain responsive to user input while it's working. The second benefit is for server-side programs: asynchronous programming enables scalability. A server application can scale somewhat just by using the thread pool, but an asynchronous server application can usually scale an order of magnitude better than that.

Both benefits of asynchronous programming derive from the same underlying aspect: asynchronous programming frees up a thread. For GUI programs, asynchronous programming frees up the UI thread; this permits the GUI application to remain responsive to user input. For server applications, asynchronous programming frees up request threads; this permits the server to use its threads to serve more requests.

Modern asynchronous .NET applications use two keywords: async and await. The async keyword is added to a method declaration, and performs a double purpose: it enables the await keyword within that method and it signals the compiler to generate a state machine for that method, similar to how yield return works. An async method may return Task<TResult> if it returns a value, Task if it doesn't return a value, or any other "task-like" type, such as ValueTask. In addition, an async method may return IAsyncEnumerable<T> or IAsyncEnumerator<T> if it returns multiple values in an enumeration. The task-like types represent futures; they can notify the calling code when the async method completes.

 Avoid async void! It is possible to have an async method return void, but you should only do this if you're writing an async event handler. A regular async method without a return value should return Task, not void.

With that background, let's take a quick look at an example:

```
async Task DoSomethingAsync()
{
    int value = 13;

    // Asynchronously wait 1 second.
    await Task.Delay(TimeSpan.FromSeconds(1));

    value *= 2;

    // Asynchronously wait 1 second.
    await Task.Delay(TimeSpan.FromSeconds(1));

    Trace.WriteLine(value);
}
```

An async method begins executing synchronously, just like any other method. Within an async method, the await keyword performs an *asynchronous wait* on its argument. First, it checks whether the operation is already complete; if it is, it continues executing (synchronously). Otherwise, it will pause the async method and return an incomplete task. When that operation completes some time later, the async method will resume executing.

You can think of an async method as having several synchronous portions, broken up by await statements. The first synchronous portion executes on whatever thread calls the method, but where do the other synchronous portions execute? The answer is a bit complicated.

When you await a task (the most common scenario), a *context* is captured when the await decides to pause the method. This is the current SynchronizationContext unless it's `null`, in which case the context is the current `TaskScheduler`. The method resumes executing within that captured context. Usually, this context is the UI context (if you're on the UI thread) or the threadpool context (most other situations). If you have an ASP.NET Classic (pre-Core) application, then the context could also be an ASP.NET request context. ASP.NET Core uses the threadpool context rather than a special request context.

So, in the preceding code, all the synchronous portions will attempt to resume on the original context. If you call `DoSomethingAsync` from a UI thread, each of its synchronous portions will run on that UI thread; but if you call it from a threadpool thread, each of its synchronous portions will run on any threadpool thread.

You can avoid this default behavior by awaiting the result of the `ConfigureAwait` extension method and passing `false` for the `continueOnCapturedContext` parameter. The following code will start on the calling thread, and after it is paused by an `await`, it'll resume on a threadpool thread:

```
async Task DoSomethingAsync()
{
  int value = 13;

  // Asynchronously wait 1 second.
  await Task.Delay(TimeSpan.FromSeconds(1)).ConfigureAwait(false);

  value *= 2;

  // Asynchronously wait 1 second.
  await Task.Delay(TimeSpan.FromSeconds(1)).ConfigureAwait(false);

  Trace.WriteLine(value);
}
```

 It's good practice to always call `ConfigureAwait` in your core "library" methods, and only resume the context when you need it —in your outer "user interface" methods.

The `await` keyword is not limited to working with tasks; it can work with any kind of *awaitable* that follows a certain pattern. As an example, the Base Class Library includes the `ValueTask<T>` type, which reduces memory allocations if the result is commonly synchronous; for example, if the result can be read from an in-memory cache. `ValueTask<T>` is not directly convertible to `Task<T>`, but it does follow the awaitable pattern, so you can directly `await` it. There are other examples, and you can build your own, but most of the time `await` will take a `Task` or `Task<TResult>`.

There are two basic ways to create a Task instance. Some tasks represent actual code that a CPU has to execute; these computational tasks should be created by calling Task.Run (or TaskFactory.StartNew if you need them to run on a particular scheduler). Other tasks represent a *notification*; these kinds of event-based tasks are created by TaskCompletionSource<TResult> (or one of its shortcuts). Most I/O tasks use TaskCompletionSource<TResult>.

Error handling is natural with async and await. In the code snippet that follows, PossibleExceptionAsync may throw a NotSupportedException, but TrySomethingAsync can catch the exception naturally. The caught exception has its stack trace properly preserved and isn't artificially wrapped in a TargetInvocationException or AggregateException:

```
async Task TrySomethingAsync()
{
  try
  {
    await PossibleExceptionAsync();
  }
  catch (NotSupportedException ex)
  {
    LogException(ex);
    throw;
  }
}
```

When an async method throws (or propagates) an exception, the exception is placed on its returned Task and the Task is completed. When that Task is awaited, the await operator will retrieve that exception and (re)throw it in a way such that its original stack trace is preserved. Thus, code such as the following example would work as expected if PossibleExceptionAsync was an async method:

```
async Task TrySomethingAsync()
{
  // The exception will end up on the Task, not thrown directly.
  Task task = PossibleExceptionAsync();

  try
  {
    // The Task's exception will be raised here, at the await.
    await task;
  }
  catch (NotSupportedException ex)
  {
    LogException(ex);
    throw;
  }
}
```

There's one other important guideline when it comes to async methods: once you start using async, it's best to allow it to grow through your code. If you call an async method, you should (eventually) await the task it returns. Resist the temptation to call Task.Wait, Task<TResult>.Result, or GetAwaiter().GetResult(); doing so could cause a deadlock. Consider the following method:

```
async Task WaitAsync()
{
  // This await will capture the current context ...
  await Task.Delay(TimeSpan.FromSeconds(1));
  // ... and will attempt to resume the method here in that context.
}

void Deadlock()
{
  // Start the delay.
  Task task = WaitAsync();

  // Synchronously block, waiting for the async method to complete.
  task.Wait();
}
```

The code in this example will deadlock if called from a UI or ASP.NET Classic context because both of those contexts only allow one thread in at a time. Deadlock will call WaitAsync, which begins the delay. Deadlock then (synchronously) waits for that method to complete, blocking the context thread. When the delay completes, await attempts to resume WaitAsync within the captured context, but it cannot because there's already a thread blocked in the context, and the context only allows one thread at a time. Deadlock can be prevented two ways: you can use ConfigureAwait(false) within WaitAsync (which causes await to ignore its context), or you can await the call to WaitAsync (making Deadlock into an async method).

 If you use async, it's best to use async all the way.

For a more complete introduction to async, the online documentation that Microsoft has provided for async is fantastic; I recommend reading at least the Asynchronous Programming overview (*http://bit.ly/async-prog*) and the Task-based Asynchronous Pattern (TAP) (*http://bit.ly/task-async-patt*) overview. If you want to go a bit deeper, there's also the Async in Depth (*http://bit.ly/async-indepth*) documentation.

Asynchronous streams take the groundwork of async and await and extend it to handle multiple values. Asynchronous streams are built around the concept of asynchronous enumerables, which are like regular enumerables, except that they enable asynchronous work to be done when retrieving the next item in the sequence. This is an extremely powerful concept that Chapter 3 covers in more detail. Asynchronous streams are especially useful whenever you have a sequence of data that arrives either one at a time or in chunks. For example, if your application processes the response of an API that uses paging with `limit` and `offset` parameters, then asynchronous streams are an ideal abstraction. As of the time of this writing, asynchronous streams are only available on the newest .NET platforms.

Introduction to Parallel Programming

Parallel programming should be used any time you have a fair amount of computation work that can be split up into independent chunks. Parallel programming increases the CPU usage temporarily to improve throughput; this is desirable on client systems where CPUs are often idle, but it's usually not appropriate for server systems. Most servers have some parallelism built in; for example, ASP.NET will handle multiple requests in parallel. Writing parallel code on the server may still be useful in some situations (if you *know* that the number of concurrent users will always be low), but in general, parallel programming on the server would work against its built-in parallelism and therefore wouldn't provide any real benefit.

There are two forms of parallelism: *data parallelism* and *task parallelism*. Data parallelism is when you have a bunch of data items to process, and the processing of each piece of data is mostly independent from the other pieces. Task parallelism is when you have a pool of work to do, and each piece of work is mostly independent from the other pieces. Task parallelism may be dynamic; if one piece of work results in several additional pieces of work, they can be added to the pool of work.

There are a few different ways to do data parallelism. `Parallel.ForEach` is similar to a `foreach` loop and should be used when possible. `Parallel.ForEach` is covered in Recipe 4.1. The `Parallel` class also supports `Parallel.For`, which is similar to a `for` loop, and can be used if the data processing depends on the index. Code that uses `Parallel.ForEach` looks like the following:

```
void RotateMatrices(IEnumerable<Matrix> matrices, float degrees)
{
  Parallel.ForEach(matrices, matrix => matrix.Rotate(degrees));
}
```

Another option is PLINQ (Parallel LINQ), which provides an `AsParallel` extension method for LINQ queries. `Parallel` is more resource friendly than PLINQ; `Parallel` will play more nicely with other processes in the system, while PLINQ will (by default) attempt to spread itself over all CPUs. The downside to `Parallel` is that it's more explicit; PLINQ in many cases has more elegant code. PLINQ is covered in Recipe 4.5 and looks like this:

```
IEnumerable<bool> PrimalityTest(IEnumerable<int> values)
{
  return values.AsParallel().Select(value => IsPrime(value));
}
```

Regardless of the method you choose, one guideline stands out when doing parallel processing.

 The chunks of work should be as independent from one another as possible.

As long as your chunk of work is independent from all other chunks, you maximize your parallelism. As soon as you start sharing state between multiple threads, you have to synchronize access to that shared state, and your application becomes less parallel. Chapter 12 covers synchronization in more detail.

The output of your parallel processing can be handled in various ways. You can place the results in some kind of a concurrent collection, or you can aggregate the results into a summary. Aggregation is common in parallel processing; this kind of map/ reduce functionality is also supported by the Parallel class method overloads. Recipe 4.2 looks at aggregation in more detail.

Now let's turn to task parallelism. Data parallelism is focused on processing data; task parallelism is just about doing work. At a high level, data parallelism and task parallelism are similar; "processing data" is a kind of "work." Many parallelism problems can be solved either way; it's convenient to use whichever API is more natural for the problem at hand.

Parallel.Invoke is one type of Parallel method that does a kind of fork/join task parallelism. This method is covered in Recipe 4.3; you just pass in the delegates you want to execute in parallel:

```
void ProcessArray(double[] array)
{
  Parallel.Invoke(
      () => ProcessPartialArray(array, 0, array.Length / 2),
      () => ProcessPartialArray(array, array.Length / 2, array.Length)
  );
}

void ProcessPartialArray(double[] array, int begin, int end)
{
  // CPU-intensive processing...
}
```

The Task type was originally introduced for task parallelism, though these days it's also used for asynchronous programming. A Task instance—as used in task parallelism—represents some work. You can use the Wait method to wait for a task to complete, and you can use the Result and Exception properties to retrieve the results of that work. Code using Task directly is more complex than code using Parallel, but it can be useful if you don't know the structure of the parallelism until runtime. With this kind of dynamic parallelism, you don't know how many pieces of work you need to do at the beginning of the processing; you find out as you go along. Generally, a dynamic piece of work should start whatever child tasks it needs and then wait for them to complete. The Task type has a special flag, TaskCreationOptions.Attached ToParent, which you could use for this. Dynamic parallelism is covered in Recipe 4.4.

Task parallelism should strive to be independent, just like data parallelism. The more independent your delegates can be, the more efficient your program can be. Also, if your delegates aren't independent, then they need to be synchronized, and it's harder to write correct code if that code needs synchronization. With task parallelism, be especially careful of variables captured in closures. Remember that closures capture references (not values), so you can end up with sharing that isn't obvious.

Error handling is similar for all kinds of parallelism. Because operations are proceeding in parallel, it's possible for multiple exceptions to occur, so they are wrapped up in an AggregateException that's thrown to your code. This behavior is consistent across Parallel.ForEach, Parallel.Invoke, Task.Wait, etc. The AggregateException type has some useful Flatten and Handle methods to simplify the error handling code:

```
try
{
  Parallel.Invoke(() => { throw new Exception(); },
      () => { throw new Exception(); });
}
catch (AggregateException ex)
{
  ex.Handle(exception =>
  {
    Trace.WriteLine(exception);
    return true; // "handled"
  });
}
```

Usually, you don't have to worry about how the work is handled by the thread pool. Data and task parallelism use dynamically adjusting partitioners to divide work among worker threads. The thread pool increases its thread count as necessary. The thread pool has a single work queue, and each threadpool thread also has its own work queue. When a threadpool thread queues additional work, it sends it to its own queue first because the work is usually related to the current work item; this behavior encourages threads to work on their own work, and maximizes cache hits. If another thread doesn't have work to do, it'll steal work from another thread's queue. Microsoft put a lot of work into making the thread pool as efficient as possible, and there are a large number of knobs you can tweak if you need maximum performance. As long as your tasks are not extremely short, they should work well with the default settings.

Tasks should neither be extremely short, nor extremely long.

If your tasks are too short, then the overhead of breaking up the data into tasks and scheduling those tasks on the thread pool becomes significant. If your tasks are too long, then the thread pool cannot dynamically adjust its work balancing efficiently. It's difficult to determine how short is too short and how long is too long; it really depends on the problem being solved and the approximate capabilities of the hardware. As a general rule, I try to make my tasks as short as possible without running into performance issues (you'll see your performance suddenly degrade when your tasks are too short). Even better, instead of using tasks directly, use the `Parallel` type or PLINQ. These higher-level forms of parallelism have partitioning built in to handle this automatically for you (and adjust as necessary at runtime).

If you want to dive deeper into parallel programming, the best book on the subject is *Parallel Programming with Microsoft .NET*, by Colin Campbell et al. (Microsoft Press).

Introduction to Reactive Programming (Rx)

Reactive programming has a higher learning curve than other forms of concurrency, and the code can be harder to maintain unless you keep up with your reactive skills. If you're willing to learn it, though, reactive programming is extremely powerful. Reactive programming enables you to treat a stream of events like a stream of data. As a rule of thumb, if you use any of the event arguments passed to an event, then your code would benefit from using System.Reactive instead of a regular event handler.

System.Reactive used to be called Reactive Extensions, which was often shortened to "Rx." All three of these terms refer to the same technology.

Reactive programming is based on the notion of observable streams. When you subscribe to an observable stream, you'll receive any number of data items (`OnNext`), and then the stream may end with a single error (OnError) or "end of stream" notification (OnCompleted). Some observable streams never end. The actual interfaces look like the following:

```
interface IObserver<in T>
{
  void OnNext(T item);
  void OnCompleted();
  void OnError(Exception error);
}

interface IObservable<out T>
{
  IDisposable Subscribe(IObserver<TResult> observer);
}
```

However, you should never implement these interfaces. The System.Reactive (Rx) library by Microsoft has all the implementations you should ever need. Reactive code ends up looking very much like LINQ; you can think of it as "LINQ to Events." System.Reactive has everything that LINQ does and adds in a large number of its own operators, particularly ones that deal with time. The following code starts with some unfamiliar operators (Interval and Timestamp) and ends with a Subscribe, but in the middle are some Where and Select operators that should be familiar from LINQ:

```
Observable.Interval(TimeSpan.FromSeconds(1))
    .Timestamp()
    .Where(x => x.Value % 2 == 0)
    .Select(x => x.Timestamp)
    .Subscribe(x => Trace.WriteLine(x));
```

The example code starts with a counter running off a periodic timer (Interval) and adds a timestamp to each event (Timestamp). It then filters the events to only include even counter values (Where), selects the timestamp values (Timestamp), and then as each resulting timestamp value arrives, writes it to the debugger (Subscribe). Don't worry if you don't understand the new operators, such as Interval: these are covered later in this book. For now, just keep in mind that this is a LINQ query very similar to the ones you're already familiar with. The main difference is that LINQ to Objects and LINQ to Entities use a *"pull" model*, where the enumeration of a LINQ query pulls the data through the query, while LINQ to Events (System.Reactive) uses a *"push" model*, where the events arrive and travel through the query by themselves.

The definition of an observable stream is independent from its subscriptions. The last example is the same as the following code:

```
IObservable<DateTimeOffset> timestamps =
    Observable.Interval(TimeSpan.FromSeconds(1))
        .Timestamp()
        .Where(x => x.Value % 2 == 0)
```

```
    .Select(x => x.Timestamp);
timestamps.Subscribe(x => Trace.WriteLine(x));
```

It is normal for a type to define the observable streams and make them available as an `IObservable<TResult>` resource. Other types can then subscribe to those streams or combine them with other operators to create another observable stream.

A System.Reactive subscription is also a resource. The `Subscribe` operators return an `IDisposable` that represents the subscription. When your code is done listening to an observable stream, it should dispose its subscription.

Subscriptions behave differently with hot and cold observables. A *hot observable* is a stream of events that is always going on, and if there are no subscribers when the events come in, they are lost. For example, mouse movement is a hot observable. A *cold observable* is an observable that doesn't have incoming events all the time. A cold observable will react to a subscription by starting the sequence of events. For example, an HTTP download is a cold observable; the subscription causes the HTTP request to be sent.

The `Subscribe` operator should always take an error handling parameter as well. The preceding examples do not; the following is a better example that will respond appropriately if the observable stream ends in an error:

```
Observable.Interval(TimeSpan.FromSeconds(1))
    .Timestamp()
    .Where(x => x.Value % 2 == 0)
    .Select(x => x.Timestamp)
    .Subscribe(x => Trace.WriteLine(x),
        ex => Trace.WriteLine(ex));
```

`Subject<TResult>` is one type that is useful when experimenting with System.Reactive. This "subject" is like a manual implementation of an observable stream. Your code can call `OnNext`, `OnError`, and `OnCompleted`, and the subject will forward those calls to its subscribers. `Subject<TResult>` is great for experimenting, but in production code, you should strive to use operators like those covered in Chapter 6.

There are tons of useful System.Reactive operators, and I only cover a few selected ones in this book. For more information on System.Reactive, I recommend the excellent online book *Introduction to Rx* (*http://www.introtorx.com/*).

Introduction to Dataflows

TPL Dataflow is an interesting mix of asynchronous and parallel technologies. It's useful when you have a sequence of processes that need to be applied to your data. For example, you may need to download data from a URL, parse it, and then process it in parallel with other data. TPL Dataflow is commonly used as a simple pipeline, where data enters one end and travels until it comes out the other. However, TPL

Dataflow is far more powerful than this; it's capable of handling any kind of mesh. You can define forks, joins, and loops in a mesh, and TPL Dataflow will handle them appropriately. Most of the time, though, TPL Dataflow meshes are used as a pipeline.

The basic building unit of a dataflow mesh is a *dataflow block*. A block can either be a target block (receiving data), a source block (producing data), or both. Source blocks can be linked to target blocks to create the mesh; linking is covered in Recipe 5.1. Blocks are semi-independent; they will attempt to process data as it arrives and push the results downstream. The usual way of using TPL Dataflow is to create all the blocks, link them together, and then start putting data in at one end. The data then comes out of the other end by itself. Again, Dataflow is more powerful than this; it's possible to break links and create new blocks and add them to the mesh *while* there is data flowing through it, but that is a very advanced scenario.

Target blocks have buffers for the data they receive. Having buffers enables them to accept new data items even if they aren't ready to process them yet; this keeps data flowing through the mesh. This buffering can cause problems in fork scenarios, where one source block is linked to two target blocks. When the source block has data to send downstream, it starts offering it to its linked blocks one at a time. By default, the first target block would just take the data and buffer it, and the second target block would never get any. The fix for this situation is to limit the target block buffers by making them nongreedy; Recipe 5.4 covers this.

A block will fault when something goes wrong, for example, if the processing delegate throws an exception when processing a data item. When a block faults, it will stop receiving data. By default, it won't take down the whole mesh; this enables you to rebuild that part of the mesh or redirect the data. However, this is an advanced scenario; most times, you want the faults to propagate along the links to the target blocks. Dataflow supports this option as well; the only tricky part is that when an exception is propagated along a link, it is wrapped in an `AggregateException`. So, if you have a long pipeline, you could end up with a deeply nested exception; the method `AggregateException.Flatten` can be used to work around this:

```
try
{
  var multiplyBlock = new TransformBlock<int, int>(item =>
  {
    if (item == 1)
      throw new InvalidOperationException("Blech.");
    return item * 2;
  });
  var subtractBlock = new TransformBlock<int, int>(item => item - 2);
  multiplyBlock.LinkTo(subtractBlock,
      new DataflowLinkOptions { PropagateCompletion = true });

  multiplyBlock.Post(1);
  subtractBlock.Completion.Wait();
```

```
  }
catch (AggregateException exception)
{
  AggregateException ex = exception.Flatten();
  Trace.WriteLine(ex.InnerException);
}
```

Recipe 5.2 covers dataflow error handling in more detail.

At first glance, dataflow meshes sound very much like observable streams, and they do have much in common. Both meshes and streams have the concept of data items passing through them. Also, both meshes and streams have the notion of a normal completion (a notification that no more data is coming), as well as a faulting completion (a notification that some error occurred during data processing). But System.Reactive (Rx) and TPL Dataflow do not have the same capabilities. Rx observables are generally better than dataflow blocks when doing anything related to timing. Dataflow blocks are generally better than Rx observables when doing parallel processing. Conceptually, Rx works more like setting up callbacks: each step in the observable directly calls the next step. In contrast, each block in a dataflow mesh is very independent from all the other blocks. Both Rx and TPL Dataflow have their own uses, with some amount of overlap. They also work quite well together; Recipe 8.8 covers interoperability between Rx and TPL Dataflow.

If you're familiar with actor frameworks, TPL Dataflow will seem to share similarities with them. Each dataflow block is independent, in the sense that it will spin up tasks to do work as needed, like executing a transformation delegate or pushing output to the next block. You can also set up each block to run in parallel, so that it'll spin up multiple tasks to deal with additional input. Due to this behavior, each block does have a certain similarity to an actor in an actor framework. However, TPL Dataflow is not a full actor framework; in particular, there's no built-in support for clean error recovery or retries of any kind. TPL Dataflow is a library with an actor-like feel, but it isn't a full-featured actor framework.

The most common TPL Dataflow block types are `TransformBlock<TInput, TOutput>` (similar to LINQ's `Select`), `TransformManyBlock<TInput, TOutput>` (similar to LINQ's `SelectMany`), and `ActionBlock<TResult>`, which executes a delegate for each data item. For more information on TPL Dataflow, I recommend the MSDN documentation (*http://bit.ly/dataflow-doc*) and the "Guide to Implementing Custom TPL Dataflow Blocks" (*http://bit.ly/tpl-dataflow*).

Introduction to Multithreaded Programming

A *thread* is an independent executor. Each process has multiple threads in it, and each of those threads can be doing different things simultaneously. Each thread has its own independent stack but shares the same memory with all the other threads in a process. In some applications, there is one thread that is special. For example, user inter-face applications have a single special UI thread, and Console applications have a sin-gle special main thread.

Every .NET application has a thread pool. The thread pool maintains a number of worker threads that are waiting to execute whatever work you have for them to do. The thread pool is responsible for determining how many threads are in the thread pool at any time. There are dozens of configuration settings you can play with to modify this behavior, but I recommend that you leave it alone; the thread pool has been carefully tuned to cover the vast majority of real-world scenarios.

There is almost no need for you to ever create a new thread yourself. The only time you should ever create a `Thread` instance is if you need an STA thread for COM interop.

A thread is a low-level abstraction. The thread pool is a slightly higher level of abstraction; when code queues work to the thread pool, the thread pool itself will take care of creating a thread if necessary. The abstractions covered in this book are higher still: parallel and dataflow processing queues work to the thread pool as necessary. Code using these higher abstractions is easier to get right than code using low-level abstractions.

For this reason, the `Thread` and `BackgroundWorker` types are not covered at all in this book. They have had their time, and that time is over.

Collections for Concurrent Applications

There are a couple of collection categories that are useful for concurrent program-ming: concurrent collections and immutable collections. Both of these collection cat-egories are covered in Chapter 9. Concurrent collections allow multiple threads to update them simultaneously in a safe way. Most concurrent collections use *snapshots* to enable one thread to enumerate the values while another thread may be adding or removing values. Concurrent collections are usually more efficient than just protect-ing a regular collection with a lock.

Immutable collections are a bit different. An immutable collection cannot actually be modified; instead, to modify an immutable collection, you create a new collection that represents the modified collection. This sounds horribly inefficient, but immuta-ble collections share as much memory as possible between collection instances, so it's not as bad as it sounds. The nice thing about immutable collections is that all opera-tions are pure, so they work very well with functional code.

Modern Design

Most concurrent technologies have one similar aspect: they are functional in nature. I don't mean *functional* as in "they get the job done," but rather *functional* as a style of programming that is based on function composition. If you adopt a functional mind-set, your concurrent designs will be less convoluted.

One principle of functional programming is *purity* (that is, avoiding side effects). Each piece of the solution takes some value(s) as input and produces some value(s) as output. As much as possible, you should avoid having these pieces depend on global (or shared) variables or update global (or shared) data structures. This is true whether the piece is an `async` method, a parallel task, a System.Reactive operation, or a data-flow block. Of course, sooner or later your computations will have to have an effect, but you'll find your code is cleaner if you can handle the *processing* with pure pieces and then perform updates with the *results*.

Another principle of functional programming is *immutability*. Immutability means that a piece of data cannot change. One reason that immutable data is useful for concurrent programs is that you never need synchronization for immutable data; the fact that it cannot change makes synchronization unnecessary. Immutable data also helps you avoid side effects. Developers are beginning to use more immutable types, and this book has several recipes covering immutable data structures.

Summary of Key Technologies

The .NET framework has had some support for asynchronous programming since the very beginning. However, asynchronous programming was difficult until 2012, when .NET 4.5 (along with C# 5.0 and VB 2012) introduced the `async` and `await` keywords. This book will use the modern `async`/`await` approach for all asynchronous recipes, and it has some recipes showing how to interoperate between `async` and the older asynchronous programming patterns. If you need support for older platforms, see Appendix A.

The Task Parallel Library was introduced in .NET 4.0 with full support for both data and task parallelism. These days, it's available even on platforms with fewer resources, such as mobile phones. The TPL is built in to .NET.

The System.Reactive team has worked hard to support as many platforms as possible. System.Reactive, like `async` and `await`, provide benefits for all sorts of applications, both client and server. System.Reactive is available in the `System.Reactive` (*http://bit.ly/sys-reactive*) NuGet package.

The TPL Dataflow library is officially distributed within the NuGet package for `System.Threading.Tasks.Dataflow` (*http://bit.ly/nuget-df*).

Most concurrent collections are built into .NET; there are some additional concurrent collections available in the System.Threading.Channels (*https://www.nuget.org/pack ages/System.Threading.Channels*) NuGet package. Immutable collections are available in the System.Collections.Immutable (*http://bit.ly/sys-coll-imm*) NuGet package.

CHAPTER 2

Async Basics

This chapter introduces you to the basics of using `async` and `await` for asynchronous operations. Here, we'll only deal with naturally asynchronous operations, which are operations such as HTTP requests, database commands, and web service calls.

If you have a CPU-intensive operation that you want to treat as though it were asynchronous (e.g., so that it doesn't block the UI thread), then see Chapter 4 and Recipe 8.4. Also, this chapter only deals with operations that are started once and complete once; if you need to handle streams of events, then see Chapters 3 and 6.

2.1 Pausing for a Period of Time

Problem

You need to (asynchronously) wait for a period of time. This is a common scenario when unit testing or implementing retry delays. It also comes up when coding simple timeouts.

Solution

The `Task` type has a static method `Delay` that returns a task that completes after the specified time.

The following example code defines a task that completes asynchronously. When faking an asynchronous operation, it's important to test synchronous success and asynchronous success, as well as asynchronous failure. The following example returns a task used for the asynchronous success case:

```
async Task<T> DelayResult<T>(T result, TimeSpan delay)
{
  await Task.Delay(delay);
```

```
      return result;
  }
```

Exponential backoff is a strategy in which you increase the delays between retries. Use it when working with web services to ensure that the server doesn't get flooded with retries. The next example is a simple implementation of exponential backoff:

```
async Task<string> DownloadStringWithRetries(HttpClient client, string uri)
{
  // Retry after 1 second, then after 2 seconds, then 4.
  TimeSpan nextDelay = TimeSpan.FromSeconds(1);
  for (int i = 0; i != 3; ++i)
  {
    try
    {
      return await client.GetStringAsync(uri);
    }
    catch
    {
    }

    await Task.Delay(nextDelay);
    nextDelay = nextDelay + nextDelay;
  }

  // Try one last time, allowing the error to propagate.
  return await client.GetStringAsync(uri);
}
```

For production code, I'd recommend a more thorough solution, such as the Polly (*http://www.thepollyproject.org/*) NuGet library; this code is just a simple example of Task.Delay usage.

You can also use Task.Delay as a simple timeout. CancellationTokenSource is the normal type used to implement a timeout (Recipe 10.3). You can wrap a cancellation token in an infinite Task.Delay to provide a task that cancels after a specified time. Finally, use that timer task with Task.WhenAny (Recipe 2.5) to implement a "soft time-out." The following example code returns null if the service doesn't respond within three seconds:

```
async Task<string> DownloadStringWithTimeout(HttpClient client, string uri)
{
  using var cts = new CancellationTokenSource(TimeSpan.FromSeconds(3));
  Task<string> downloadTask = client.GetStringAsync(uri);
  Task timeoutTask = Task.Delay(Timeout.InfiniteTimeSpan, cts.Token);

  Task completedTask = await Task.WhenAny(downloadTask, timeoutTask);
  if (completedTask == timeoutTask)
```

```
      return null;
    return await downloadTask;
}
```

While it's possible to use `Task.Delay` as a "soft timeout," this approach has limitations. If the operation times out, it's not canceled; in the previous example, the download task continues downloading and will download the full response before discarding it. The preferred approach is to use a cancellation token as the timeout and pass it directly to the operation (`GetStringAsync` in the last example). That said, sometimes the operation is not cancelable, and in that case `Task.Delay` may be used by other code to *act like* the operation timed out.

Discussion

`Task.Delay` is a fine option for unit testing asynchronous code or for implementing retry logic. However, if you need to implement a timeout, a `CancellationToken` is usually a better choice.

See Also

Recipe 2.5 covers how `Task.WhenAny` is used to determine which task completes first.

Recipe 10.3 covers using `CancellationToken` as a timeout.

2.2 Returning Completed Tasks

Problem

You need to implement a synchronous method with an asynchronous signature. This situation can arise if you're inheriting from an asynchronous interface or base class but want to implement it synchronously. This technique is particularly useful when unit testing asynchronous code, when you need a simple stub or mock for an asynchronous interface.

Solution

You can use `Task.FromResult` to create and return a new `Task<T>` that is already completed with the specified value:

```
interface IMyAsyncInterface
{
  Task<int> GetValueAsync();
}

class MySynchronousImplementation : IMyAsyncInterface
{
  public Task<int> GetValueAsync()
```

```
  {
    return Task.FromResult(13);
  }
}
```

For methods that don't have a return value, you can use Task.CompletedTask, which is a cached Task that is successfully completed:

```
interface IMyAsyncInterface
{
  Task DoSomethingAsync();
}

class MySynchronousImplementation : IMyAsyncInterface
{
  public Task DoSomethingAsync()
  {
    return Task.CompletedTask;
  }
}
```

Task.FromResult provides completed tasks only for successful results. If you need a task with a different kind of result (e.g., a task that is completed with a NotImplementedException), then you can use Task.FromException:

```
Task<T> NotImplementedAsync<T>()
{
  return Task.FromException<T>(new NotImplementedException());
}
```

Similarly, there's a Task.FromCanceled for creating tasks that have already been canceled from a given CancellationToken:

```
Task<int> GetValueAsync(CancellationToken cancellationToken)
{
  if (cancellationToken.IsCancellationRequested)
    return Task.FromCanceled<int>(cancellationToken);
  return Task.FromResult(13);
}
```

If it is possible for your synchronous implementation to fail, then you should capture exceptions and use Task.FromException to return them, as such:

```
interface IMyAsyncInterface
{
  Task DoSomethingAsync();
}

class MySynchronousImplementation : IMyAsyncInterface
{
  public Task DoSomethingAsync()
  {
    try
```

```
    {
      DoSomethingSynchronously();
      return Task.CompletedTask;
    }
    catch (Exception ex)
    {
      return Task.FromException(ex);
    }
  }
}
```

Discussion

If you're implementing an asynchronous interface with synchronous code, avoid any form of blocking. It isn't ideal for an asynchronous method to block and then return a completed task, when it is possible for the method to be implemented asynchronously. For a counterexample, consider the Console text readers in the .NET BCL. Console.In.ReadLineAsync will actually block the calling thread until a line is read, and then it will return a completed task. This behavior isn't intuitive and has surprised many developers. If an asynchronous method blocks, it prevents the calling thread from starting other tasks, which interferes with concurrency and may even cause a deadlock.

If you regularly use Task.FromResult with the same value, consider caching the actual task. For example, if you create a Task<int> with a zero result once, then you avoid creating extra instances that will have to be garbage-collected:

```
private static readonly Task<int> zeroTask = Task.FromResult(0);
Task<int> GetValueAsync()
{
  return zeroTask;
}
```

Logically, Task.FromResult, Task.FromException, and Task.FromCanceled are all helper methods and shortcuts for the general-purpose TaskCompletionSource<T>. TaskCompletionSource<T> is a lower-level type that is useful for interoperating with other forms of asynchronous code. Generally, you should use the shorthand Task.FromResult and friends if you want to return a task that's already been completed. Use TaskCompletionSource<T> to return a task that is completed at some future time.

See Also

Recipe 7.1 covers unit testing asynchronous methods.

Recipe 11.1 covers inheritance of async methods.

Recipe 8.3 shows how `TaskCompletionSource<T>` can be used for general-purpose interop with other asynchronous code.

2.3 Reporting Progress

Problem

You need to respond to progress while an operation is executing.

Solution

Use the provided `IProgress<T>` and `Progress<T>` types. Your `async` method should take an `IProgress<T>` argument; the `T` is whatever type of progress you need to report:

```
async Task MyMethodAsync(IProgress<double> progress = null)
{
  bool done = false;
  double percentComplete = 0;
  while (!done)
  {
    ...
    progress?.Report(percentComplete);
  }
}
```

Calling code can use it as such:

```
async Task CallMyMethodAsync()
{
  var progress = new Progress<double>();
  progress.ProgressChanged += (sender, args) =>
  {
    ...
  };
  await MyMethodAsync(progress);
}
```

Discussion

By convention, the `IProgress<T>` parameter may be `null` if the caller doesn't need progress reports, so be sure to check for this in your `async` method.

Bear in mind that the `IProgress<T>.Report` method is usually asynchronous. This means that `MyMethodAsync` may continue executing before the progress is reported. For this reason, it's best to define `T` as an *immutable type* or at least a value type. If `T` is a mutable reference type, then you'll have to create a separate copy yourself each time you call `IProgress<T>.Report`.

`Progress<T>` will capture the current context when it is constructed and will invoke its callback within that context. This means that if you construct the `Progress<T>` on the UI thread, then you can update the UI from its callback, even if the asynchronous method is invoking `Report` from a background thread.

When a method supports progress reporting, it should also make a best effort to support cancellation.

`IProgress<T>` is not exclusively for asynchronous code; both progress and cancellation can (and should) be used in long-running synchronous code as well.

See Also

Recipe 10.4 covers how to support cancellation in an asynchronous method.

2.4 Waiting for a Set of Tasks to Complete

Problem

You have several tasks and need to wait for them all to complete.

Solution

The framework provides a `Task.WhenAll` method for this purpose. This method takes several tasks and returns a task that completes when all of those tasks have completed:

```
Task task1 = Task.Delay(TimeSpan.FromSeconds(1));
Task task2 = Task.Delay(TimeSpan.FromSeconds(2));
Task task3 = Task.Delay(TimeSpan.FromSeconds(1));

await Task.WhenAll(task1, task2, task3);
```

If all the tasks have the same result type and they all complete successfully, then the `Task.WhenAll` task will return an array containing all the task results:

```
Task<int> task1 = Task.FromResult(3);
Task<int> task2 = Task.FromResult(5);
Task<int> task3 = Task.FromResult(7);

int[] results = await Task.WhenAll(task1, task2, task3);

// "results" contains { 3, 5, 7 }
```

There is an overload of `Task.WhenAll` that takes an `IEnumerable` of tasks; however, I don't recommend that you use it. Whenever I mix asynchronous code with LINQ, I find the code is clearer when I explicitly "reify" the sequence (i.e., evaluate the sequence, creating a collection):

```
async Task<string> DownloadAllAsync(HttpClient client,
    IEnumerable<string> urls)
{
  // Define the action to do for each URL.
  var downloads = urls.Select(url => client.GetStringAsync(url));
  // Note that no tasks have actually started yet
  //   because the sequence is not evaluated.

  // Start all URLs downloading simultaneously.
  Task<string>[] downloadTasks = downloads.ToArray();
  // Now the tasks have all started.

  // Asynchronously wait for all downloads to complete.
  string[] htmlPages = await Task.WhenAll(downloadTasks);

  return string.Concat(htmlPages);
}
```

Discussion

If any of the tasks throws an exception, then `Task.WhenAll` will fault its returned task
with that exception. If multiple tasks throw an exception, then all of those exceptions
are placed on the `Task` returned by `Task.WhenAll`. However, when that task is awaited, only one of them will be thrown. If you need each specific exception, you can
examine the `Exception` property on the `Task` returned by `Task.WhenAll`:

```
async Task ThrowNotImplementedExceptionAsync()
{
  throw new NotImplementedException();
}

async Task ThrowInvalidOperationExceptionAsync()
{
  throw new InvalidOperationException();
}

async Task ObserveOneExceptionAsync()
{
  var task1 = ThrowNotImplementedExceptionAsync();
  var task2 = ThrowInvalidOperationExceptionAsync();

  try
  {
    await Task.WhenAll(task1, task2);
  }
  catch (Exception ex)
  {
    // "ex" is either NotImplementedException or InvalidOperationException.
    ...
  }
}
```

```
async Task ObserveAllExceptionsAsync()
{
  var task1 = ThrowNotImplementedExceptionAsync();
  var task2 = ThrowInvalidOperationExceptionAsync();

  Task allTasks = Task.WhenAll(task1, task2);
  try
  {
    await allTasks;
  }
  catch
  {
    AggregateException allExceptions = allTasks.Exception;
    ...
  }
}
```

Most of the time, I do *not* observe all the exceptions when using `Task.WhenAll`. It's usually sufficient to respond to only the first error that was thrown, rather than all of them.

Note that in the preceding example, the `ThrowNotImplementedExceptionAsync` and `ThrowInvalidOperationExceptionAsync` methods don't throw their exceptions directly; they use the `async` keyword, so their exceptions are captured and placed on a task that is returned normally. This is the normal and expected behavior of methods that return awaitable types.

See Also

Recipe 2.5 covers a way to wait for *any* of a collection of tasks to complete.

Recipe 2.6 covers waiting for a collection of tasks to complete and performing actions as each one completes.

Recipe 2.8 covers exception handling for `async Task` methods.

2.5 Waiting for Any Task to Complete

Problem

You have several tasks and need to respond to just one of them that's completing. You'll encounter this problem most commonly when you have multiple independent attempts at an operation, with a first-one-takes-all kind of structure. For example, you could request stock quotes from multiple web services simultaneously, but you only care about the first one that responds.

Solution

Use the `Task.WhenAny` method. The `Task.WhenAny` method takes a sequence of tasks and returns a task that completes when any of the tasks complete. The result of the returned task is the task that completed. Don't worry if that sounds confusing; it's one of those things that's difficult to explain but is easier to understand with code:

```
// Returns the length of data at the first URL to respond.
async Task<int> FirstRespondingUrlAsync(HttpClient client,
    string urlA, string urlB)
{
  // Start both downloads concurrently.
  Task<byte[]> downloadTaskA = client.GetByteArrayAsync(urlA);
  Task<byte[]> downloadTaskB = client.GetByteArrayAsync(urlB);

  // Wait for either of the tasks to complete.
  Task<byte[]> completedTask =
      await Task.WhenAny(downloadTaskA, downloadTaskB);

  // Return the length of the data retrieved from that URL.
  byte[] data = await completedTask;
  return data.Length;
}
```

Discussion

The task returned by `Task.WhenAny` never completes in a faulted or canceled state. This "outer" task always completes successfully, and its result value is the first `Task` to complete (the "inner" task). If the inner task completed with an exception, then that exception is not propagated to the outer task (the one returned by `Task.WhenAny`). You should usually `await` the inner task after it has completed to ensure any exceptions are observed.

When the first task completes, consider whether to cancel the remaining tasks. If the other tasks aren't canceled but are also never awaited, then they are abandoned. Abandoned tasks will run to completion, and their results will be ignored. Any exceptions from those abandoned tasks will also be ignored. If these tasks aren't canceled, they do continue to run and can use resources unnecessarily, such as HTTP connections, DB connections, or timers.

It is possible to use `Task.WhenAny` to implement timeouts (e.g., using `Task.Delay` as one of the tasks), but it's not recommended. It's more natural to express timeouts with cancellation, and cancellation has the added benefit that it can actually *cancel* the operation(s) if they time out.

Another anti-pattern for `Task.WhenAny` is handling tasks as they complete. At first it seems reasonable to keep a list of tasks and remove each task from the list as it completes. The problem with this approach is that it executes in $O(N^2)$ time, when an $O(N)$ algorithm exists. The proper $O(N)$ algorithm is discussed in Recipe 2.6.

See Also

Recipe 2.4 covers asynchronously waiting for *all* of a collection of tasks to complete.

Recipe 2.6 covers waiting for a collection of tasks to complete and performing actions as each one completes.

Recipe 10.3 covers using a cancellation token to implement timeouts.

2.6 Processing Tasks as They Complete

Problem

You have a collection of tasks to await, and you want to do some processing on each task after it completes. However, you want to do the processing for each one as soon as it completes, not waiting for any of the other tasks.

The following example code kicks off three delay tasks and then awaits each one:

```
async Task<int> DelayAndReturnAsync(int value)
{
  await Task.Delay(TimeSpan.FromSeconds(value));
  return value;
}

// Currently, this method prints "2", "3", and "1".
// The desired behavior is for this method to print "1", "2", and "3".
async Task ProcessTasksAsync()
{
  // Create a sequence of tasks.
  Task<int> taskA = DelayAndReturnAsync(2);
  Task<int> taskB = DelayAndReturnAsync(3);
  Task<int> taskC = DelayAndReturnAsync(1);
  Task<int>[] tasks = new[] { taskA, taskB, taskC };

  // Await each task in order.
  foreach (Task<int> task in tasks)
  {
    var result = await task;
    Trace.WriteLine(result);
  }
}
```

The code currently awaits each task in sequence order, even though the third task in the sequence is the first one to complete. You want the code to do the processing (e.g., `Trace.WriteLine`) as each task completes without waiting for the others.

Solution

There are a few different approaches you can take to solve this problem. The one described first in this recipe is the recommended approach; another is described in the "Discussion" section.

The easiest solution is to restructure the code by introducing a higher-level async method that handles awaiting the task and processing its result. Once the processing is factored out, the code is significantly simplified:

```
async Task<int> DelayAndReturnAsync(int value)
{
  await Task.Delay(TimeSpan.FromSeconds(value));
  return value;
}

async Task AwaitAndProcessAsync(Task<int> task)
{
  int result = await task;
  Trace.WriteLine(result);
}

// This method now prints "1", "2", and "3".
async Task ProcessTasksAsync()
{
  // Create a sequence of tasks.
  Task<int> taskA = DelayAndReturnAsync(2);
  Task<int> taskB = DelayAndReturnAsync(3);
  Task<int> taskC = DelayAndReturnAsync(1);
  Task<int>[] tasks = new[] { taskA, taskB, taskC };

  IEnumerable<Task> taskQuery =
      from t in tasks select AwaitAndProcessAsync(t);
  Task[] processingTasks = taskQuery.ToArray();

  // Await all processing to complete
  await Task.WhenAll(processingTasks);
}
```

Alternatively, this code can be written like this:

```
async Task<int> DelayAndReturnAsync(int value)
{
  await Task.Delay(TimeSpan.FromSeconds(value));
  return value;
}

// This method now prints "1", "2", and "3".
async Task ProcessTasksAsync()
{
  // Create a sequence of tasks.
  Task<int> taskA = DelayAndReturnAsync(2);
```

```
  Task<int> taskB = DelayAndReturnAsync(3);
  Task<int> taskC = DelayAndReturnAsync(1);
  Task<int>[] tasks = new[] { taskA, taskB, taskC };

  Task[] processingTasks = tasks.Select(async t =>
  {
    var result = await t;
    Trace.WriteLine(result);
  }).ToArray();

  // Await all processing to complete
  await Task.WhenAll(processingTasks);
}
```

The refactoring shown is the cleanest and most portable way to solve this problem.
Note that it is subtly different than the original code. This solution will do the task
processing concurrently, whereas the original code would do the task processing one
at a time. Typically this isn't a problem, but if it's not acceptable for your situation,
then consider using locks (Recipe 12.2) or the following alternative solution.

Discussion

If refactoring isn't a palatable solution, then there is an alternative. Stephen Toub and
Jon Skeet have both developed an extension method that returns an array of tasks
that will complete in order. Stephen Toub's solution is available on the Parallel Programming with .NET blog (*http://bit.ly/toub-task*), and Jon Skeet's solution is available on his coding blog (*http://bit.ly/skeet_blog*).

> The OrderByCompletion extension method is also available in the
> open source AsyncEx library (*https://github.com/StephenCleary/
> AsyncEx*), in the Nito.AsyncEx NuGet package (*http://bit.ly/nito-
> async*).

Using an extension method like OrderByCompletion minimizes the changes to the
original code:

```
async Task<int> DelayAndReturnAsync(int value)
{
  await Task.Delay(TimeSpan.FromSeconds(value));
  return value;
}

// This method now prints "1", "2", and "3".
async Task UseOrderByCompletionAsync()
{
  // Create a sequence of tasks.
  Task<int> taskA = DelayAndReturnAsync(2);
  Task<int> taskB = DelayAndReturnAsync(3);
```

```
    Task<int> taskC = DelayAndReturnAsync(1);
    Task<int>[] tasks = new[] { taskA, taskB, taskC };

    // Await each one as they complete.
    foreach (Task<int> task in tasks.OrderByCompletion())
    {
      int result = await task;
      Trace.WriteLine(result);
    }
}
```

See Also

Recipe 2.4 covers asynchronously waiting for a sequence of tasks to complete.

2.7 Avoiding Context for Continuations

Problem

When an `async` method resumes after an `await`, by default it will resume executing within the same context. This can cause performance problems if that context was a UI context and a large number of `async` methods are resuming on the UI context.

Solution

To avoid resuming on a context, `await` the result of `ConfigureAwait` and pass `false` for its `continueOnCapturedContext` parameter:

```
async Task ResumeOnContextAsync()
{
  await Task.Delay(TimeSpan.FromSeconds(1));

  // This method resumes within the same context.
}

async Task ResumeWithoutContextAsync()
{
  await Task.Delay(TimeSpan.FromSeconds(1)).ConfigureAwait(false);

  // This method discards its context when it resumes.
}
```

Discussion

Having too many continuations run on the UI thread can cause a performance problem. This type of performance problem is difficult to diagnose, since it's not a single method that is slowing down the system. Rather, the UI performance begins to suffer from "thousands of paper cuts" as the application grows more complex.

The real question is, *how many* continuations on the UI thread are *too many?* There's no hard-and-fast answer, but Lucian Wischik of Microsoft has publicized the guideline (*http://bit.ly/new-async*) used by the Universal Windows team: a hundred or so per second is OK, but a thousand or so per second is too many.

It's best to avoid this problem right at the beginning. For every `async` method you write, if it doesn't *need* to resume to its original context, then use `ConfigureAwait`. There's no disadvantage to doing so.

It's also a good idea to be aware of context when writing `async` code. Normally, an `async` method should *either* require context (dealing with UI elements or ASP.NET requests/responses) or be free from context (doing background operations). If you have an `async` method that has parts requiring context and parts free from context, consider splitting it up into two (or more) `async` methods. This approach helps keep your code better organized into layers.

See Also

Chapter 1 covers an introduction to asynchronous programming.

2.8 Handling Exceptions from async Task Methods

Problem

Exception handling is a critical part of any design. It's easy to design for the success case, but a design isn't correct until it also handles the failure cases. Fortunately, handling exceptions from `async Task` methods is straightforward.

Solution

Exceptions can be caught by a simple `try/catch`, just like you would do for synchronous code:

```
async Task ThrowExceptionAsync()
{
  await Task.Delay(TimeSpan.FromSeconds(1));
  throw new InvalidOperationException("Test");
}

async Task TestAsync()
{
  try
  {
    await ThrowExceptionAsync();
  }
  catch (InvalidOperationException)
  {
```

```
    }
  }
```

Exceptions raised from `async Task` methods are placed on the returned `Task`. They are only raised when the returned `Task` is awaited:

```
async Task ThrowExceptionAsync()
{
  await Task.Delay(TimeSpan.FromSeconds(1));
  throw new InvalidOperationException("Test");
}

async Task TestAsync()
{
  // The exception is thrown by the method and placed on the task.
  Task task = ThrowExceptionAsync();
  try
  {
    // The exception is re-raised here, where the task is awaited.
    await task;
  }
  catch (InvalidOperationException)
  {
    // The exception is correctly caught here.
  }
}
```

Discussion

When an exception is thrown out of an `async Task` method, that exception is captured and put on the returned `Task`. Since `async void` methods don't have a `Task` to put their exception on, their behavior is different; catching exceptions from `async void` methods is covered in Recipe 2.9.

When you `await` a faulted `Task`, the first exception on that task is re-thrown. If you're familiar with the problems of re-throwing exceptions, you may be wondering about stack traces. Rest assured: when the exception is re-thrown, the original stack trace is correctly preserved.

This setup sounds somewhat complicated, but all this complexity works together so that the simple scenario has simple code. Most of the time, your code should propagate exceptions from asynchronous methods that it calls; all it has to do is `await` the task returned from that asynchronous method, and the exception will be propagated naturally.

There are some situations (such as `Task.WhenAll`) where a `Task` may have multiple exceptions, and `await` will only rethrow the first one. See Recipe 2.4 for an example of handling all exceptions.

See Also

Recipe 2.4 covers waiting for multiple tasks.

Recipe 2.9 covers techniques for catching exceptions from `async void` methods.

Recipe 7.2 covers unit testing exceptions thrown from `async Task` methods.

2.9 Handling Exceptions from async void Methods

Problem

You have an `async void` method and need to handle exceptions propagated out of that method.

Solution

There is no good solution. If at all possible, change the method to return `Task` instead of `void`. In some situations, doing that isn't possible; for example, let's say you need to unit test an `ICommand` implementation (which *must* return `void`). In this case, you can provide a `Task`-returning overload of your `Execute` method:

```
sealed class MyAsyncCommand : ICommand
{
  async void ICommand.Execute(object parameter)
  {
    await Execute(parameter);
  }

  public async Task Execute(object parameter)
  {
    ... // Asynchronous command implementation goes here.
  }

  ... // Other members (CanExecute, etc.)
}
```

It's best to avoid propagating exceptions out of `async void` methods. If you must use an `async void` method, consider wrapping all of its code in a `try` block and handling the exception directly.

There is another solution for handling exceptions from `async void` methods. When an `async void` method propagates an exception, that exception is then raised on the `SynchronizationContext` that was active at the time the `async void` method started executing. If your execution environment provides a `SynchronizationContext`, then it usually has a way to handle these top-level exceptions at a global scope. For example, WPF has `Application.DispatcherUnhandledException`, Universal Windows has `Application.UnhandledException`, and ASP.NET has the `UseExceptionHandler` middleware.

It is also possible to handle exceptions from `async void` methods by controlling the `SynchronizationContext`. Writing your own `SynchronizationContext` isn't easy, but you can use the `AsyncContext` type from the free `Nito.AsyncEx` NuGet helper library. `AsyncContext` is particularly useful for applications that don't have a built-in Synchronization Context, such as Console applications and Win32 services. The next example uses `AsyncContext` to run and handle exceptions from an `async void` method:

```
static class Program
{
  static void Main(string[] args)
  {
    try
    {
      AsyncContext.Run(() => MainAsync(args));
    }
    catch (Exception ex)
    {
      Console.Error.WriteLine(ex);
    }
  }

  // BAD CODE!!!
  // In the real world, do not use async void unless you have to.
  static async void MainAsync(string[] args)
  {
    ...
  }
}
```

Discussion

One reason to prefer `async Task` over `async void` is that Task-returning methods are easier to test. At the very least, overloading void-returning methods with Task-returning methods will give you a testable API surface.

If you do need to provide your own `SynchronizationContext` type (for example, `AsyncContext`), be sure not to install that `SynchronizationContext` on any threads that don't belong to you. As a general rule, you shouldn't place this type on any thread that already has one (such as UI or ASP.NET classic request threads); nor should you place a `SynchronizationContext` on threadpool threads. The main thread of a Console application does belong to you, and so do any threads you manually create yourself.

The `AsyncContext` type is in the `Nito.AsyncEx` (*http://bit.ly/nito-async*) NuGet package.

See Also

Recipe 2.8 covers exception handling with `async Task` methods.

Recipe 7.3 covers unit testing `async void` methods.

2.10 Creating a ValueTask

Problem

You need to implement a method that returns `ValueTask<T>`.

Solution

`ValueTask<T>` is used as a return type in scenarios where there's usually a synchronous result that can be returned and asynchronous behavior is more rare. As a general rule, for your own application code, you should use `Task<T>` as a return type and not `ValueTask<T>`. Only consider using `ValueTask<T>` as a return type in your own application after profiling shows that you'd see a performance increase. That said, there are situations where you need to implement a method that returns `Value Task<T>`. One such situation is `IAsyncDisposable`, whose `DisposeAsync` method returns `ValueTask`. See Recipe 11.6 for a more detailed discussion of asynchronous disposal.

The easiest way to implement a method that returns `ValueTask<T>` is to use `async` and `await` just like a normal `async` method:

```
public async ValueTask<int> MethodAsync()
{
  await Task.Delay(100); // asynchronous work.
  return 13;
}
```

Many times a method returning `ValueTask<T>` is capable of returning a value immediately; in that case, you can optimize for that scenario using the `ValueTask<T>` constructor, and then forward to the slow asynchronous method only if necessary:

```
public ValueTask<int> MethodAsync()
{
  if (CanBehaveSynchronously)
    return new ValueTask<int>(13);
  return new ValueTask<int>(SlowMethodAsync());
```

```
  }

  private Task<int> SlowMethodAsync();
```

A similar approach is possible for the nongeneric ValueTask. Here, the ValueTask default constructor is used to return a successfully completed ValueTask. The following example shows an IAsyncDisposable implementation that only runs its asynchronous disposal logic once; on future invocations, the DisposeAsync method completes successfully and synchronously:

```
  private Func<Task> _disposeLogic;

  public ValueTask DisposeAsync()
  {
    if (_disposeLogic == null)
      return default;

    // Note: this simple example is not threadsafe;
    //  if multiple threads call DisposeAsync,
    //  the logic could run more than once.
    Func<Task> logic = _disposeLogic;
    _disposeLogic = null;
    return new ValueTask(logic());
  }
```

Discussion

Most of your methods should return Task<T>, since consuming Task<T> has fewer pitfalls than consuming ValueTask<T>. See Recipe 2.11 for details on these pitfalls.

Most often, if you're just implementing interfaces that use ValueTask or Value Task<T>, then you can simply use async and await. The more advanced implementations are for when you want to use ValueTask<T> yourself.

The approaches covered in this recipe are the simpler and more common approaches to creating ValueTask<T> and ValueTask instances. There is another approach more suitable to more advanced scenarios, when you need to absolutely minimize the allocations used. This more advanced approach enables you to cache or pool an IValue TaskSource<T> implementation and reuse it for multiple asynchronous method invocations. To get started with the advanced scenario, see the Microsoft docs for the Man ualResetValueTaskSourceCore<T> type (*http://bit.ly/man-reset-type-doc*).

See Also

Recipe 2.11 covers limitations of consuming ValueTask<T> and ValueTask types.

Recipe 11.6 covers asynchronous disposal.

2.11 Consuming a ValueTask

Problem

You need to consume a `ValueTask<T>` value.

Solution

Using `await` is the most straightforward and common way to consume a Value
Task<T> or ValueTask value. The majority of the time, this is all you need to do:

```
ValueTask<int> MethodAsync();

async Task ConsumingMethodAsync()
{
  int value = await MethodAsync();
}
```

You can also do the `await` after doing a concurrent operation, as with Task<T>:

```
ValueTask<int> MethodAsync();

async Task ConsumingMethodAsync()
{
  ValueTask<int> valueTask = MethodAsync();
  ... // other concurrent work
  int value = await valueTask;
}
```

Both of these are appropriate because the `ValueTask` is only awaited a single time.
This is one of the restrictions of ValueTask.

> A ValueTask or ValueTask<T> may only be awaited once.

To do anything more complex, convert the `ValueTask<T>` into a `Task<T>` by calling
AsTask:

```
ValueTask<int> MethodAsync();

async Task ConsumingMethodAsync()
{
  Task<int> task = MethodAsync().AsTask();
  ... // other concurrent work
  int value = await task;
  int anotherValue = await task;
}
```

It's perfectly safe to `await` a `Task<T>` multiple times. You can do other things with it, too, like asynchronously wait for multiple operations to complete (see Recipe 2.4):

```
ValueTask<int> MethodAsync();

async Task ConsumingMethodAsync()
{
  Task<int> task1 = MethodAsync().AsTask();
  Task<int> task2 = MethodAsync().AsTask();
  int[] results = await Task.WhenAll(task1, task2);
}
```

However, for each `ValueTask<T>`, you can only call `AsTask` once. The usual approach is to convert it to a `Task<T>` immediately and then ignore the `ValueTask<T>`. Also note that you cannot both `await` and call `AsTask` on the same `ValueTask<T>`.

Most code should either immediately `await` a `ValueTask<T>` or convert it to a `Task<T>`.

Discussion

Other properties on `ValueTask<T>` are for more advanced usage. They don't tend to act like other properties you may be familiar with; in particular, `Value Task<T>.Result` has more restrictions than `Task<T>.Result`. Code that synchronously retrieves a result from a `ValueTask<T>` may call `ValueTask<T>.Result` or `Val ueTask<T>.GetAwaiter().GetResult()`, but these members must not be called until the `ValueTask<T>` is complete. Synchronously retrieving a result from `Task<T>` blocks the calling thread until the task completes; `ValueTask<T>` makes no such guarantees.

 Synchronously getting results from a `ValueTask` or `ValueTask<T>` may only be done once, after the `ValueTask` has completed, and that same `ValueTask` cannot be awaited or converted to a task.

At the risk of being repetitive, when your code calls a method returning `ValueTask` or `ValueTask<T>`, it should either immediately `await` that `ValueTask` or immediately call `AsTask` to convert it to a `Task`. This simple guideline doesn't cover all the advanced scenarios, but most applications will never need to do more than that.

See Also

Recipe 2.10 covers how to return `ValueTask<T>` and `ValueTask` values from your methods.

Recipes 2.4 and 2.5 cover waiting for multiple tasks simultaneously.

CHAPTER 3

Asynchronous Streams

Asynchronous streams are a way to asynchronously receive multiple data items. They're built on *asynchronous enumerables* (IAsyncEnumerable<T>). An asynchronous enumerable is an asynchronous version of an enumerable; that is, it can produce items on demand for a consumer, and each item may be produced asynchronously.

I find it useful to contrast asynchronous streams with other types that may be more familiar and to consider the differences. This helps me remember when to use asynchronous streams and when other types would be more appropriate.

Asynchronous Streams and Task<T>

The standard asynchronous approach with Task<T> is only sufficient for asynchronously handling a single data value. Once a given Task<T> completes, that's it; a single Task<T> cannot provide more than one value of T for its consumers. Even if T is a collection, the value can only be provided once. See "Introduction to Asynchronous Programming" on page 3 and Chapter 2 for more on using async with Task<T>.

When comparing Task<T> to asynchronous streams, the asynchronous streams are more similar to enumerables. Specifically, an IAsyncEnumerator<T> may provide any number of T values, one at a time. Like IEnumerator<T>, an IAsyncEnumerator<T> may be infinite in length.

Asynchronous Streams and IEnumerable<T>

IAsyncEnumerable<T>, as the name would imply, is similar to IEnumerable<T>. This is perhaps not a surprise; they both enable consumers to retrieve elements from them one at a time. The big difference is in the name: one is asynchronous and the other is not.

When your code iterates over an IEnumerable<T>, it blocks as it retrieves each element from the enumerable. If the IEnumerable<T> is representing some I/O-bound operation, such as a database query or API call, then the consuming code ends up blocking on I/O, which is not ideal. IAsyncEnumerable<T> works just like an IEnumerable<T>, except that it asynchronously retrieves each next element.

Asynchronous Streams and Task<IEnumerable<T>>

It is entirely possible to asynchronously return a collection with more than one item; one common example is Task<List<T>>. Still, async methods that return List<T> only get one return statement; the collection must be completely populated before it is returned. Even methods returning Task<IEnumerable<T>> may asynchronously return an enumerable, but then that enumerable is evaluated synchronously. Consider that LINQ-to-Entities has a ToListAsync LINQ method that returns Task<List<T>>. When a LINQ provider executes this, it has to communicate with the database and get *all* the matching responses back before it can finish populating the list and return it.

The limitation of Task<IEnumerable<T>> is that it cannot return items as it gets them; if returning a collection, it has to load all of its items into memory, populate the collection, and then return the entire collection all at once. Even if it returns a LINQ query, it can asynchronously build that query, but once the query is returned, each item is retrieved from that query synchronously. IAsyncEnumerable<T> also returns multiple items asynchronously, but the difference is that IAsyncEnumerable<T> can act asynchronously for *each* item returned. It's a true asynchronous stream of items.

Asynchronous Streams and IObservable<T>

Observables are a true notion of asynchronous streams; they produce their notifications one at a time with true support for asynchronous production (no blocking). But the consumption pattern for IObservable<T> is completely different than that of IAsyncEnumerable<T>. See Chapter 6 for more details about IObservable<T>.

To consume an IObservable<T>, code needs to define a LINQ-like query through which the observable notifications will flow, and then subscribe to the observable in order to start the flow. When working with observables, the code first defines how it will *react* to the incoming notifications, and then it turns them on (hence the name "reactive"). In contrast, consuming an IAsyncEnumerable<T> is done very similarly to consuming an IEnumerable<T>, except that the consumption is asynchronous.

There is also a backpressure problem; all notifications in System.Reactive are synchronous, so as soon as one item notification is sent to its subscribers, the observable continues execution and retrieves the next item to publish, possibly calling the API again. If the consuming code is consuming the stream asynchronously (i.e., doing some asynchronous action for each notification as it arrives), then the observable will race ahead of the consuming code.

A nice way of thinking about the difference between them is that IObservable<T> is push-based and IAsyncEnumerable<T> is pull-based. An observable stream will push notifications at your code, but an asynchronous stream will passively let your code (asynchronously) pull data items out of it. Only when the consuming code requests the next item does the observable stream resume execution.

Summary

A theoretical example may be useful. Many APIs take offset and limit parameters to enable paging of results. Let's say we wanted to define a method that retrieves results from an API that does paging, and we want our method to handle the paging so that our higher-level methods don't have to deal with that.

If our method returns Task<T>, we are limited to returning only a single T. This is fine for a single call to the API where the T is the result of the API, but it doesn't work well as a return type if we want our method to call the API multiple times.

If our method returns IEnumerable<T>, we can create a loop, paging through the API results by calling it multiple times. Each time the method calls the API, it would yield return the results of that page. Further API calls are only necessary if the enumeration continues. Unfortunately, methods returning IEnumerable<T> cannot be asynchronous, so all our API calls are forced to be synchronous.

If our method returns Task<List<T>>, then we can have a loop that pages through the API results, calling the API asynchronously. However, the code cannot return each item as it gets the response; it would have to build up all the results and return them all at once.

If our method returns IObservable<T>, we can use System.Reactive to implement an observable stream that begins requests when subscribed to and publishes each item as we get them. The abstraction is push-based; it appears to consuming code that the API results are being pushed to them, which is more awkward to handle. IObservable<T> would be a better fit for scenarios like receiving and responding to WebSocket/SignalR messages.

If our method returns IAsyncEnumerable<T>, we can have a natural loop that uses both await and yield return to create a true pull-based asynchronous stream. IAsyncEnumerable<T> is the natural fit for this kind of scenario.

Table 3-1 summarizes the different roles of common types.

Table 3-1. Type classifications

Type	Single or multiple value	Asynchronous or synchronous	Push or pull
T	Single value	Synchronous	N/A
IEnumerable<T>	Multiple values	Synchronous	N/A
Task<T>	Single value	Asynchronous	Pull
IAsyncEnumerable<T>	Multiple values	Asynchronous	Pull
IObservable<T>	Single or multiple	Asynchronous	Push

 As this book goes to press, .NET Core 3.0 is still in beta, so the details around asynchronous streams may change.

3.1 Creating Asynchronous Streams

Problem

You need to return multiple values, and each value may require some asynchronous work. This point is commonly reached from one of two paths:

- You have multiple values to return (as an IEnumerable<T>), and then need to add asynchronous work.

- You have a single asynchronous return (as a Task<T>), and then need to add other return values.

Solution

Returning multiple values from a method can be done with `yield return`, and asynchronous methods use `async` and `await`. With asynchronous streams, you can combine these two; just use a return type of IAsyncEnumerable<T>:

```
async IAsyncEnumerable<int> GetValuesAsync()
{
  await Task.Delay(1000); // some asynchronous work
  yield return 10;
  await Task.Delay(1000); // more asynchronous work
  yield return 13;
}
```

This simple example illustrates how `await` can be used with `yield return` to create an asynchronous stream.

A more real-world example is asynchronously enumerating over all the results of an API that uses parameters for paging:

```
async IAsyncEnumerable<string> GetValuesAsync(HttpClient client)
{
  int offset = 0;
  const int limit = 10;
  while (true)
  {
    // Get the current page of results and parse them.
    string result = await client.GetStringAsync(
        $"https://example.com/api/values?offset={offset}&limit={limit}");
    string[] valuesOnThisPage = result.Split('\n');

    // Produce the results for this page.
    foreach (string value in valuesOnThisPage)
      yield return value;

    // If this is the last page, we're done.
    if (valuesOnThisPage.Length != limit)
      break;

    // Otherwise, proceed to the next page.
    offset += limit;
  }
}
```

When GetValuesAsync starts, it does an asynchronous request for the first page of data, and then produces the first element. When the second element is then requested, GetValuesAsync produces it immediately, since it is also in that same first page of data. The next element is also in that page, and so on, up to 10 elements. Then, when the 11th element is requested, all the values in valuesOnThisPage will have been produced, so there are no more elements on the first page. GetValuesAsync will continue executing its while loop, proceed to the next page, do an asynchronous request for the second page of data, receive back a new batch of values, and then it'll produce the 11th element.

Discussion

Ever since async and await were introduced, users have been wondering how to use them with yield return. For many years, that wasn't possible, but asynchronous streams has now brought this capability to C# and modern versions of .NET.

One thing you may notice with the more realistic example is that only some of the results need any asynchronous work. In that example, with a page length of 10, only about 1 out of every 10 elements will need asynchronous work. If the page size is 20, then only 1 out of every 20 elements will need asynchronous work.

This is a normal pattern with asynchronous streams. For many streams, the majority of asynchronous iteration is actually synchronous; asynchronous streams merely *allow* any next item to be retrieved asynchronously. Asynchronous streams were designed with both asynchronous and synchronous code in mind; this is why asynchronous streams are built on `ValueTask<T>`. By using `ValueTask<T>` under the hood, asynchronous streams maximize their efficiency, whether items are retrieved synchronously or asynchronously. See Recipe 2.10 for more about `ValueTask<T>` and when it is appropriate to use.

When you do implement asynchronous streams, consider supporting cancellation. See Recipe 3.4 for a detailed discussion of cancellation with asynchronous streams. Some scenarios do not require actual cancellation; the consuming code can always choose not to retrieve the next element. That is a perfectly fine approach if there's no external source for the cancellation. If you have an asynchronous stream where you want to cancel the asynchronous stream, even if it's in the middle of getting the next element, then you'd want to support proper cancellation using a `CancellationToken`.

See Also

Recipe 3.2 covers consuming asynchronous streams.

Recipe 3.4 covers handling cancellation for asynchronous streams.

Recipe 2.10 has more detail about `ValueTask<T>` and when it is appropriate to use.

3.2 Consuming Asynchronous Streams

Problem

You need to process the results of an asynchronous stream, also known as an asynchronous enumerable.

Solution

Consuming an asynchronous operation is done via `await`, and consuming an enumerable is usually done via `foreach`. Consuming an asynchronous enumerable is done by combining these two into `await foreach`. For example, given an asynchronous enumerable that pages over API responses, you can consume it and write each element to the console:

```
IAsyncEnumerable<string> GetValuesAsync(HttpClient client);

public async Task ProcessValueAsync(HttpClient client)
{
  await foreach (string value in GetValuesAsync(client))
  {
```

```
    Console.WriteLine(value);
  }
}
```

Conceptually, what is happening here is that `GetValuesAsync` is invoked, and it returns an `IAsyncEnumerable<T>`. The `foreach` then creates an asynchronous enumerator from that asynchronous enumerable. Asynchronous enumerators are logically similar to regular enumerators, except that their "get next element" operation may be asynchronous. So, the `await foreach` will `await` for the next element to arrive or for the asynchronous enumerator to complete. If an element arrived, `await foreach` will execute its loop body; if the asynchronous enumerator is complete, then the loop will exit.

It is also natural to do asynchronous processing of each element:

```
IAsyncEnumerable<string> GetValuesAsync(HttpClient client);

public async Task ProcessValueAsync(HttpClient client)
{
  await foreach (string value in GetValuesAsync(client))
  {
    await Task.Delay(100); // asynchronous work
    Console.WriteLine(value);
  }
}
```

In this case, the `await foreach` won't proceed to the next element until the loop body is complete. So, the `await foreach` will asynchronously receive the first element, then asynchronously execute the loop body for that first element, then asynchronously receive the next element, then asynchronously execute the loop body for that next element, and so on.

There is an `await` buried in the `await foreach`: the "get next element" operation is awaited. With a regular `await`, you can avoid the implicitly captured context by using `ConfigureAwait(false)`, as described in Recipe 2.7. Asynchronous streams also support `ConfigureAwait(false)`, which is passed to the hidden `await` statements:

```
IAsyncEnumerable<string> GetValuesAsync(HttpClient client);

public async Task ProcessValueAsync(HttpClient client)
{
  await foreach (string value in GetValuesAsync(client).ConfigureAwait(false))
  {
    await Task.Delay(100).ConfigureAwait(false); // asynchronous work
    Console.WriteLine(value);
  }
}
```

Discussion

`await foreach` is the most natural way to consume asynchronous streams. The language supports `ConfigureAwait(false)` for avoiding context in `await foreach`.

It's also possible to pass in cancellation tokens; this is a bit more advanced due to the complexity of asynchronous streams, so you can find it covered in Recipe 3.4.

While it's possible and natural to use `await foreach` to consume asynchronous streams, there's an exhaustive library of asynchronous LINQ operators available; some of the more popular ones are covered in Recipe 3.3.

The body of `await foreach` can be either synchronous or asynchronous. For the asynchronous example in particular, this is something that is much trickier to get right when working with other streaming abstractions, such as `IObservable<T>`. This is because observable subscriptions must be synchronous, but `await foreach` permits natural asynchronous processing.

The `await foreach` generates an `await` used for the "get next element" operation; it also generates an `await` used to asynchronously dispose the enumerable.

See Also

Recipe 3.1 covers producing asynchronous streams.

Recipe 3.4 covers handling cancellation for asynchronous streams.

Recipe 3.3 covers common LINQ methods for asynchronous streams.

Recipe 11.6 covers asynchronous disposal.

3.3 Using LINQ with Asynchronous Streams

Problem

You want to process an asynchronous stream using well-defined and well-tested operators.

Solution

`IEnumerable<T>` has LINQ to Objects, and `IObservable<T>` has LINQ to Events. Both of these have libraries of extension methods that define operators you can use to build queries. `IAsyncEnumerable<T>` also has LINQ support, provided by the .NET community in the `System.Linq.Async` NuGet package.

As an example, one of the common questions about LINQ is how to use the `Where` operator if the predicate for `Where` is asynchronous. In other words, you want to filter a sequence based on some asynchronous condition—e.g., you need to look up each element in a database or API to see if it should be included in the result sequence. Where doesn't work with an asynchronous condition because the Where operator requires that its delegate return an immediate, synchronous answer.

Asynchronous streams have a support library that defines many useful operators. In the following example, WhereAwait is the proper choice:

```
IAsyncEnumerable<int> values = SlowRange().WhereAwait(
    async value =>
    {
      // Do some asynchronous work to determine
      //  if this element should be included.
      await Task.Delay(10);
      return value % 2 == 0;
    });

await foreach (int result in values)
{
  Console.WriteLine(result);
}

// Produce sequence that slows down as it progresses.
async IAsyncEnumerable<int> SlowRange()
{
  for (int i = 0; i != 10; ++i)
  {
    await Task.Delay(i * 100);
    yield return i;
  }
}
```

LINQ operators for asynchronous streams also include synchronous versions; it does make sense to apply a synchronous Where (or Select, or whatever) to an asynchronous stream. The result is still an asynchronous stream:

```
IAsyncEnumerable<int> values = SlowRange().Where(
    value => value % 2 == 0);

await foreach (int result in values)
{
  Console.WriteLine(result);
}
```

All of your old LINQ friends are here: Where, Select, SelectMany, and even Join. Most LINQ operators now also take asynchronous delegates, like the WhereAwait example above.

Discussion

Asynchronous streams are pull-based, so there's no time-related operators like there are for observables. `Throttle` and `Sample` don't make sense in this world, since the elements are pulled out of the asynchronous stream on demand.

LINQ methods for asynchronous streams can also be useful for regular enumerables. If you find yourself in this situation, you can call `ToAsyncEnumerable()` on any `IEnumerable<T>`, and then you'll have an asynchronous stream interface that you can use with `WhereAwait`, `SelectAwait`, and other operators that support asynchronous delegates.

Before you dive in, a word on naming is in order. The example in this recipe used `WhereAwait` as the asynchronous equivalent of `Where`. As you explore the LINQ operators for asynchronous streams, you'll find that some end in `Async` and others end in `Await`. The operators that end in `Async` return an awaitable; they represent a regular value, not an asynchronous sequence. The operators that end in `Await` take an asynchronous delegate; the `Await` in their name implies that they actually perform an `await` on the delegate you pass to them.

We already looked at an example of the `Await` suffix with `Where` and `WhereAwait`. The `Async` suffix only applies to *termination operators*—operators that extract some value or perform some calculation and return an asynchronous scalar value instead of an asynchronous sequence. An example of a termination operator is `CountAsync`, the asynchronous stream version of `Count`, which can count the number of elements that match some predicate:

```
int count = await SlowRange().CountAsync(
    value => value % 2 == 0);
```

That predicate can *also* be asynchronous, in which case you would then use the `CountAwaitAsync` operator, since it both takes an asynchronous delegate (which it will `await`) and produces a single terminal value, the count:

```
int count = await SlowRange().CountAwaitAsync(
    async value =>
    {
        await Task.Delay(10);
        return value % 2 == 0;
    });
```

In summary, operators that can take delegates have two names: one with an `Await` suffix and one without. In addition, operators that return a terminal value rather than an asynchronous stream end in `Async`. If an operator takes an asynchronous delegate *and* returns a terminal value, then it has both suffixes.

The LINQ operators for asynchronous streams are in the NuGet package for `System.Linq.Async` (*http://bit.ly/sys-linq-async*). Additional LINQ operators for asynchronous streams can be found in the NuGet package for `System.Interactive.Async` (*http://bit.ly/sys-int-async*).

See Also

Recipe 3.1 covers producing asynchronous streams.

Recipe 3.2 covers consuming asynchronous streams.

3.4 Asynchronous Streams and Cancellation

Problem

You want a way to cancel asynchronous streams.

Solution

Not all asynchronous streams require cancellation. It's possible to simply stop enumerating when a condition is reached. If that is the only kind of "cancellation" necessary, then a true cancellation isn't required, as the following example shows:

```
await foreach (int result in SlowRange())
{
  Console.WriteLine(result);
  if (result >= 8)
    break;
}

// Produce sequence that slows down as it progresses.
async IAsyncEnumerable<int> SlowRange()
{
  for (int i = 0; i != 10; ++i)
  {
    await Task.Delay(i * 100);
    yield return i;
  }
}
```

That said, it's often useful to cancel asynchronous streams, as some operators pass cancellation tokens to their source streams. In this scenario, you' would want to use a `CancellationToken` to stop the `await foreach` from external code.

An `async` method returning `IAsyncEnumerable<T>` may take a cancellation token by defining a parameter marked with the `EnumeratorCancellation` attribute. It can then use the token naturally, which is usually done by passing it to other APIs that take cancellation tokens, like this:

```
using var cts = new CancellationTokenSource(500);
CancellationToken token = cts.Token;
await foreach (int result in SlowRange(token))
{
  Console.WriteLine(result);
}

// Produce sequence that slows down as it progresses.
async IAsyncEnumerable<int> SlowRange(
    [EnumeratorCancellation] CancellationToken token = default)
{
  for (int i = 0; i != 10; ++i)
  {
    await Task.Delay(i * 100, token);
    yield return i;
  }
}
```

Discussion

The example solution here passes the `CancellationToken` directly to the method returning the asynchronous enumerator. This is the most common usage.

There are other scenarios where your code will be given an asynchronous enumerator and will want to apply a `CancellationToken` to the enumerators it uses. Cancellation tokens are used when starting a new enumeration of an enumerable, so it makes sense to apply a `CancellationToken` in this way. The enumerable itself is *defined* by the `SlowRange` method, but it's not started until it is consumed. There are even some scenarios where different cancellation tokens should be passed to different enumerations of the enumerable.

Briefly; it is not the enumerable that is cancelable, but the enumerator created by that enumerable. This is an uncommon but important use case, and it's the reason asynchronous streams support a `WithCancellation` extension method that you can use to attach a `CancellationToken` to a specific iteration of an asynchronous stream:

```
async Task ConsumeSequence(IAsyncEnumerable<int> items)
{
  using var cts = new CancellationTokenSource(500);
  CancellationToken token = cts.Token;
  await foreach (int result in items.WithCancellation(token))
  {
    Console.WriteLine(result);
  }
}

// Produce sequence that slows down as it progresses.
```

```
async IAsyncEnumerable<int> SlowRange(
    [EnumeratorCancellation] CancellationToken token = default)
{
  for (int i = 0; i != 10; ++i)
  {
    await Task.Delay(i * 100, token);
    yield return i;
  }
}

await ConsumeSequence(SlowRange());
```

With the EnumeratorCancellation parameter attribute in place, the compiler takes care of passing the token from WithCancellation to the token parameter marked by EnumeratorCancellation, and the cancellation request now causes await foreach to raise an OperationCanceledException after it has processed the first few items.

The WithCancellation extension method doesn't prevent ConfigureAwait(false). Both extension methods can be chained together:

```
async Task ConsumeSequence(IAsyncEnumerable<int> items)
{
  using var cts = new CancellationTokenSource(500);
  CancellationToken token = cts.Token;
  await foreach (int result in items
      .WithCancellation(token).ConfigureAwait(false))
  {
    Console.WriteLine(result);
  }
}
```

See Also

Recipe 3.1 covers producing asynchronous streams.

Recipe 3.2 covers consuming asynchronous streams.

Chapter 10 covers cooperative cancellation across multiple technologies.

CHAPTER 4

Parallel Basics

This chapter covers patterns for parallel programming. Parallel programming is used to split up CPU-bound pieces of work and divide them among multiple threads. These parallel processing recipes only consider CPU-bound work. If you have naturally asynchronous operations (such as I/O-bound work) that you want to execute in parallel, then see Chapter 2, and Recipe 2.4 in particular.

The parallel processing abstractions covered in this chapter are part of the Task Parallel Library (TPL). The TPL is built into the .NET framework.

4.1 Parallel Processing of Data

Problem

You have a collection of data, and you need to perform the same operation on each element of the data. This operation is CPU-bound and may take some time.

Solution

The `Parallel` type contains a `ForEach` method specifically designed for this problem. The following example takes a collection of matrices and rotates them all:

```
void RotateMatrices(IEnumerable<Matrix> matrices, float degrees)
{
  Parallel.ForEach(matrices, matrix => matrix.Rotate(degrees));
}
```

There are some situations where you'll want to stop the loop early, such as if you encounter an invalid value. The following example inverts each matrix, but if an invalid matrix is encountered, it'll abort the loop:

```
void InvertMatrices(IEnumerable<Matrix> matrices)
{
  Parallel.ForEach(matrices, (matrix, state) =>
  {
    if (!matrix.IsInvertible)
      state.Stop();
    else
      matrix.Invert();
  });
}
```

This code uses `ParallelLoopState.Stop` to stop the loop, preventing any further invocations of the loop body. Bear in mind that this is a parallel loop, so other invocations of the loop body may already be running, including invocations for items after the current item. In this code example, if the third matrix isn't invertible, the loop is stopped and no new matrixes will be processed, but other matrixes (such as the fourth and fifth) may already be processing.

A more common situation is when you want the ability to cancel a parallel loop. This is different than stopping the loop; a loop is *stopped* from inside the loop, and it is *canceled* from outside the loop. To show an example, a cancel button may cancel a `CancellationTokenSource`, canceling a parallel loop as in this code example:

```
void RotateMatrices(IEnumerable<Matrix> matrices, float degrees,
    CancellationToken token)
{
  Parallel.ForEach(matrices,
      new ParallelOptions { CancellationToken = token },
      matrix => matrix.Rotate(degrees));
}
```

One thing to keep in mind is that each parallel task may run on a different thread, so any shared state must be protected. The following example inverts each matrix and counts the number of matrices that couldn't be inverted:

```
// Note: this is not the most efficient implementation.
// This is just an example of using a lock to protect shared state.
int InvertMatrices(IEnumerable<Matrix> matrices)
{
  object mutex = new object();
  int nonInvertibleCount = 0;
  Parallel.ForEach(matrices, matrix =>
  {
    if (matrix.IsInvertible)
    {
      matrix.Invert();
    }
    else
    {
      lock (mutex)
      {
```

```
        ++nonInvertibleCount;
      }
    }
  });
  return nonInvertibleCount;
}
```

Discussion

The `Parallel.ForEach` method enables parallel processing over a sequence of values. A similar solution is Parallel LINQ (PLINQ), which provides much of the same capabilities with a LINQ-like syntax. One difference between `Parallel` and PLINQ is that PLINQ assumes it can use all the cores on the computer, while `Parallel` will dynamically react to changing CPU conditions.

`Parallel.ForEach` is a parallel `foreach` loop. If you need to do a parallel `for` loop, the `Parallel` class also supports a `Parallel.For` method. `Parallel.For` is especially useful if you have multiple arrays of data that all take the same index.

See Also

Recipe 4.2 covers aggregating a series of values in parallel, including sums and averages.

Recipe 4.5 covers the basics of PLINQ.

Chapter 10 covers cancellation.

4.2 Parallel Aggregation

Problem

At the conclusion of a parallel operation, you need to aggregate the results. Examples of aggregation are summing up values or finding their average.

Solution

The `Parallel` class supports aggregation through the concept of *local values*, which are variables that exist locally within a parallel loop. This means that the body of the loop can just access the value directly, without needing synchronization. When the loop is ready to aggregate each of its local results, it does so with the `localFinally` delegate. Note that the `localFinally` delegate *does* need to synchronize access to the variable that holds the final result. Here's an example of a parallel sum:

```
// Note: this is not the most efficient implementation.
// This is just an example of using a lock to protect shared state.
int ParallelSum(IEnumerable<int> values)
```

```
{
  object mutex = new object();
  int result = 0;
  Parallel.ForEach(source: values,
      localInit: () => 0,
      body: (item, state, localValue) => localValue + item,
      localFinally: localValue =>
      {
        lock (mutex)
          result += localValue;
      });
  return result;
}
```

Parallel LINQ has more natural aggregation support than the `Parallel` class:

```
int ParallelSum(IEnumerable<int> values)
{
  return values.AsParallel().Sum();
}
```

OK, that was a cheap shot, since PLINQ has built-in support for many common operators (for example, `Sum`). PLINQ also has generic aggregation support via the `Aggregate` operator:

```
int ParallelSum(IEnumerable<int> values)
{
  return values.AsParallel().Aggregate(
      seed: 0,
      func: (sum, item) => sum + item
  );
}
```

Discussion

If you're already using the `Parallel` class, you may want to use its aggregation support. Otherwise, in most scenarios, the PLINQ support is more expressive and has shorter code.

See Also

Recipe 4.5 covers the basics of PLINQ.

4.3 Parallel Invocation

Problem

You have a number of methods to call in parallel, and these methods are (mostly) independent of one another.

Solution

The `Parallel` class contains a simple `Invoke` member that is designed for this scenario. This example splits an array in half and processes each half independently:

```
void ProcessArray(double[] array)
{
  Parallel.Invoke(
      () => ProcessPartialArray(array, 0, array.Length / 2),
      () => ProcessPartialArray(array, array.Length / 2, array.Length)
  );
}

void ProcessPartialArray(double[] array, int begin, int end)
{
  // CPU-intensive processing...
}
```

You can also pass an array of delegates to the `Parallel.Invoke` method if the number of invocations isn't known until runtime:

```
void DoAction20Times(Action action)
{
  Action[] actions = Enumerable.Repeat(action, 20).ToArray();
  Parallel.Invoke(actions);
}
```

`Parallel.Invoke` supports cancellation just like the other members of the `Parallel` class:

```
void DoAction20Times(Action action, CancellationToken token)
{
  Action[] actions = Enumerable.Repeat(action, 20).ToArray();
  Parallel.Invoke(new ParallelOptions { CancellationToken = token }, actions);
}
```

Discussion

`Parallel.Invoke` is a great solution for simple parallel invocation. Note that it will not be a perfect fit if you want to invoke an action for each item of input data (use `Parallel.ForEach` instead) or if each action produces some output (use Parallel LINQ instead).

See Also

Recipe 4.1 covers `Parallel.ForEach`, which invokes an action for each item of data.

Recipe 4.5 covers Parallel LINQ.

4.4 Dynamic Parallelism

Problem

You have a more complex parallel situation where the structure and number of parallel tasks depend on information known only at runtime.

Solution

The Task Parallel Library (TPL) is centered around the `Task` type. The `Parallel` class and Parallel LINQ are just convenience wrappers around the powerful `Task`. When you need dynamic parallelism, it's easiest to use the `Task` type directly.

Here is an example in which some expensive processing needs to be done for each node of a binary tree. The structure of the tree won't be known until runtime, so this is a good scenario for dynamic parallelism. The `Traverse` method processes the current node and then creates two child tasks, one for each branch underneath the node (for this example, I'm assuming that the parent nodes must be processed before the children). The `ProcessTree` method starts the processing by creating a top-level parent task and waiting for it to complete:

```
void Traverse(Node current)
{
  DoExpensiveActionOnNode(current);
  if (current.Left != null)
  {
    Task.Factory.StartNew(
        () => Traverse(current.Left),
        CancellationToken.None,
        TaskCreationOptions.AttachedToParent,
        TaskScheduler.Default);
  }
  if (current.Right != null)
  {
    Task.Factory.StartNew(
        () => Traverse(current.Right),
        CancellationToken.None,
        TaskCreationOptions.AttachedToParent,
        TaskScheduler.Default);
  }
}

void ProcessTree(Node root)
{
  Task task = Task.Factory.StartNew(
      () => Traverse(root),
      CancellationToken.None,
      TaskCreationOptions.None,
      TaskScheduler.Default);
```

```
    task.Wait();
}
```

The `AttachedToParent` flag ensures that the `Task` for each branch is linked to the `Task` for their parent node. This creates parent/child relationships among the `Task` instances that mirror the parent/child relationships in the tree nodes. Parent tasks execute their delegate and then wait for their child tasks to complete. Exceptions from child tasks are then propagated from the child tasks to their parent task. So, `ProcessTree` can wait for the tasks for the entire tree just by calling `Wait` on the single `Task` at the root of the tree.

If you don't have a parent/child kind of situation, you can schedule any task to run after another by using a task *continuation*. The continuation is a separate task that executes when the original task completes:

```
Task task = Task.Factory.StartNew(
    () => Thread.Sleep(TimeSpan.FromSeconds(2)),
    CancellationToken.None,
    TaskCreationOptions.None,
    TaskScheduler.Default);
Task continuation = task.ContinueWith(
    t => Trace.WriteLine("Task is done"),
    CancellationToken.None,
    TaskContinuationOptions.None,
    TaskScheduler.Default);
// The "t" argument to the continuation is the same as "task".
```

Discussion

`CancellationToken.None` and `TaskScheduler.Default` are used in the preceding code example. Cancellation tokens are covered in Recipe 10.2, and task schedulers are covered in Recipe 13.3. It's always a good idea to explicitly specify the `TaskScheduler` used by `StartNew` and `ContinueWith`.

This arrangement of parent and child tasks is common with dynamic parallelism, although it's not required. It's equally possible to store each new task in a threadsafe collection and then wait for them all to complete using `Task.WaitAll`.

 Using `Task` for parallel processing is completely different than using `Task` for asynchronous processing.

The `Task` type serves two purposes in concurrent programming: it can be a parallel task or an asynchronous task. Parallel tasks may use blocking members, such as `Task.Wait`, `Task.Result`, `Task.WaitAll`, and `Task.WaitAny`. Parallel tasks also commonly use `AttachedToParent` to create parent/child relationships between tasks. Parallel tasks should be created with `Task.Run` or `Task.Factory.StartNew`.

In contrast, asynchronous tasks should avoid blocking members, and prefer `await`, `Task.WhenAll`, and `Task.WhenAny`. Asynchronous tasks should not use `AttachedToParent`, but they can form an implicit kind of parent/child relationship by awaiting another task.

See Also

Recipe 4.3 covers invoking a sequence of methods in parallel, when all the methods are known at the start of the parallel work.

4.5 Parallel LINQ

Problem

You need to perform parallel processing on a sequence of data to produce another sequence of data or a summary of that data.

Solution

Most developers are familiar with LINQ, which you can use to write pull-based calculations over sequences. Parallel LINQ (PLINQ) extends this LINQ support with parallel processing.

PLINQ works well in streaming scenarios, when you have a sequence of inputs and are producing a sequence of outputs. Here's a simple example that just multiplies each element in a sequence by two (real-world scenarios will be much more CPU-intensive than a simple multiply):

```
IEnumerable<int> MultiplyBy2(IEnumerable<int> values)
{
  return values.AsParallel().Select(value => value * 2);
}
```

The example may produce its outputs in any order; this behavior is the default for Parallel LINQ. You can also specify the order to be preserved. The following example is still processed in parallel, but it preserves the original order:

```
IEnumerable<int> MultiplyBy2(IEnumerable<int> values)
{
  return values.AsParallel().AsOrdered().Select(value => value * 2);
}
```

Another natural use of Parallel LINQ is to aggregate or summarize the data in parallel. The following code performs a parallel summation:

```
int ParallelSum(IEnumerable<int> values)
{
  return values.AsParallel().Sum();
}
```

Discussion

The `Parallel` class is good for many scenarios, but PLINQ code is simpler when doing aggregation or transforming one sequence to another. Bear in mind that the `Parallel` class is more friendly to other processes on the system than PLINQ; this is especially a consideration if the parallel processing is done on a server machine.

PLINQ provides parallel versions of a wide variety of operators, including filtering (`Where`), projection (`Select`), and a variety of aggregations, such as `Sum`, `Average`, and the more generic `Aggregate`. In general, anything you can do with regular LINQ you can do in parallel with PLINQ. This makes PLINQ a great choice if you have existing LINQ code that would benefit from running in parallel.

See Also

Recipe 4.1 covers how to use the `Parallel` class to execute code for each element in a sequence.

Recipe 10.5 covers how to cancel PLINQ queries.

CHAPTER 5

Dataflow Basics

TPL Dataflow is a powerful library that enables you to create a mesh or pipeline and then (asynchronously) send your data through it. Dataflow is a very declarative style of coding: normally, you completely define the mesh first and then start processing data. The mesh ends up being a structure through which your data flows. This requires you to think about your application a bit differently, but once you make that leap, dataflow becomes a natural fit for many scenarios.

Each mesh is comprised of various blocks that are linked to each other. The individual blocks are simple and are responsible for a single step in the data processing. When a block finishes working on its data, it will pass its result along to any linked blocks.

To use TPL Dataflow, install the NuGet package System.Threading.Tasks.Dataflow (*http://bit.ly/nuget-df*) into your application.

5.1 Linking Blocks

Problem

You need to link dataflow blocks to one another to create a mesh.

Solution

The blocks provided by the TPL Dataflow library define only the most basic members. Many of the useful TPL Dataflow methods are actually extension methods. The LinkTo extension method provides an easy way to link dataflow blocks together:

```
var multiplyBlock = new TransformBlock<int, int>(item => item * 2);
var subtractBlock = new TransformBlock<int, int>(item => item - 2);
```

```
// After linking, values that exit multiplyBlock will enter subtractBlock.
multiplyBlock.LinkTo(subtractBlock);
```

By default, linked dataflow blocks only propagate data; they do not propagate completion (or errors). If your dataflow is linear (like a pipeline), then you will probably want to propagate completion. To propagate completion (and errors), you can set the PropagateCompletion option on the link:

```
var multiplyBlock = new TransformBlock<int, int>(item => item * 2);
var subtractBlock = new TransformBlock<int, int>(item => item - 2);

var options = new DataflowLinkOptions { PropagateCompletion = true };
multiplyBlock.LinkTo(subtractBlock, options);

...

// The first block's completion is automatically propagated to the second block.
multiplyBlock.Complete();
await subtractBlock.Completion;
```

Discussion

Once linked, data will flow automatically from the source block to the target block. The PropagateCompletion option flows completion in addition to data; however, at each step in the pipeline, a faulting block will propagate its exception to the next block wrapped in an AggregateException. So, if you have a long pipeline that propagates completions, the original error may be nested in multiple AggregateException instances. AggregateException has several members, such as Flatten, that assist with error handling in this situation.

It is possible to link dataflow blocks in many ways; your mesh can have forks and joins and even loops. However, the simple, linear pipeline is sufficient for most scenarios. We'll be dealing mainly with pipelines (and briefly cover forks); more advanced scenarios are beyond the scope of this book.

The DataflowLinkOptions type gives you several different options you can set on a link (such as the PropagateCompletion option used in this solution), and the LinkTo overload can also take a predicate that you can use to filter which data can go over a link. If data doesn't pass the filter, it is not dropped. Data that passes the filter travels over that link; data that doesn't pass the filter attempts to pass over an alternate link, and stays in the block if there's no other link for it to take. If a data item gets stuck in a block like this, then that block won't produce any other data items; the entire block becomes stalled until that data item is removed.

See Also

Recipe 5.2 covers propagating errors along links.

Recipe 5.3 covers removing links between blocks.

Recipe 8.8 covers how to link dataflow blocks to System.Reactive observable streams.

5.2 Propagating Errors

Problem

You need a way to respond to errors that can happen in your dataflow mesh.

Solution

If a delegate passed to a dataflow block throws an exception, then that block will enter a faulted state. When a block is in a faulted state, it will drop all of its data (and stop accepting new data). The block in the following code will never produce any output data; the first value raises an exception, and the second value is just dropped:

```
var block = new TransformBlock<int, int>(item =>
{
  if (item == 1)
    throw new InvalidOperationException("Blech.");
  return item * 2;
});
block.Post(1);
block.Post(2);
```

To catch exceptions from a dataflow block, you should `await` its `Completion` property. The `Completion` property returns a `Task` that will complete when the block is completed, and if the block faults, the `Completion` task is also faulted:

```
try
{
  var block = new TransformBlock<int, int>(item =>
  {
    if (item == 1)
      throw new InvalidOperationException("Blech.");
    return item * 2;
  });
  block.Post(1);
  await block.Completion;
}
catch (InvalidOperationException)
{
  // The exception is caught here.
}
```

When you propagate completion using the `PropagateCompletion` link option, errors are also propagated. However, the exception is passed to the next block wrapped in an `AggregateException`. The following example catches the exception from the end of a pipeline, so it would catch `AggregateException` if an exception was propagated from earlier blocks:

```
try
{
  var multiplyBlock = new TransformBlock<int, int>(item =>
  {
    if (item == 1)
      throw new InvalidOperationException("Blech.");
    return item * 2;
  });
  var subtractBlock = new TransformBlock<int, int>(item => item - 2);
  multiplyBlock.LinkTo(subtractBlock,
      new DataflowLinkOptions { PropagateCompletion = true });
  multiplyBlock.Post(1);
  await subtractBlock.Completion;
}
catch (AggregateException)
{
  // The exception is caught here.
}
```

Each block wraps incoming errors in an `AggregateException`, even if the incoming error is already an `AggregateException`. If an error occurs early in a pipeline and travels down several links before it's observed, the original error will be wrapped in multiple layers of `AggregateException`. The `AggregateException.Flatten` method simplifies error handling in this scenario.

Discussion

When you build your mesh (or pipeline), consider how errors should be handled. In simpler situations, it can be best to just propagate the errors and catch them once at the end. In more complex meshes, you may need to observe each block when the dataflow has completed.

Alternatively, if you want your blocks to remain viable in the face of exceptions, you can choose to treat exceptions as another kind of data and let them flow through your mesh along with your correctly processed data items. Using that pattern, you can keep your dataflow mesh operational, since the blocks themselves don't fault and continue processing the next data item. See Recipe 14.6 for more details.

See Also

Recipe 5.1 covers establishing links between blocks.

Recipe 5.3 covers breaking links between blocks.

Recipe 14.6 covers flowing exceptions alongside data in a dataflow mesh.

5.3 Unlinking Blocks

Problem

During processing, you need to dynamically change the structure of your dataflow. This is an advanced scenario that is hardly ever needed.

Solution

You can link or unlink dataflow blocks at any time; data can be freely passing through the mesh and it's still safe to link or unlink at any time. Both linking and unlinking are fully threadsafe.

When you create a dataflow block link, keep the IDisposable returned by the LinkTo method, and dispose of it when you want to unlink the blocks:

```
var multiplyBlock = new TransformBlock<int, int>(item => item * 2);
var subtractBlock = new TransformBlock<int, int>(item => item - 2);

IDisposable link = multiplyBlock.LinkTo(subtractBlock);
multiplyBlock.Post(1);
multiplyBlock.Post(2);

// Unlink the blocks.
// The data posted above may or may not have already gone through the link.
// In real-world code, consider a using block rather than calling Dispose.
link.Dispose();
```

Discussion

Unless you can guarantee that the link is idle, there will be race conditions when you unlink it. However, these race conditions are usually not a concern; data will either flow over the link before the link is broken, or it won't. There are no race conditions that would cause duplication or loss of data.

Unlinking is an advanced scenario, but it can be useful in a handful of situations. As one example, there's no way to change the filter for a link. To change the filter on an existing link, you'd have to unlink the old one and create a new link with the new filter (optionally setting DataflowLinkOptions.Append to false). As another example, unlinking at a strategic point can be used to pause a dataflow mesh.

See Also

Recipe 5.1 covers establishing links between blocks.

5.4 Throttling Blocks

Problem

You have a fork scenario in your dataflow mesh and want the data to flow in a load-balancing way.

Solution

By default, when a block produces output data, it'll examine all of its links (in the order they were created) and attempt to flow the data down each link one at a time. Also, by default, each block will maintain an input buffer and accept any amount of data before it's ready to process it.

This causes a problem in a fork scenario, where one source block is linked to two target blocks: the second block is then starved. As the source block produces data, it will try to flow the data down each link. The first target block would always accept the data and buffer it, and so the source block would never try to flow the data to the second target block. This problem can be fixed by throttling the target blocks using the `BoundedCapacity` block option. By default, `BoundedCapacity` is set to `Dataflow BlockOptions.Unbounded`, which causes the first target block to buffer *all* the data even if it isn't ready to process it yet.

`BoundedCapacity` can be set to any value greater than zero (or, of course, `Dataflow BlockOptions.Unbounded`). As long as the target blocks can keep up with the data coming from the source blocks, a simple value of 1 will suffice:

```
var sourceBlock = new BufferBlock<int>();
var options = new DataflowBlockOptions { BoundedCapacity = 1 };
var targetBlockA = new BufferBlock<int>(options);
var targetBlockB = new BufferBlock<int>(options);

sourceBlock.LinkTo(targetBlockA);
sourceBlock.LinkTo(targetBlockB);
```

Discussion

Throttling is useful for load balancing in fork scenarios, but it can be used anywhere else you want throttling behavior. For example, if you're populating your dataflow mesh with data from an I/O operation, you can apply `BoundedCapacity` to the blocks in your mesh. That way, you won't read too much I/O data until your mesh is ready for it, and your mesh won't end up buffering all the input data before it's able to process it.

See Also

Recipe 5.1 covers linking blocks together.

5.5 Parallel Processing with Dataflow Blocks

Problem

You want to perform some parallel processing within your dataflow mesh.

Solution

By default, each dataflow block is independent from each other block. When you link two blocks together, they will process independently. So, every dataflow mesh has some natural parallelism built in.

If you need to go beyond this—for example, if you have one particular block that does heavy CPU computations—then you can instruct that block to operate in parallel on its input data by setting the MaxDegreeOfParallelism option. By default, this option is set to 1, so each dataflow block will only process one piece of data at a time.

BoundedCapacity can be set to DataflowBlockOptions.Unbounded or any value greater than zero. The following example permits any number of tasks to be multiplying data simultaneously:

```
var multiplyBlock = new TransformBlock<int, int>(
    item => item * 2,
    new ExecutionDataflowBlockOptions
    {
      MaxDegreeOfParallelism = DataflowBlockOptions.Unbounded
    });
var subtractBlock = new TransformBlock<int, int>(item => item - 2);
multiplyBlock.LinkTo(subtractBlock);
```

Discussion

The MaxDegreeOfParallelism option makes parallel processing within a block easy to do. What is not so easy is determining which blocks need it. One technique is to pause dataflow execution in the debugger, where you can see the number of data items queued up (i.e., the ones that haven't yet been processed by the block). An unexpected number of data items can be an indication that some restructuring or parallelization would be helpful.

MaxDegreeOfParallelism also works if the dataflow block does asynchronous processing. In this case, the MaxDegreeOfParallelism option specifies the level of concurrency—a certain number of *slots*. Each data item takes up a slot when the block begins processing it and only leaves that slot when the asynchronous processing is fully completed.

See Also

Recipe 5.1 covers linking blocks together.

5.6 Creating Custom Blocks

Problem

You have reusable logic that you want to place into a custom dataflow block. Doing so enables you to create larger blocks that contain complex logic.

Solution

You can cut out any part of a dataflow mesh that has a single input and output block by using the `Encapsulate` method. `Encapsulate` will create a single block out of the two endpoints. Propagating data *and completion* between those endpoints is your responsibility. The following code creates a custom dataflow block out of two blocks, propagating data and completion:

```
IPropagatorBlock<int, int> CreateMyCustomBlock()
{
  var multiplyBlock = new TransformBlock<int, int>(item => item * 2);
  var addBlock = new TransformBlock<int, int>(item => item + 2);
  var divideBlock = new TransformBlock<int, int>(item => item / 2);

  var flowCompletion = new DataflowLinkOptions { PropagateCompletion = true };
  multiplyBlock.LinkTo(addBlock, flowCompletion);
  addBlock.LinkTo(divideBlock, flowCompletion);

  return DataflowBlock.Encapsulate(multiplyBlock, divideBlock);
}
```

Discussion

When you encapsulate a mesh into a custom block, consider what kind of options you want to expose to your users. Consider how each block option should (or shouldn't) be passed on to your inner mesh; in many cases, some block options don't apply or don't make sense. For this reason, it's common for custom blocks to define their own custom options instead of accepting a `DataflowBlockOptions` parameter.

`DataflowBlock.Encapsulate` will only encapsulate a mesh with one input block and one output block. If you have a reusable mesh with multiple inputs and/or outputs, you should encapsulate it within a custom object and expose the inputs and outputs as properties of type `ITargetBlock<T>` (for inputs) and `IReceivableSourceBlock<T>` (for outputs).

These examples all use `Encapsulate` to create a custom block. It is also possible to implement the dataflow interfaces yourself, but it's much more difficult. Microsoft has a paper (*http://bit.ly/tpl-dataflow*) that describes advanced techniques for creating your own custom dataflow blocks.

See Also

Recipe 5.1 covers linking blocks together.

Recipe 5.2 covers propagating errors along block links.

CHAPTER 6

System.Reactive Basics

LINQ is a set of language features that enable developers to query sequences. The two most common LINQ providers are the built-in LINQ to Objects (which is based on `IEnumerable<T>`) and LINQ to Entities (based on `IQueryable<T>`). There are many other providers available, and most providers have the same general structure. Queries are lazily evaluated, and the sequences produce values as necessary. Conceptually, this is a pull model; during evaluation, value items are pulled from the query one at a time.

System.Reactive (Rx) treats events as sequences of data that arrive over time. As such, you can think of Rx as LINQ to Events (based on `IObservable<T>`). The main difference between observables and other LINQ providers is that Rx is a "push" model, meaning that the query defines how the program reacts as events arrive. Rx builds on top of LINQ, adding some powerful new operators as extension methods.

This chapter looks at some of the more common Rx operations. Bear in mind that all of the LINQ operators are also available, so simple operations, such as filtering (`Where`) and projection (`Select`), work conceptually the same as they do with any other LINQ provider. We won't cover these common LINQ operations here; we'll focus on the new capabilities that Rx builds on top of LINQ, particularly those dealing with *time*.

To use System.Reactive, install the NuGet package for `System.Reactive` (*http://bit.ly/sys-reactive*) into your application.

6.1 Converting .NET Events

Problem

You have an event that you need to treat as a System.Reactive input stream, producing some data via OnNext each time the event is raised.

Solution

The Observable class defines several event converters. Most .NET framework events are compatible with FromEventPattern, but if you have events that don't follow the common pattern, you can use FromEvent instead.

FromEventPattern works best if the event delegate type is EventHandler<T>. Many newer framework types use this event delegate type. For example, the Progress<T> type defines a ProgressChanged event, which is of type EventHandler<T>, so it can be easily wrapped with FromEventPattern:

```
var progress = new Progress<int>();
IObservable<EventPattern<int>> progressReports =
    Observable.FromEventPattern<int>(
        handler => progress.ProgressChanged += handler,
        handler => progress.ProgressChanged -= handler);
progressReports.Subscribe(data => Trace.WriteLine("OnNext: " + data.EventArgs));
```

Note here that the data.EventArgs is strongly typed to be an int. The type argument to FromEventPattern (int in the previous example) is the same as the type T in EventHandler<T>. The two lambda arguments to FromEventPattern enable System.Reactive to subscribe and unsubscribe from the event.

The newer user interface frameworks use EventHandler<T>, and can easily be used with FromEventPattern, but older types often define a unique delegate type for each event. These can also be used with FromEventPattern, but it takes a bit more work. For example, the System.Timers.Timer type defines an Elapsed event, which is of type ElapsedEventHandler. You can wrap older events like this with FromEventPattern:

```
var timer = new System.Timers.Timer(interval: 1000) { Enabled = true };
IObservable<EventPattern<ElapsedEventArgs>> ticks =
    Observable.FromEventPattern<ElapsedEventHandler, ElapsedEventArgs>(
        handler => (s, a) => handler(s, a),
        handler => timer.Elapsed += handler,
        handler => timer.Elapsed -= handler);
ticks.Subscribe(data => Trace.WriteLine("OnNext: " + data.EventArgs.SignalTime));
```

Note that in this example that data.EventArgs is still strongly typed. The type arguments to FromEventPattern are now the unique handler type and the derived Even

tArgs type. The first lambda argument to FromEventPattern is a converter from
EventHandler<ElapsedEventArgs> to ElapsedEventHandler; the converter should
do nothing more than pass along the event.

That syntax is definitely getting awkward. Here's another option, which uses reflection:

```
var timer = new System.Timers.Timer(interval: 1000) { Enabled = true };
IObservable<EventPattern<object>> ticks =
    Observable.FromEventPattern(timer, nameof(Timer.Elapsed));
ticks.Subscribe(data => Trace.WriteLine("OnNext: "
    + ((ElapsedEventArgs)data.EventArgs).SignalTime));
```

With this approach, the call to FromEventPattern is much easier. Note that there's
one drawback to this approach: the consumer doesn't get strongly typed data. Because
data.EventArgs is of type object, you have to cast it to ElapsedEventArgs yourself.

Discussion

Events are a common source of data for System.Reactive streams. This recipe covers
wrapping any events that conform to the standard event pattern (where the first argument is the sender and the second argument is the event arguments type). If you have
unusual event types, you can still use the Observable.FromEvent method overloads
to wrap them into an observable.

When events are wrapped into an observable, OnNext is called each time the event is
raised. When you're dealing with AsyncCompletedEventArgs, this can cause surpris-
ing behavior, because any exception is passed along as data (OnNext), not as an error
(OnError). Consider this wrapper for WebClient.DownloadStringCompleted, for
example:

```
var client = new WebClient();
IObservable<EventPattern<object>> downloadedStrings =
    Observable.
    FromEventPattern(client, nameof(WebClient.DownloadStringCompleted));
downloadedStrings.Subscribe(
    data =>
    {
      var eventArgs = (DownloadStringCompletedEventArgs)data.EventArgs;
      if (eventArgs.Error != null)
        Trace.WriteLine("OnNext: (Error) " + eventArgs.Error);
      else
        Trace.WriteLine("OnNext: " + eventArgs.Result);
    },
    ex => Trace.WriteLine("OnError: " + ex.ToString()),
    () => Trace.WriteLine("OnCompleted"));
client.DownloadStringAsync(new Uri("http://invalid.example.com/"));
```

When `WebClient.DownloadStringAsync` completes with an error, the event is raised with an exception in `AsyncCompletedEventArgs.Error`. Unfortunately, System.Reactive sees this as a data event, so if you then run the preceding code you will see `OnNext: (Error)` printed instead of `OnError:`.

Some event subscriptions and unsubscriptions must be done from a particular context. For example, events on many UI controls must be subscribed to from the UI thread. System.Reactive provides an operator that will control the context for subscribing and unsubscribing: `SubscribeOn`. The `SubscribeOn` operator isn't necessary in most situations because most of the time a UI-based subscription is done from the UI thread.

 `SubscribeOn` controls the context for the code that adds and removes the event handlers. Don't confuse this with `ObserveOn`, which controls the context for the observable notifications (the delegates passed to `Subscribe`).

See Also

Recipe 6.2 covers how to change the context in which events are raised.

Recipe 6.4 covers how to throttle events so subscribers aren't overwhelmed.

6.2 Sending Notifications to a Context

Problem

System.Reactive does its best to be thread agnostic. So, it'll raise notifications (e.g., `OnNext`) in whatever thread happens to be current. Each `OnNext` notification will happen sequentially, but not necessarily on the same thread.

You often want these notifications raised in a particular context. For example, UI elements should only be manipulated from the UI thread that owns them, so if you're updating a UI in response to a notification that is arriving on a threadpool thread, then you'll need to move over to the UI thread.

Solution

System.Reactive provides the `ObserveOn` operator to move notifications to another scheduler.

Consider the following example, which uses the `Interval` operator to create `OnNext` notifications once a second:

```
private void Button_Click(object sender, RoutedEventArgs e)
{
  Trace.WriteLine($"UI thread is {Environment.CurrentManagedThreadId}");
  Observable.Interval(TimeSpan.FromSeconds(1))
      .Subscribe(x => Trace.WriteLine(
          $"Interval {x} on thread {Environment.CurrentManagedThreadId}"));
}
```

On my machine, the output looks like the following:

```
UI thread is 9
Interval 0 on thread 10
Interval 1 on thread 10
Interval 2 on thread 11
Interval 3 on thread 11
Interval 4 on thread 10
Interval 5 on thread 11
Interval 6 on thread 11
```

Since `Interval` is based on a timer (without a specific thread), the notifications are raised on a threadpool thread, rather than the UI thread. If you need to update a UI element, you can pipe those notifications through `ObserveOn` and pass a synchronization context representing the UI thread:

```
private void Button_Click(object sender, RoutedEventArgs e)
{
  SynchronizationContext uiContext = SynchronizationContext.Current;
  Trace.WriteLine($"UI thread is {Environment.CurrentManagedThreadId}");
  Observable.Interval(TimeSpan.FromSeconds(1))
      .ObserveOn(uiContext)
      .Subscribe(x => Trace.WriteLine(
          $"Interval {x} on thread {Environment.CurrentManagedThreadId}"));
}
```

Another common usage of `ObserveOn` is to move *off* the UI thread when necessary. Consider a situation where you need to do some CPU-intensive computation whenever the mouse moves. By default, all mouse moves are raised on the UI thread, so you can use `ObserveOn` to move those notifications to a threadpool thread, do the computation, and then move the result notifications back to the UI thread:

```
SynchronizationContext uiContext = SynchronizationContext.Current;
Trace.WriteLine($"UI thread is {Environment.CurrentManagedThreadId}");
Observable.FromEventPattern<MouseEventHandler, MouseEventArgs>(
        handler => (s, a) => handler(s, a),
        handler => MouseMove += handler,
        handler => MouseMove -= handler)
    .Select(evt => evt.EventArgs.GetPosition(this))
    .ObserveOn(Scheduler.Default)
    .Select(position =>
    {
      // Complex calculation
      Thread.Sleep(100);
```

```
    var result = position.X + position.Y;
    var thread = Environment.CurrentManagedThreadId;
    Trace.WriteLine($"Calculated result {result} on thread {thread}");
    return result;
})
.ObserveOn(uiContext)
.Subscribe(x => Trace.WriteLine(
    $"Result {x} on thread {Environment.CurrentManagedThreadId}"));
```

If you execute this sample, you'll see the calculations done on a threadpool thread and the results printed on the UI thread. However, you'll also notice that the calculations and results will lag behind the input; they'll queue up because the mouse location updates more often than every 100 ms. System.Reactive has several techniques for handling this situation; one common one covered in Recipe 6.4 is throttling the input.

Discussion

ObserveOn actually moves notifications to a System.Reactive *scheduler*. This recipe covered the default (thread pool) scheduler and one way of creating a UI scheduler. The most common uses for the ObserveOn operator are moving on or off the UI thread, but schedulers are also useful in other scenarios. A more advanced scenario where schedulers are useful is faking the passage of time when unit testing, which you'll find covered in Recipe 7.6.

 ObserveOn controls the context for the observable notifications. This is not to be confused with SubscribeOn, which controls the context for the code that adds and removes the event handlers.

See Also

Recipe 6.1 covers how to create sequences from events, and using SubscribeOn.

Recipe 6.4 covers throttling event streams.

Recipe 7.6 covers the special scheduler used for testing your System.Reactive code.

6.3 Grouping Event Data with Windows and Buffers

Problem

You have a sequence of events, and you want to group the incoming events as they arrive. As an example, you need to react to pairs of inputs. As another example, you need to react to all inputs within a two-second window.

Solution

System.Reactive provides a pair of operators that group incoming sequences: `Buffer` and `Window`. `Buffer` will hold on to the incoming events until the group is complete, at which time it forwards them all at once as a collection of events. `Window` will logically group the incoming events but will pass them along as they arrive. The return type of `Buffer` is `IObservable<IList<T>>` (an event stream of collections); the return type of `Window` is `IObservable<IObservable<T>>` (an event stream of event streams).

The following example uses the `Interval` operator to create `OnNext` notifications once a second and then buffers them two at a time:

```
Observable.Interval(TimeSpan.FromSeconds(1))
    .Buffer(2)
    .Subscribe(x => Trace.WriteLine(
        $"{DateTime.Now.Second}: Got {x[0]} and {x[1]}"));
```

On my machine, this code produces a pair of outputs every two seconds:

```
13: Got 0 and 1
15: Got 2 and 3
17: Got 4 and 5
19: Got 6 and 7
21: Got 8 and 9
```

The following is a similar example of using `Window` to create groups of two events:

```
Observable.Interval(TimeSpan.FromSeconds(1))
    .Window(2)
    .Subscribe(group =>
    {
      Trace.WriteLine($"{DateTime.Now.Second}: Starting new group");
      group.Subscribe(
          x => Trace.WriteLine($"{DateTime.Now.Second}: Saw {x}"),
          () => Trace.WriteLine($"{DateTime.Now.Second}: Ending group"));
    });
```

On my machine, this `Window` example produces this output:

```
17: Starting new group
18: Saw 0
19: Saw 1
19: Ending group
19: Starting new group
20: Saw 2
21: Saw 3
21: Ending group
21: Starting new group
22: Saw 4
23: Saw 5
23: Ending group
23: Starting new group
```

These examples illustrate the difference between Buffer and Window. Buffer waits for all the events in its group and then publishes a single collection. Window groups events the same way, but publishes the events as they come in; Window immediately publishes an observable that will publish the events for that window.

Both Buffer and Window also work with time spans. The following code is an example where all mouse move events are collected in windows of one second:

```
private void Button_Click(object sender, RoutedEventArgs e)
{
  Observable.FromEventPattern<MouseEventHandler, MouseEventArgs>(
        handler => (s, a) => handler(s, a),
        handler => MouseMove += handler,
        handler => MouseMove -= handler)
    .Buffer(TimeSpan.FromSeconds(1))
    .Subscribe(x => Trace.WriteLine(
        $"{DateTime.Now.Second}: Saw {x.Count} items."));
}
```

Depending on how you move the mouse, you should see output like the following:

```
49: Saw 93 items.
50: Saw 98 items.
51: Saw 39 items.
52: Saw 0 items.
53: Saw 4 items.
54: Saw 0 items.
55: Saw 58 items.
```

Discussion

Buffer and Window are some of the tools you have for taming input and shaping it the way you want it to look. Another useful technique is throttling, which you'll learn about in Recipe 6.4.

Both Buffer and Window have other overloads that can be used in more advanced scenarios. The overloads with skip and timeShift parameters enable you to create groups that overlap other groups or skip elements in between groups. There are also overloads that take delegates, which enable you to dynamically define the boundary of the groups.

See Also

Recipe 6.1 covers how to create sequences from events.

Recipe 6.4 covers throttling event streams.

6.4 Taming Event Streams with Throttling and Sampling

Problem

A common problem with writing reactive code is when the events come in too quickly. A fast-moving stream of events can overwhelm your program's processing.

Solution

System.Reactive provides operators specifically for dealing with a flood of event data. The `Throttle` and `Sample` operators give us two different ways to tame fast input events.

The `Throttle` operator establishes a sliding timeout window. When an incoming event arrives, it resets the timeout window. When the timeout window expires, it publishes the last event value that arrived within the window.

The following example monitors mouse movements and uses `Throttle` to only report updates once the mouse has stayed still for a full second:

```
private void Button_Click(object sender, RoutedEventArgs e)
{
  Observable.FromEventPattern<MouseEventHandler, MouseEventArgs>(
        handler => (s, a) => handler(s, a),
        handler => MouseMove += handler,
        handler => MouseMove -= handler)
    .Select(x => x.EventArgs.GetPosition(this))
    .Throttle(TimeSpan.FromSeconds(1))
    .Subscribe(x => Trace.WriteLine(
        $"{DateTime.Now.Second}: Saw {x.X + x.Y}"));
}
```

The output varies considerably based on mouse movement, but one example run on my machine looked like this:

```
47: Saw 139
49: Saw 137
51: Saw 424
56: Saw 226
```

`Throttle` is often used in situations such as autocomplete, when the user is typing text into a text box, and you don't want to do the actual lookup until the user stops typing.

`Sample` takes a different approach to taming fast-moving sequences. `Sample` establishes a regular timeout period and publishes the most recent value within that window each time the timeout expires. If no values were received within the sample period, then no results are published for that period.

The following example captures mouse movements and samples them in one-second intervals. Unlike the `Throttle` example, this `Sample` example doesn't require you to hold the mouse still to see data:

```
private void Button_Click(object sender, RoutedEventArgs e)
{
  Observable.FromEventPattern<MouseEventHandler, MouseEventArgs>(
        handler => (s, a) => handler(s, a),
        handler => MouseMove += handler,
        handler => MouseMove -= handler)
      .Select(x => x.EventArgs.GetPosition(this))
      .Sample(TimeSpan.FromSeconds(1))
      .Subscribe(x => Trace.WriteLine(
          $"{DateTime.Now.Second}: Saw {x.X + x.Y}"));
}
```

Here's the output on my machine when I first left the mouse still for a few seconds and then continuously moved it:

```
12: Saw 311
17: Saw 254
18: Saw 269
19: Saw 342
20: Saw 224
21: Saw 277
```

Discussion

Throttling and sampling are essential tools for taming the flood of input. Don't forget that you can also easily do filtering with the standard LINQ `Where` operator. You can think of the `Throttle` and `Sample` operators as similar to `Where`, only they filter on time windows instead of filtering on event data. All three of these operators help you tame fast-moving input streams in different ways.

See Also

Recipe 6.1 covers how to create sequences from events.

Recipe 6.2 covers how to change the context in which events are raised.

6.5 Timeouts

Problem

You expect an event to arrive within a certain time and need to ensure that your program will respond in a timely fashion, even if the event doesn't arrive. Most commonly, this kind of expected event is a single asynchronous operation (e.g., expecting the response from a web service request).

Solution

The Timeout operator establishes a sliding timeout window on its input stream. Whenever a new event arrives, the timeout window is reset. If the timeout expires without seeing an event in that window, the Timeout operator will end the stream with an OnError notification containing a TimeoutException.

The following example issues a web request for the example domain and applies a timeout of one second. To get the web request started, the code uses ToObservable to convert a Task<T> to an IObservable<T> (see Recipe 8.6):

```
void GetWithTimeout(HttpClient client)
{
  client.GetStringAsync("http://www.example.com/").ToObservable()
      .Timeout(TimeSpan.FromSeconds(1))
      .Subscribe(
          x => Trace.WriteLine($"{DateTime.Now.Second}: Saw {x.Length}"),
          ex => Trace.WriteLine(ex));
}
```

Timeout is ideal for asynchronous operations, such as web requests, but it can be applied to any event stream. The following example applies Timeout to mouse movements, which are easier to play around with:

```
private void Button_Click(object sender, RoutedEventArgs e)
{
  Observable.FromEventPattern<MouseEventHandler, MouseEventArgs>(
          handler => (s, a) => handler(s, a),
          handler => MouseMove += handler,
          handler => MouseMove -= handler)
      .Select(x => x.EventArgs.GetPosition(this))
      .Timeout(TimeSpan.FromSeconds(1))
      .Subscribe(
          x => Trace.WriteLine($"{DateTime.Now.Second}: Saw {x.X + x.Y}"),
          ex => Trace.WriteLine(ex));
}
```

On my machine, I moved the mouse a bit and then kept it still for a second, and got these results:

```
16: Saw 180
16: Saw 178
16: Saw 177
16: Saw 176
System.TimeoutException: The operation has timed out.
```

Note that once the TimeoutException is sent to OnError, the stream is finished. No more mouse movements come through. You may not want exactly this behavior, so the Timeout operator has overloads that substitute a second stream when the timeout occurs instead of ending the stream with an exception.

The code in the following example observes mouse movements until there's a time-out. After the timeout, the code observes mouse clicks:

```
private void Button_Click(object sender, RoutedEventArgs e)
{
  IObservable<Point> clicks =
      Observable.FromEventPattern<MouseButtonEventHandler, MouseButtonEventArgs>(
          handler => (s, a) => handler(s, a),
          handler => MouseDown += handler,
          handler => MouseDown -= handler)
      .Select(x => x.EventArgs.GetPosition(this));

  Observable.FromEventPattern<MouseEventHandler, MouseEventArgs>(
          handler => (s, a) => handler(s, a),
          handler => MouseMove += handler,
          handler => MouseMove -= handler)
      .Select(x => x.EventArgs.GetPosition(this))
      .Timeout(TimeSpan.FromSeconds(1), clicks)
      .Subscribe(
          x => Trace.WriteLine($"{DateTime.Now.Second}: Saw {x.X},{x.Y}"),
          ex => Trace.WriteLine(ex));
}
```

On my machine, I moved the mouse a bit, then held it still for a second, and then clicked a couple of different points. The following outputs shows the mouse movements quickly moving through until the timeout, and then the two clicks:

```
49: Saw 95,39
49: Saw 94,39
49: Saw 94,38
49: Saw 94,37
53: Saw 130,141
55: Saw 469,4
```

Discussion

Timeout is an essential operator in nontrivial applications because you always want your program to be responsive even if the rest of the world isn't. It's particularly useful when you have asynchronous operations, but it can be applied to any event stream. Note that the underlying operation is not actually canceled; in the case of a timeout, the operation will continue executing until it succeeds or fails.

See Also

Recipe 6.1 covers how to create sequences from events.

Recipe 8.6 covers wrapping asynchronous code as an observable event stream.

Recipe 10.6 covers unsubscribing from sequences as a result of a CancellationToken.

Recipe 10.3 covers using a CancellationToken as a timeout.

CHAPTER 7

Testing

Testing is an essential part of software quality. Unit testing advocates have become common in recent years; it seems that you read or hear about it everywhere. Some promote *test-driven development*, a style of coding that ensures you have comprehensive tests when the application is complete. The benefits of unit testing on code quality and overall time to completion are well known, and yet many developers still don't write unit tests.

I encourage you to write at least some unit tests. Start with the code in which you feel the least confidence. In my experience, unit tests have given me two main advantages:

- **Better understanding of the code.** You know that part of the application that works but you have no idea how? It's always kind of in the back of your mind when the really weird bug reports come in. Writing unit tests for code you find difficult is a great way to get a clear understanding of how it works. After writing unit tests describing its behavior, the code is no longer mysterious; you end up with a set of unit tests that describe its behavior and the dependencies that code has on the rest of the code.

- **Greater confidence to make changes.** Sooner or later, you'll get that feature request that requires you to change the code that scares you, and you'll no longer be able to pretend it isn't there (I know how that feels; I've been there!). It's best to be proactive: write the unit tests for the scary code before the feature request comes in. Once your unit tests are complete, you'll have an early warning system that will alert you immediately if your changes break existing behavior. When you have a pull request, unit tests also give you greater confidence that the code changes don't break existing behavior.

Both of these advantages apply to your own code just as much as others' code. I'm sure there are other advantages, too. Does unit testing decrease the frequency of bugs? Most likely. Does unit testing reduce the overall time on a project? Possibly. But the advantages I've described are definite; I experience them every time I write unit tests. So, that's my sales pitch for unit testing.

This chapter contains recipes that are all about testing. A lot of developers (even ones who normally write unit tests) shy away from testing concurrent code because they assume it's hard. However, as these recipes will show, unit testing concurrent code isn't as difficult as they think. Modern features and libraries, such as async and System.Reactive, have put a lot of thought into testing, and it shows. I encourage you to use these recipes to write unit tests, especially if you're new to concurrency (i.e., the new concurrent code appears hard or scary).

7.1 Unit Testing async Methods

Problem

You have an async method that you need to unit test.

Solution

Most modern unit test frameworks support async Task unit test methods, including MSTest, NUnit, and xUnit. MSTest began support for these tests with Visual Studio 2012. If you use another unit test framework, you may have to upgrade to the latest version.

Here is an example of an async MSTest unit test:

```
[TestMethod]
public async Task MyMethodAsync_ReturnsFalse()
{
    var objectUnderTest = ...;
    bool result = await objectUnderTest.MyMethodAsync();
    Assert.IsFalse(result);
}
```

The unit test framework will notice that the return type of the method is Task and will intelligently wait for the task to complete before marking the test "successful" or "failed."

If your unit test framework doesn't support async Task unit tests, then it'll need some help to wait for the asynchronous operation under test. One option is that you can use GetAwaiter().GetResult() to synchronously block on the task; if you then use GetAwaiter().GetResult() instead of Wait(), it avoids the AggregateException wrapper if the task has an exception. However, I prefer to use the AsyncContext type from the Nito.AsyncEx NuGet package:

```
[TestMethod]
public void MyMethodAsync_ReturnsFalse()
{
  AsyncContext.Run(async () =>
  {
    var objectUnderTest = ...;
    bool result = await objectUnderTest.MyMethodAsync();
    Assert.IsFalse(result);
  });
}
```

AsyncContext.Run will wait until all asynchronous methods complete.

Discussion

Mocking asynchronous dependencies can be a bit awkward at first. It's a good idea to at least test how your methods respond to synchronous success (mocking with Task.FromResult), synchronous errors (mocking with Task.FromException), and asynchronous success (mocking with Task.Yield and a return value). You'll find coverage of Task.FromResult and Task.FromException in Recipe 2.2. Task.Yield can be used to force asynchronous behavior, and is primarily useful for unit tests:

```
interface IMyInterface
{
  Task<int> SomethingAsync();
}

class SynchronousSuccess : IMyInterface
{
  public Task<int> SomethingAsync()
  {
    return Task.FromResult(13);
  }
}

class SynchronousError : IMyInterface
{
  public Task<int> SomethingAsync()
  {
    return Task.FromException<int>(new InvalidOperationException());
  }
}

class AsynchronousSuccess : IMyInterface
{
  public async Task<int> SomethingAsync()
  {
    await Task.Yield(); // Force asynchronous behavior.
    return 13;
  }
}
```

When testing asynchronous code, deadlocks and race conditions may surface more often than when testing synchronous code. I find the per-test timeout setting useful; in Visual Studio, you can add a test settings file to your solution that enables you to set individual test timeouts. The default value is quite high; I usually have a per-test timeout setting of two seconds.

 The AsyncContext type is in the Nito.AsyncEx (*http://bit.ly/nito-async*) NuGet package.

See Also

Recipe 7.2 covers unit testing asynchronous methods expected to fail.

7.2 Unit Testing async Methods Expected to Fail

Problem

You need to write a unit test that checks for a specific failure of an `async` `Task` method.

Solution

If you're doing desktop or server development, MSTest does support failure testing via the regular `ExpectedExceptionAttribute`:

```
// Not a recommended solution; see below.
[TestMethod]
[ExpectedException(typeof(DivideByZeroException))]
public async Task Divide_WhenDenominatorIsZero_ThrowsDivideByZero()
{
  await MyClass.DivideAsync(4, 0);
}
```

However, this solution isn't the best: `ExpectedException` is actually a poor design. The exception it expects may be thrown by *any* of the methods called by your unit test method. A better design checks that a *particular* piece of code throws that exception, not the unit test as a whole.

Most modern unit test frameworks include `Assert.ThrowsAsync<TException>` in some form. For example, you can use xUnit's `ThrowsAsync` like this:

```
[Fact]
public async Task Divide_WhenDenominatorIsZero_ThrowsDivideByZero()
{
  await Assert.ThrowsAsync<DivideByZeroException>(async () =>
```

```
  {
    await MyClass.DivideAsync(4, 0);
  });
}
```

 Do not forget to await the task returned by ThrowsAsync! The await will propagate any assertion failures that it detects. If you forget the await and ignore the compiler warning, your unit test will always silently succeed regardless of your method's behavior.

Unfortunately, several other unit test frameworks don't include an equivalent async-compatible ThrowsAsync. If you find yourself in this boat, create your own:

```
/// <summary>
/// Ensures that an asynchronous delegate throws an exception.
/// </summary>
/// <typeparam name="TException">
/// The type of exception to expect.
/// </typeparam>
/// <param name="action">The asynchronous delegate to test.</param>
/// <param name="allowDerivedTypes">
/// Whether derived types should be accepted.
/// </param>
public static async Task<TException> ThrowsAsync<TException>(Func<Task> action,
    bool allowDerivedTypes = true)
    where TException : Exception
{
  try
  {
    await action();
    var name = typeof(Exception).Name;
    Assert.Fail($"Delegate did not throw expected exception {name}.");
    return null;
  }
  catch (Exception ex)
  {
    if (allowDerivedTypes && !(ex is TException))
      Assert.Fail($"Delegate threw exception of type {ex.GetType().Name}" +
          $", but {typeof(TException).Name} or a derived type was expected.");
    if (!allowDerivedTypes && ex.GetType() != typeof(TException))
      Assert.Fail($"Delegate threw exception of type {ex.GetType().Name}" +
          $", but {typeof(TException).Name} was expected.");
    return (TException)ex;
  }
}
```

You can use the method just like it was any other Assert.ThrowsAsync<TException> method. Don't forget to await the return value!

Discussion

Testing error handling is just as important as testing the successful scenarios. Some would even say more important, since the successful scenario is the one that everyone tries before the software is released. If your application behaves strangely, it will be due to an unexpected error situation.

However, I encourage developers to move away from ExpectedException. It's better to test for an exception thrown at a specific point rather than testing for an exception at any time during the test. Instead of ExpectedException, use ThrowsAsync (or its equivalent in your unit test framework), or use the ThrowsAsync implementation, as in the last code example.

See Also

Recipe 7.1 covers the basics of unit testing asynchronous methods.

7.3 Unit Testing async void Methods

Problem

You have an async void method that you need to unit test.

Solution

Stop.

Rather than solving this problem, you should do your dead-level best to avoid it. If it's possible to change your async void method to an async Task method, then do so.

If your method *must* be async void (e.g., to satisfy an interface method signature), then consider writing two methods: an async Task method that contains all the logic, and an async void wrapper that just calls the async Task method and awaits the result. The async void method satisfies the architecture requirements, while the async Task method (with all the logic) is testable.

If it's impossible to change your method and you *must* unit test an async void method, then there is a way to do it. You can use the AsyncContext class from the Nito.AsyncEx library:

```
// Not a recommended solution; see the rest of this section.
[TestMethod]
public void MyMethodAsync_DoesNotThrow()
{
  AsyncContext.Run(() =>
  {
    var objectUnderTest = new Sut(); // ...;
```

```
    objectUnderTest.MyVoidMethodAsync();
  });
}
```

The `AsyncContext` type will wait until all asynchronous operations complete (including `async void` methods) and will propagate exceptions that they raise.

 The `AsyncContext` type is in the `Nito.AsyncEx` (*http://bit.ly/nito-async*) NuGet package.

Discussion

One of the key guidelines in `async` code is to avoid `async void`. I strongly recommend you refactor your code instead of using `AsyncContext` for unit testing `async void` methods.

See Also

Recipe 7.1 covers unit testing `async Task` methods.

7.4 Unit Testing Dataflow Meshes

Problem

You have a dataflow mesh in your application, and you need to verify it works correctly.

Solution

Dataflow meshes are independent: they have a lifetime of their own and are asynchronous by nature. So, the most natural way to test them is with an asynchronous unit test. The following unit test verifies the custom dataflow block from Recipe 5.6:

```
[TestMethod]
public async Task MyCustomBlock_AddsOneToDataItems()
{
  var myCustomBlock = CreateMyCustomBlock();

  myCustomBlock.Post(3);
  myCustomBlock.Post(13);
  myCustomBlock.Complete();

  Assert.AreEqual(4, myCustomBlock.Receive());
  Assert.AreEqual(14, myCustomBlock.Receive());
```

```
    await myCustomBlock.Completion;
}
```

Unit testing failures isn't quite as straightforward, unfortunately. This is because exceptions in dataflow meshes are wrapped in another `AggregateException` each time they are propagated to the next block. The following example uses a helper method to ensure that an exception will discard data and propagate through the custom block:

```
[TestMethod]
public async Task MyCustomBlock_Fault_DiscardsDataAndFaults()
{
    var myCustomBlock = CreateMyCustomBlock();

    myCustomBlock.Post(3);
    myCustomBlock.Post(13);
    (myCustomBlock as IDataflowBlock).Fault(new InvalidOperationException());

    try
    {
        await myCustomBlock.Completion;
    }
    catch (AggregateException ex)
    {
        AssertExceptionIs<InvalidOperationException>(
            ex.Flatten().InnerException, false);
    }
}

public static void AssertExceptionIs<TException>(Exception ex,
    bool allowDerivedTypes = true)
{
    if (allowDerivedTypes && !(ex is TException))
        Assert.Fail($"Exception is of type {ex.GetType().Name}, but " +
            $"{typeof(TException).Name} or a derived type was expected.");
    if (!allowDerivedTypes && ex.GetType() != typeof(TException))
        Assert.Fail($"Exception is of type {ex.GetType().Name}, but " +
            $"{typeof(TException).Name} was expected.");
}
```

Discussion

Unit testing of dataflow meshes directly is doable, but somewhat awkward. If your mesh is a part of a larger component, then you may find that it's easier to just unit test the larger component (implicitly testing the mesh). But if you're developing a reusable custom block or mesh, then unit tests like the preceding ones should be used.

See Also

Recipe 7.1 covers unit testing async methods.

7.5 Unit Testing System.Reactive Observables

Problem

Part of your program is using IObservable<T>, and you need to find a way to unit test it.

Solution

System.Reactive has a number of operators that produce sequences (e.g., Return) and other operators that can convert a reactive sequence into a regular collection or item (e.g., SingleAsync). You can use operators like Return to create stubs for observable dependencies, and operators like SingleAsync to test the output.

Consider the following code, which takes an HTTP service as a dependency and applies a timeout to the HTTP call:

```
public interface IHttpService
{
  IObservable<string> GetString(string url);
}

public class MyTimeoutClass
{
  private readonly IHttpService _httpService;

  public MyTimeoutClass(IHttpService httpService)
  {
    _httpService = httpService;
  }

  public IObservable<string> GetStringWithTimeout(string url)
  {
    return _httpService.GetString(url)
        .Timeout(TimeSpan.FromSeconds(1));
  }
}
```

The system under test is MyTimeoutClass, which consumes an observable dependency and produces an observable as output.

The Return operator creates a cold sequence with a single element in it; you can use Return to build a simple stub. The SingleAsync operator returns a Task<T> that is completed when the next event arrives. SingleAsync can be used for simple unit tests like the following:

```
class SuccessHttpServiceStub : IHttpService
{
  public IObservable<string> GetString(string url)
```

```
    {
      return Observable.Return("stub");
    }
  }

  [TestMethod]
  public async Task MyTimeoutClass_SuccessfulGet_ReturnsResult()
  {
    var stub = new SuccessHttpServiceStub();
    var my = new MyTimeoutClass(stub);

    var result = await my.GetStringWithTimeout("http://www.example.com/")
        .SingleAsync();

    Assert.AreEqual("stub", result);
  }
```

Another operator important in stub code is Throw, which returns an observable that ends with an error. The operator enables us to unit test the error case as well. The following example uses the ThrowsAsync helper from Recipe 7.2:

```
  private class FailureHttpServiceStub : IHttpService
  {
    public IObservable<string> GetString(string url)
    {
      return Observable.Throw<string>(new HttpRequestException());
    }
  }

  [TestMethod]
  public async Task MyTimeoutClass_FailedGet_PropagatesFailure()
  {
    var stub = new FailureHttpServiceStub();
    var my = new MyTimeoutClass(stub);

    await ThrowsAsync<HttpRequestException>(async () =>
    {
      await my.GetStringWithTimeout("http://www.example.com/")
          .SingleAsync();
    });
  }
```

Discussion

Return and Throw are great for creating observable stubs, and SingleAsync is an easy way to test observables with async unit tests. They're a good combination for simple observables, but they don't hold up well once you start dealing with *time*. For example, if you wanted to test the timeout capability of MyTimeoutClass, the unit test would have to wait for that amount of time. That, however, would be a poor approach: it makes your unit tests unreliable by introducing a race condition, and it doesn't scale well as you add more unit tests. Recipe 7.6 covers a special way that System.Reactive empowers you to stub out time itself.

See Also

Recipe 7.1 covers unit testing `async` methods, which is very similar to unit tests that await `SingleAsync`.

Recipe 7.6 covers unit testing observable sequences that depend on time passing.

7.6 Unit Testing System.Reactive Observables with Faked Scheduling

Problem

You have an observable that is dependent on time, and want to write a unit test that is not dependent on time. Observables that depend on time include ones that use timeouts, windowing/buffering, and throttling/sampling. You want to unit test these but do not want your unit tests to have excessive runtimes.

Solution

It's certainly possible to put delays in your unit tests; however, there are two problems with that approach: 1) the unit tests take a long time to run, and 2) there are race conditions because the unit tests all run at the same time, making timing unpredictable.

The System.Reactive (Rx) library was designed with testing in mind; in fact, the Rx library itself is extensively unit tested. To enable thorough unit testing, Rx introduced a concept called a *scheduler*, and *every* Rx operator that deals with time is implemented using this abstract scheduler.

To make your observables testable, you need to allow your caller to specify the scheduler. For example, you can take the `MyTimeoutClass` from Recipe 7.5 and add a scheduler:

```
public interface IHttpService
{
  IObservable<string> GetString(string url);
}

public class MyTimeoutClass
{
  private readonly IHttpService _httpService;

  public MyTimeoutClass(IHttpService httpService)
  {
```

```
    _httpService = httpService;
  }

  public IObservable<string> GetStringWithTimeout(string url,
      IScheduler scheduler = null)
  {
    return _httpService.GetString(url)
        .Timeout(TimeSpan.FromSeconds(1), scheduler ?? Scheduler.Default);
  }
}
```

Next, you can modify your HTTP service stub so that it also understands scheduling, then introduce a variable delay:

```
private class SuccessHttpServiceStub : IHttpService
{
  public IScheduler Scheduler { get; set; }
  public TimeSpan Delay { get; set; }

  public IObservable<string> GetString(string url)
  {
    return Observable.Return("stub")
        .Delay(Delay, Scheduler);
  }
}
```

Now you can go ahead and use TestScheduler, a type included in the System.Reactive library. TestScheduler gives you powerful control over (virtual) time.

 TestScheduler is in a separate NuGet package from the rest of System.Reactive; you'll need to install the Microsoft.Reactive.Testing (*http://bit.ly/ms-react-test*) NuGet package.

TestScheduler gives you complete control over time, but you often just need to set up your code and then call TestScheduler.Start. Start will virtually advance time until everything is done. A simple success test case could look like the following:

```
[TestMethod]
public void MyTimeoutClass_SuccessfulGetShortDelay_ReturnsResult()
{
  var scheduler = new TestScheduler();
  var stub = new SuccessHttpServiceStub
  {
    Scheduler = scheduler,
    Delay = TimeSpan.FromSeconds(0.5),
  };
  var my = new MyTimeoutClass(stub);
  string result = null;
```

```
my.GetStringWithTimeout("http://www.example.com/", scheduler)
    .Subscribe(r => { result = r; });

scheduler.Start();

Assert.AreEqual("stub", result);
}
```

The code simulates a network delay of half a second. It's important to note that this unit test *does not* take half a second to run; on my machine, it takes about 70 milliseconds. The half-second delay only exists in virtual time. The other notable difference in this unit test is that it isn't asynchronous; since you're using TestScheduler, all your tests can complete immediately.

Now that everything is using test schedulers, it's easy to test timeout situations:

```
[TestMethod]
public void MyTimeoutClass_SuccessfulGetLongDelay_ThrowsTimeoutException()
{
  var scheduler = new TestScheduler();
  var stub = new SuccessHttpServiceStub
  {
    Scheduler = scheduler,
    Delay = TimeSpan.FromSeconds(1.5),
  };
  var my = new MyTimeoutClass(stub);
  Exception result = null;

  my.GetStringWithTimeout("http://www.example.com/", scheduler)
      .Subscribe(_ => Assert.Fail("Received value"), ex => { result = ex; });

  scheduler.Start();

  Assert.IsInstanceOfType(result, typeof(TimeoutException));
}
```

Once again, the preceding unit test does not take 1 second (or 1.5 seconds) to run; it executes immediately using virtual time.

Discussion

In this recipe we've just scratched the surface on System.Reactive schedulers and virtual time. I recommend that you start unit testing when you start writing System.Reactive code; as your code grows more and more complex, you can rest assured that Microsoft.Reactive.Testing is capable of handling it.

TestScheduler also has AdvanceTo and AdvanceBy methods, which enable you to gradually step through virtual time. These may be useful in some situations, but you should strive to have your unit tests only test one thing. To test a timeout, you could write a single unit test that partially advanced the TestScheduler and ensured that the timeout didn't happen early, and then advanced the `TestScheduler` past the time-out value and ensured that the timeout did happen. However, I prefer to run separate unit tests as much as possible; for example, one unit test ensuring that the timeout didn't happen early, and a different unit test ensuring that the timeout did happen later.

See Also

Recipe 7.5 covers the basics of unit testing observable sequences.

CHAPTER 8

Interop

Asynchronous, parallel, reactive—each of these has its place, but how well do they work together?

In this chapter, we'll look at various *interop* scenarios where you'll learn how to combine these different approaches. You'll learn that they complement each other, rather than compete; there's very little friction at the boundaries where one approach meets another.

8.1 Async Wrappers for "Async" Methods with "Completed" Events

Problem

There is an older asynchronous pattern that uses methods named *Operation*Async along with events named *Operation*Completed. You want to perform an operation using the older asynchronous pattern and await the result.

 The *Operation*Async and *Operation*Completed pattern is called the Event-based Asynchronous Pattern (EAP). You're going to wrap those into a Task-returning method that follows the Task-based Asynchronous Pattern (TAP).

Solution

By using the TaskCompletionSource<TResult> type, you can create wrappers for asynchronous operations. The TaskCompletionSource<TResult> type controls a Task<TResult> and enables you to complete the task at the appropriate time.

This example defines an extension method for WebClient that downloads a string. The WebClient type defines DownloadStringAsync and DownloadStringCompleted. Using those, you can define a DownloadStringTaskAsync method, like this:

```
public static Task<string> DownloadStringTaskAsync(this WebClient client,
    Uri address)
{
  var tcs = new TaskCompletionSource<string>();

  // The event handler will complete the task and unregister itself.
  DownloadStringCompletedEventHandler handler = null;
  handler = (_, e) =>
  {
    client.DownloadStringCompleted -= handler;
    if (e.Cancelled)
      tcs.TrySetCanceled();
    else if (e.Error != null)
      tcs.TrySetException(e.Error);
    else
      tcs.TrySetResult(e.Result);
  };

  // Register for the event and *then* start the operation.
  client.DownloadStringCompleted += handler;
  client.DownloadStringAsync(address);

  return tcs.Task;
}
```

Discussion

This particular example is not very useful because WebClient already is defining a DownloadStringTaskAsync, and there's a more async-friendly HttpClient that could be used. However, this same technique can be used to interface with older asynchronous code that hasn't yet been updated to use Task.

 For new code, always use HttpClient. Only use WebClient if you're working with legacy code.

Normally, a TAP method for downloading strings would be named *Operation*Async (e.g., DownloadStringAsync); however, that naming convention won't work in this case because EAP already defines a method with that name. Here the convention is to name the TAP method *Operation*TaskAsync (e.g., DownloadStringTaskAsync).

When wrapping EAP methods, there's the possibility that the "start" method may throw an exception; in the previous example, DownloadStringAsync may throw. In that case, you'll need to decide whether to allow the exception to propagate or to catch the exception and call TrySetException. Most of the time, exceptions thrown at that point are usage errors, so it doesn't matter which option you choose. If you're unsure whether the exceptions are usage errors, then I recommend catching the exception and calling TrySetException.

See Also

Recipe 8.2 covers TAP wrappers for APM methods (Begin*Operation* and End*Operation*).

Recipe 8.3 covers TAP wrappers for any kind of notification.

8.2 Async Wrappers for "Begin/End" Methods

Problem

An older asynchronous pattern uses pairs of methods named Begin*Operation* and End*Operation*, with the IAsyncResult representing the asynchronous operation. You have an operation that follows the older asynchronous pattern and want to consume it with await.

The Begin*Operation* and End*Operation* pattern is called the Asynchronous Programming Model (APM). You're going to wrap those into a Task-returning method that follows the Task-based Asynchronous Pattern (TAP).

Solution

The best approach for wrapping APM is to use one of the FromAsync methods on the TaskFactory type. FromAsync uses TaskCompletionSource<TResult> under the hood, but when you're wrapping APM, FromAsync is much easier to use.

This example defines an extension method for WebRequest that sends an HTTP request and gets the response. The WebRequest type defines BeginGetResponse and EndGetResponse; you can define a GetResponseAsync method like this:

```
public static Task<WebResponse> GetResponseAsync(this WebRequest client)
{
  return Task<WebResponse>.Factory.FromAsync(client.BeginGetResponse,
      client.EndGetResponse, null);
}
```

Discussion

`FromAsync` has a downright confusing number of overloads!

As a general rule, it's best to call `FromAsync`, as in the example. First, pass the `Begin`*`Operation`* method (without calling it), then pass the `End`*`Operation`* method (without calling it). Next, pass all arguments that `Begin`*`Operation`* takes except for the last `AsyncCallback` and `object` arguments. Finally, pass `null`.

In particular, do not call the `Begin`*`Operation`* method before calling `FromAsync`. You can call `FromAsync`, passing the `IAsyncOperation` that you get from `Begin`*`Operation`*, but if you call it that way, `FromAsync` is forced to use a less efficient implementation.

You might be wondering why the recommended pattern always passes a `null` at the end. `FromAsync` was introduced along with the `Task` type in .NET 4.0, before `async` was around. At the time, it was common to use `state` objects in asynchronous callbacks, and the `Task` type supports this via its `AsyncState` member. In the new `async` pattern, state objects are no longer necessary, so it's normal to always pass `null` for the `state` parameter. These days, `state` is only used to avoid a closure instance when optimizing memory usage.

See Also

Recipe 8.3 covers writing TAP wrappers for any kind of notification.

8.3 Async Wrappers for Anything

Problem

You have an unusual or nonstandard asynchronous operation or event and want to consume it via `await`.

Solution

The `TaskCompletionSource<T>` type can be used to construct `Task<T>` objects in any scenario. Using a `TaskCompletionSource<T>`, you can complete a task in three different ways: with a successful result, faulted, or canceled.

Before `async` was on the scene, there were two other asynchronous patterns recommended by Microsoft: APM (Recipe 8.2) and EAP (Recipe 8.1). However, both APM and EAP were rather awkward and in some cases difficult to get right. So, an unofficial convention arose that used callbacks, with methods like the following:

```
public interface IMyAsyncHttpService
{
```

```
    void DownloadString(Uri address, Action<string, Exception> callback);
}
```

Methods like these follow the convention that `DownloadString` will start the (asynchronous) download, and when it completes, the `callback` is invoked with either the result or the exception. Usually, `callback` is invoked on a background thread.

A nonstandard kind of asynchronous method like the previous example can be wrapped using `TaskCompletionSource<T>` so that it naturally works with `await`, as this next example shows:

```
public static Task<string> DownloadStringAsync(
    this IMyAsyncHttpService httpService, Uri address)
{
  var tcs = new TaskCompletionSource<string>();
  httpService.DownloadString(address, (result, exception) =>
  {
    if (exception != null)
      tcs.TrySetException(exception);
    else
      tcs.TrySetResult(result);
  });
  return tcs.Task;
}
```

Discussion

You can use this same `TaskCompletionSource<T>` pattern to wrap *any* asynchronous method, no matter how nonstandard. Create the `TaskCompletionSource<T>` instance first. Next, arrange a callback so that the `TaskCompletionSource<T>` completes its task appropriately. Then, start the actual asynchronous operation. Finally, return the `Task<T>` that is attached to that `TaskCompletionSource<T>`.

It is important for this pattern that you make *sure* that the `TaskCompletionSource<T>` is always completed. Think through your error handling in particular, and ensure that the `TaskCompletionSource<T>` will be completed appropriately. In the last example, exceptions are explicitly passed into the callback, so you don't need a `catch` block; but some nonstandard patterns might need you to catch exceptions in your callbacks and place them on the `TaskCompletionSource<T>`.

See Also

Recipe 8.1 has coverage of TAP wrappers for EAP members (*Operation*Async, *Operation*Completed).

Recipe 8.2 covers TAP wrappers for APM members (Begin*Operation*, End*Operation*).

8.4 Async Wrappers for Parallel Code

Problem

You have (CPU-bound) parallel processing that you want to consume using `await`. Usually, this is desirable so that your UI thread doesn't block waiting for the parallel processing to complete.

Solution

The `Parallel` type and Parallel LINQ use the thread pool to do parallel processing. They will also include the calling thread as one of the parallel processing threads, so if you call a parallel method from the UI thread, the UI will be unresponsive until the processing completes.

To keep the UI responsive, wrap the parallel processing in a `Task.Run` and `await` the result:

```
await Task.Run(() => Parallel.ForEach(...));
```

The key behind this recipe is that parallel code *includes the calling thread* in its pool of threads that it uses to do the parallel processing. This is true for both Parallel LINQ and the `Parallel` class.

Discussion

This is a simple recipe but one that is often overlooked. By using `Task.Run`, you're pushing all of the parallel processing off to the thread pool. `Task.Run` returns a `Task` that then represents that parallel work, and the UI thread can (asynchronously) wait for it to complete.

This recipe only applies to UI code. On the server side (e.g., ASP.NET), parallel processing is rarely done because the server host already does parallelism. For this reason, server-side code shouldn't perform parallel processing, nor should it push work off to the thread pool.

See Also

Chapter 4 covers the basics of parallel code.

Chapter 2 covers the basics of asynchronous code.

8.5 Async Wrappers for System.Reactive Observables

Problem

You have an observable stream that you want to consume using `await`.

Solution

First, you need to decide *which* of the observable events in the event stream you're interested in. These are common situations:

- The last event before the stream ends
- The next event
- All the events

To capture the *last* event in the stream, you can either `await` the result of `LastAsync` or just `await` the observable directly:

```
IObservable<int> observable = ...;
int lastElement = await observable.LastAsync();
// or:  int lastElement = await observable;
```

When you `await` an observable or `LastAsync`, the code (asynchronously) waits until the stream completes and then returns the last element. Under the covers, the `await` is subscribing to the stream.

To capture the *next* event in the stream, use `FirstAsync`. In the following code, the `await` subscribes to the stream and then completes (and unsubscribes) as soon as the first event arrives:

```
IObservable<int> observable = ...;
int nextElement = await observable.FirstAsync();
```

To capture *all* events in the stream, you can use `ToList`:

```
IObservable<int> observable = ...;
IList<int> allElements = await observable.ToList();
```

Discussion

The System.Reactive library provides all the tools you need to consume streams using `await`. The only tricky part is that you have to think about whether the awaitable will wait until the stream completes. Of the examples in this recipe, `LastAsync`, `ToList`, and the direct `await` will wait until the stream completes; `FirstAsync` will only wait for the next event.

If these examples don't satisfy your needs, remember that you have the full power of LINQ as well as the System.Reactive manipulators. Operators such as `Take` and `Buffer` can also help you asynchronously wait for the elements you need without having to wait for the entire stream to complete.

Some of the operators for use with `await`—such as `FirstAsync` and `LastAsync`—don't actually return a `Task<T>`. If you plan to use `Task.WhenAll` or `Task.WhenAny`, then you'll need an actual `Task<T>`, which you can get by calling `ToTask` on any observable. `ToTask` will return a `Task<T>` that completes with the last value in the stream.

See Also

Recipe 8.6 covers using asynchronous code within an observable stream.

Recipe 8.8 covers using observable streams as an input to a dataflow block (which can perform asynchronous work).

Recipe 6.3 covers windows and buffering for observable streams.

8.6 System.Reactive Observable Wrappers for async Code

Problem

You have an asynchronous operation that you want to combine with an observable.

Solution

Any asynchronous operation can be treated as an observable stream that does one of two things:

- Produces a single element and then completes
- Faults without producing any elements

To implements this transformation, the System.Reactive library has a simple conversion from `Task<T>` to `IObservable<T>`. The following code starts an asynchronous download of a web page, treating it as an observable sequence:

```
IObservable<HttpResponseMessage> GetPage(HttpClient client)
{
  Task<HttpResponseMessage> task =
      client.GetAsync("http://www.example.com/");
  return task.ToObservable();
}
```

The ToObservable approach assumes you have already called the async method and have a Task to convert.

Another approach is to call StartAsync. StartAsync also calls the async method immediately but supports cancellation: if a subscription is disposed of, the async method is canceled:

```
IObservable<HttpResponseMessage> GetPage(HttpClient client)
{
  return Observable.StartAsync(
      token => client.GetAsync("http://www.example.com/", token));
}
```

Both ToObservable and StartAsync immediately start the asynchronous operation without waiting for a subscription; the observable is "hot." To create a "cold" observable that only starts the operation when subscribed to, use FromAsync (which also supports cancellation just like StartAsync):

```
IObservable<HttpResponseMessage> GetPage(HttpClient client)
{
  return Observable.FromAsync(
      token => client.GetAsync("http://www.example.com/", token));
}
```

FromAsync is notably different than ToObservable and StartAsync, which return an observable for an async operation that has already started. FromAsync starts a new, independent async operation every time it is subscribed to.

Finally, you can use special overloads of SelectMany to start asynchronous operations for each event in a source stream as they arrive. SelectMany also supports cancellation.

The following example takes an existing event stream of URLs and then initiates a request as each URL arrives:

```
IObservable<HttpResponseMessage> GetPages(
    IObservable<string> urls, HttpClient client)
{
  return urls.SelectMany(
      (url, token) => client.GetAsync(url, token));
}
```

Discussion

System.Reactive existed before the introduction of async but added these operators (and others) so that it could interoperate well with async code. I recommend that you use the operators described even though you can build the same functionality using other System.Reactive operators.

See Also

Recipe 8.5 covers consuming observable streams with asynchronous code.

Recipe 8.8 covers using dataflow blocks (which can contain asynchronous code) as sources of observable streams.

8.7 Asynchronous Streams and Dataflow Meshes

Problem

Part of your solution uses asynchronous streams, and part of your solution uses dataflow meshes, and you need to pass data between them.

Solution

Consuming a Channel as an asynchronous stream is built right into the Channel types; see Recipe 9.8 for details. Consuming a TPL Dataflow block as an asynchronous stream is a bit more awkward, but certainly doable. I find it easiest to first define an extension method for dataflow blocks that make their API more similar to Channels, and then consume them as an asynchronous stream using that extension method:

```
public static class DataflowExtensions
{
  public static bool TryReceiveItem<T>(this ISourceBlock<T> block, out T value)
  {
    if (block is IReceivableSourceBlock<T> receivableSourceBlock)
      return receivableSourceBlock.TryReceive(out value);

    try
    {
      value = block.Receive(TimeSpan.Zero);
      return true;
    }
    catch (TimeoutException)
    {
      // There is no item available right now.
      value = default;
      return false;
    }
    catch (InvalidOperationException)
    {
      // The block is complete and there are no more items.
      value = default;
      return false;
    }
  }
}
```

```
public static async IAsyncEnumerable<T> ReceiveAllAsync<T>(
    this ISourceBlock<T> block,
    [EnumeratorCancellation] CancellationToken cancellationToken = default)
{
  while (await block
      .OutputAvailableAsync(cancellationToken).ConfigureAwait(false))
  {
    while (block.TryReceiveItem(out var value))
    {
      yield return value;
    }
  }
}
```

See Recipe 3.4 for the details on the EnumeratorCancellation attribute.

Using the extension method in the previous code example, it's possible to consume any output dataflow block as an asynchronous stream:

```
var multiplyBlock = new TransformBlock<int, int>(value => value * 2);

multiplyBlock.Post(5);
multiplyBlock.Post(2);
multiplyBlock.Complete();

await foreach (int item in multiplyBlock.ReceiveAllAsync())
{
  Console.WriteLine(item);
}
```

It is also possible to use an asynchronous stream as a source of items for a dataflow block. All you need is a loop to pull the items out and place them into the block. There are a couple of assumptions in the following code that may not be appropriate in every scenario. First, the code assumes you want the block to complete when the stream completes. Second, it begins running on its calling thread; some scenarios may want to always run the entire loop on a threadpool thread:

```
public static async Task WriteToBlockAsync<T>(
    this IAsyncEnumerable<T> enumerable,
    ITargetBlock<T> block, CancellationToken token = default)
{
  try
  {
    await foreach (var item in enumerable
        .WithCancellation(token).ConfigureAwait(false))
    {
      await block.SendAsync(item, token).ConfigureAwait(false);
    }

    block.Complete();
  }
```

```
  catch (Exception ex)
  {
    block.Fault(ex);
  }
}
```

Discussion

The extension methods in this recipe are intended as a starting point. In particular, the `WriteToBlockAsync` extension method does make some assumptions; be sure to consider the behavior of these methods and ensure that their behavior is appropriate for your scenario before using them.

See Also

Recipe 9.8 covers consuming a Channel as an asynchronous stream.

Recipe 3.4 covers canceling asynchronous streams.

Chapter 5 covers recipes for TPL Dataflow.

Chapter 3 covers recipes for asynchronous streams.

8.8 System.Reactive Observables and Dataflow Meshes

Problem

Part of your solution uses System.Reactive observables, and part of your solution uses dataflow meshes, and you need them to communicate.

System.Reactive observables and dataflow meshes each have their own uses, with some conceptual overlap; this recipe shows how easily they work together so that you can use the best tool for each part of the job.

Solution

First, let's consider using a dataflow block as an input to an observable stream. The following code creates a buffer block (which does no processing) and creates an observable interface from that block by calling `AsObservable`:

```
var buffer = new BufferBlock<int>();
IObservable<int> integers = buffer.AsObservable();
integers.Subscribe(data => Trace.WriteLine(data),
    ex => Trace.WriteLine(ex),
    () => Trace.WriteLine("Done"));

buffer.Post(13);
```

Buffer blocks and observable streams can be completed normally or with error, and the `AsObservable` method will translate the block completion (or fault) into the completion of the observable stream. However, if the block faults with an exception, that exception will be wrapped in an `AggregateException` when it's passed to the observable stream. This is similar to how linked blocks propagate their faults.

It's only a little more complicated to take a mesh and treat it as a destination for an observable stream. The following code calls `AsObserver` to enable a block to subscribe to an observable stream:

```
IObservable<DateTimeOffset> ticks =
    Observable.Interval(TimeSpan.FromSeconds(1))
        .Timestamp()
        .Select(x => x.Timestamp)
        .Take(5);

var display = new ActionBlock<DateTimeOffset>(x => Trace.WriteLine(x));
ticks.Subscribe(display.AsObserver());

try
{
  display.Completion.Wait();
  Trace.WriteLine("Done.");
}
catch (Exception ex)
{
  Trace.WriteLine(ex);
}
```

Just as before, the completion of the observable stream is translated to the completion of the block, and any errors from the observable stream are translated to a fault of the block.

Discussion

Dataflow blocks and observable streams share a lot of conceptual ground. They both have data pass through them, and they both understand completion and faults. They were designed for different scenarios; TPL Dataflow is intended for a mixture of asynchronous and parallel programming, while System.Reactive is intended for reactive programming. However, the conceptual overlap is compatible enough that they work very well and naturally together.

See Also

Recipe 8.5 covers consuming observable streams with asynchronous code.

Recipe 8.6 covers using asynchronous code within an observable stream.

8.9 Converting System.Reactive Observables to Asynchronous Streams

Problem

Part of your solution uses System.Reactive observables, and you want to consume them as asynchronous streams.

Solution

System.Reactive observables are push-based, and asynchronous streams are pull-based. So right off the bat, you need to realize there's a conceptual mismatch. You need a way to remain responsive to the observable stream, storing its notifications until the consuming code requests them.

The most straightforward solution is already included in the `System.Linq.Async` library:

```
IObservable<long> observable =
    Observable.Interval(TimeSpan.FromSeconds(1));

// WARNING: May consume unbounded memory; see discussion!
IAsyncEnumerable<long> enumerable =
    observable.ToAsyncEnumerable();
```

> The `ToAsyncEnumerable` extension method is in the `Sys tem.Linq.Async` (*http://bit.ly/sys-linq-async*) NuGet package.

However, it's important to recognize that this simple `ToAsyncEnumerable` extension method is using an unbounded producer/consumer queue under the hood. It is essentially the same as an extension method you can write yourself using a Channel as an unbounded producer/consumer queue:

```
// WARNING: May consume unbounded memory; see discussion!
public static async IAsyncEnumerable<T> ToAsyncEnumerable<T>(
    this IObservable<T> observable)
{
  Channel<T> buffer = Channel.CreateUnbounded<T>();
  using (observable.Subscribe(
      value => buffer.Writer.TryWrite(value),
      error => buffer.Writer.Complete(error),
      () => buffer.Writer.Complete()))
  {
    await foreach (T item in buffer.Reader.ReadAllAsync())
      yield return item;
```

```
    }
}
```

These are simple solutions, but they use unbounded queues, so they should only be used if you're sure that the consumer can (eventually) keep up with the observable events. It's fine if the producer runs faster than the consumer for a while; during that time, the observable events go into the buffer. As long as the producer eventually catches up, the preceding solutions will work. But if the producer always runs faster than the consumer, the observable events will continue to arrive, expanding the buffer, and eventually use up all the memory for the process.

You can avoid the memory issue by using a bounded queue. The trade-off is that you must decide how to handle extra items if the observable events fill up the queue. One option is to discard the extra items; the following example code uses a bounded channel to throw away the oldest observable notification when the buffer is full:

```
// WARNING: May discard items; see discussion!
public static async IAsyncEnumerable<T> ToAsyncEnumerable<T>(
    this IObservable<T> observable, int bufferSize)
{
  var bufferOptions = new BoundedChannelOptions(bufferSize)
  {
    FullMode = BoundedChannelFullMode.DropOldest,
  };
  Channel<T> buffer = Channel.CreateBounded<T>(bufferOptions);
  using (observable.Subscribe(
      value => buffer.Writer.TryWrite(value),
      error => buffer.Writer.Complete(error),
      () => buffer.Writer.Complete()))
  {
    await foreach (T item in buffer.Reader.ReadAllAsync())
      yield return item;
  }
}
```

Discussion

When you have a producer that runs faster than a consumer, your options are to either buffer the producer items (assuming that the producer eventually catches up), or limit the producer's items. The second solution in this recipe limits the producer's items by dropping ones that don't fit in the buffer. You can also limit the producer's items by using observable operators designed for that, such as Throttle or Sample; see Recipe 6.4 for details. Depending on your needs, it may be best to Throttle or Sample the input observable before converting it to an IAsyncEnumerable<T> using one of the techniques in this recipe.

Aside from bounded queues and unbounded queues, there's a third option not covered here: use backpressure to notify the observable stream that it must stop producing notifications until the buffer is ready to receive them. Unfortunately, System.Reactive hasn't yet standardized on a backpressure pattern, so this isn't a viable option at the time of writing. Backpressure is complex and nuanced, and reactive libraries for other languages have implemented different patterns for backpressure. It remains to be seen whether System.Reactive will adopt one of these, invent its own backpressure pattern, or just leave backpressure unsolved.

See Also

Recipe 6.4 covers System.Reactive operators designed to throttle input.

Recipe 9.8 covers using Channel as an unbounded producer/consumer queue.

Recipe 9.10 covers using Channel as a sampling queue, dropping items when it is full.

CHAPTER 9

Collections

Using the proper collections is essential in concurrent applications. I'm not talking about the standard collections like List<T>; I assume you already know about those. The purpose of this chapter is to introduce newer collections that are specifically intended for concurrent or asynchronous use.

Immutable collections are collection instances that can never change. At first glance, this sounds completely useless; but they're actually very useful, even in single-threaded, nonconcurrent applications. Read-only operations (such as enumeration) act directly on the immutable instance. Write operations (such as adding an item) return a new immutable instance instead of changing the existing instance. This isn't as wasteful as it first sounds because most of the time immutable collections share most of their memory. Furthermore, immutable collections have the advantage of being implicitly safe to access from multiple threads; since they cannot change, they are threadsafe.

Immutable collections are in the System.Collections.Immutable (*http://bit.ly/sys-coll-imm*) NuGet package.

Immutable collections are new, but they should be considered for new development unless you *need* a mutable instance. If you're not familiar with immutable collections, I recommend that you start with Recipe 9.1, even if you don't need a stack or queue, because I'll cover several common patterns that all immutable collections follow.

There are special ways to more efficiently construct an immutable collection with lots of existing elements; the example code in these recipes only adds elements one at a time. The MSDN documentation has details on how to efficiently construct immutable collections if you need to speed up your initialization.

Threadsafe collections

These mutable collection instances can be changed by multiple threads simultaneously. Threadsafe collections use a mixture of fine-grained locks and lock-free techniques to ensure that threads are blocked for a minimal amount of time (and usually aren't blocked at all). For many threadsafe collections, enumeration of the collection creates a snapshot of the collection and then enumerates that snapshot. The key advantage of threadsafe collections is that they can be accessed safely from multiple threads, yet the operations will only block your code for a short time, if at all.

Producer/consumer collections

These mutable collection instances are designed with a specific purpose in mind: to allow (possibly multiple) producers to push items to the collection while allowing (possibly multiple) consumers to pull items out of the collection. So they act as a bridge between producer code and consumer code, and they also have an option to limit the number of items in the collection. Producer/consumer collections can either have a blocking or asynchronous API. For example, when the collection is empty, a blocking producer/consumer collection will block the calling consumer thread until another item is added; but an asynchronous producer/consumer collection will allow the calling consumer thread to asynchronously wait until another item is added.

There are a number of different producer/consumer collections used in the recipes in this chapter, and different producer/consumer collections have different advantages. Table 9-1 may be helpful in determining which one you should use.

Table 9-1. Producer/consumer collections

Feature	Channels	BlockingCollection\<T>	BufferBlock\<T>	AsyncProducer-ConsumerQueue\<T>	AsyncCollection\<T>
Queue semantics	✓	✓	✓	✓	✓
Stack/bag semantics	✗	✓	✗	✗	✓
Synchronous API	✓	✓	✓	✓	✓
Asynchronous API	✓	✗	✓	✓	✓
Drop items when full	✓	✗	✗	✗	✗
Tested by Microsoft	✓	✓	✓	✗	✗

Channels can be found in the System.Threading.Channels (*http://bit.ly/sys-thrd-chanls*) NuGet package, BufferBlock<T> in the NuGet package for System.Threading.Tasks.Dataflow (*http://bit.ly/nuget-df*), and AsyncProducerConsumerQueue<T> and AsyncCollection<T> in the NuGet package for Nito.AsyncEx (*http://bit.ly/nito-async*).

9.1 Immutable Stacks and Queues

Problem

You need a stack or queue that does not change very often and can be accessed by multiple threads safely.

For example, a queue can be used as a sequence of operations to perform, and a stack can be used as a sequence of undo operations.

Solution

Immutable stacks and queues are the simplest immutable collections. They behave very similarly to the standard Stack<T> and Queue<T>. Performance-wise, immutable stacks and queues have the same time complexity as standard stacks and queues; however, in simple scenarios where the collections are updated frequently, the standard stacks and queues are faster.

Stacks are a first-in, last-out data structure. The following code creates an empty immutable stack, pushes two items, enumerates the items, and then pops an item:

```
ImmutableStack<int> stack = ImmutableStack<int>.Empty;
stack = stack.Push(13);
stack = stack.Push(7);

// Displays "7" followed by "13".
foreach (int item in stack)
  Trace.WriteLine(item);

int lastItem;
stack = stack.Pop(out lastItem);
// lastItem == 7
```

Note in the example that we keep overwriting the local variable stack. Immutable collections follow a pattern where they return an updated collection; the original collection reference is unchanged. This means that once you have a reference to a particular immutable collection instance, it'll never change. Consider the following example:

```
ImmutableStack<int> stack = ImmutableStack<int>.Empty;
stack = stack.Push(13);
```

```
ImmutableStack<int> biggerStack = stack.Push(7);

// Displays "7" followed by "13".
foreach (int item in biggerStack)
  Trace.WriteLine(item);

// Only displays "13".
foreach (int item in stack)
  Trace.WriteLine(item);
```

Under the covers, the two stacks are sharing the memory used to contain the item 13. This kind of implementation is very efficient while enabling you to easily snapshot the current state. Each immutable collection instance is naturally threadsafe, but immutable collections can also be used in single-threaded applications. In my experience, immutable collections are especially useful when the code is more functional or when you need to store a large number of snapshots and want them to share memory as much as possible.

Queues are similar to stacks, except they are a first-in, first-out data structure. The following code creates an empty immutable queue, enqueues two items, enumerates the items, and then dequeues an item:

```
ImmutableQueue<int> queue = ImmutableQueue<int>.Empty;
queue = queue.Enqueue(13);
queue = queue.Enqueue(7);

// Displays "13" followed by "7".
foreach (int item in queue)
  Trace.WriteLine(item);

int nextItem;
queue = queue.Dequeue(out nextItem);
// Displays "13".
Trace.WriteLine(nextItem);
```

Discussion

This recipe introduced the two simplest immutable collections, the stack and the queue. It also covered several important design philosophies that are true for *all* immutable collections:

- An instance of an immutable collection never changes.
- Since it never changes, it is naturally threadsafe.
- When you call a modifying method on an immutable collection, the new modified collection is returned.

Even though immutable collections are threadsafe, *references* to immutable collections are *not* threadsafe. A variable that refers to an immutable collection needs the same synchronization protections as any other variable (see Chapter 12).

Immutable collections are ideal for sharing state. They don't, however, work as well as communication conduits. In particular, don't use an immutable queue to communicate between threads; producer/consumer queues work much better for that.

`ImmutableStack<T>` and `ImmutableQueue<T>` can be found in the `System.Collections.Immutable` (*http://bit.ly/sys-coll-imm*) NuGet package.

See Also

Recipe 9.6 covers threadsafe (blocking) mutable queues.

Recipe 9.7 covers threadsafe (blocking) mutable stacks.

Recipe 9.8 covers async-compatible mutable queues.

Recipe 9.11 covers async-compatible mutable stacks.

Recipe 9.12 covers blocking/asynchronous mutable queues.

9.2 Immutable Lists

Problem

You need a data structure you can index into that does not change very often and can be accessed by multiple threads safely.

Solution

A list is a general-purpose data structure that can be used for all kinds of application states. Immutable lists do allow indexing, but you need to be aware of the performance characteristics. They're not just a drop-in replacement for `List<T>`.

`ImmutableList<T>` does support similar methods as `List<T>`, as the following example shows:

```
ImmutableList<int> list = ImmutableList<int>.Empty;
list = list.Insert(0, 13);
list = list.Insert(0, 7);
```

```
// Displays "7" followed by "13".
foreach (int item in list)
  Trace.WriteLine(item);

list = list.RemoveAt(1);
```

The immutable list is internally organized as a binary tree so that immutable list instances may maximize the amount of memory they share with other instances. As a result, there are performance differences between ImmutableList<T> and List<T> for some common operations (Table 9-2).

Table 9-2. Performance difference of immutable lists

Operation	List<T>	ImmutableList<T>
Add	amortized O(1)	O(log N)
Insert	O(N)	O(log N)
RemoveAt	O(N)	O(log N)
Item[index]	O(1)	O(log N)

Of note, the indexing operation for ImmutableList<T> is O(log N), not O(1), as you may expect. If you're replacing List<T> with ImmutableList<T> in existing code, you'll need to consider how your algorithms access items in the collection.

This means that you should use foreach instead of for whenever possible. A foreach loop over an ImmutableList<T> executes in O(N) time, while a for loop over the same collection executes in O(N * log N) time:

```
// The best way to iterate over an ImmutableList<T>.
foreach (var item in list)
  Trace.WriteLine(item);

// This will also work, but it will be much slower.
for (int i = 0; i != list.Count; ++i)
  Trace.WriteLine(list[i]);
```

Discussion

ImmutableList<T> is a good general-purpose data structure, but because of its performance differences, you can't blindly replace all your List<T> uses with it. List<T> is commonly used by default—it's the one you use unless you *need* a different collection. ImmutableList<T> isn't quite that ubiquitous; you'll need to consider the other immutable collections carefully and choose the one that makes the most sense for your situation.

ImmutableList<T> is in the System.Collections.Immutable (*http://bit.ly/sys-coll-imm*) NuGet package.

See Also

Recipe 9.1 covers immutable stacks and queues, which are like lists that only allow certain elements to be accessed.

The MSDN documentation on ImmutableList<T>.Builder (*http://bit.ly/msdn-iml*) covers an efficient way to populate an immutable list.

9.3 Immutable Sets

Problem

You need a data structure that does not need to store duplicates, does not change very often, and can be accessed by multiple threads safely.

For example, an index of words from a file would be a good use case for a set.

Solution

There are two immutable set types: ImmutableHashSet<T> is a collection of unique items, and ImmutableSortedSet<T> is a *sorted* collection of unique items. Both types have a similar interface:

```
ImmutableHashSet<int> hashSet = ImmutableHashSet<int>.Empty;
hashSet = hashSet.Add(13);
hashSet = hashSet.Add(7);

// Displays "7" and "13" in an unpredictable order.
foreach (int item in hashSet)
  Trace.WriteLine(item);

hashSet = hashSet.Remove(7);
```

Only the sorted set allows indexing into it like a list:

```
ImmutableSortedSet<int> sortedSet = ImmutableSortedSet<int>.Empty;
sortedSet = sortedSet.Add(13);
sortedSet = sortedSet.Add(7);

// Displays "7" followed by "13".
foreach (int item in sortedSet)
  Trace.WriteLine(item);
int smallestItem = sortedSet[0];
// smallestItem == 7
```

```
sortedSet = sortedSet.Remove(7);
```

Unsorted sets and sorted sets have similar performance (see Table 9-3).

Table 9-3. Performance of immutable sets

Operation	ImmutableHashSet<T>	ImmutableSortedSet<T>
Add	O(log N)	O(log N)
Remove	O(log N)	O(log N)
Item[index]	n/a	O(log N)

However, I recommend you use an unsorted set unless you know it needs to be sorted. Many types only support basic equality and not full comparison, so an unsorted set can be used for many more types than a sorted set.

One important note about the sorted set is that its indexing is O(log N), not O(1), just like `ImmutableList<T>`, which is covered in Recipe 9.2. This means that the same caveat applies in this situation: you should use `foreach` instead of `for` whenever possible with an `ImmutableSortedSet<T>`.

Discussion

Immutable sets are useful data structures, but populating a large immutable set can be slow. Most immutable collections have special builders that can be used to construct them quickly in a mutable way and then convert them into an immutable collection. This is true for many immutable collections, but I've found them most useful for immutable sets.

> `ImmutableHashSet<T>` and `ImmutableSortedSet<T>` are in the NuGet System.Collections.Immutable (*http://bit.ly/sys-coll-imm*) package.

See Also

Recipe 9.7 covers threadsafe mutable bags, which are similar to sets.

Recipe 9.11 covers async-compatible mutable bags.

The MSDN documentation on `ImmutableHashSet<T>.Builder` (*http://bit.ly/msdn-imh*) covers an efficient way to populate an immutable hash set.

The MSDN documentation on `ImmutableSortedSet<T>.Builder` (*http://bit.ly/msdn-ims*) covers an efficient way to populate an immutable sorted set.

9.4 Immutable Dictionaries

Problem

You need a key/value collection that does not change very often and can be accessed by multiple threads safely. For example, you may want to store reference data in a *lookup collection*; the reference data rarely changes but should be available to different threads.

Solution

There are two immutable dictionary types: `ImmutableDictionary<TKey, TValue>` and `ImmutableSortedDictionary<TKey, TValue>`. As you may be able to guess from their names, while the items in `ImmutableDictionary` have an unpredictable order, `ImmutableSortedDictionary` ensures that its elements are sorted.

Both of these collection types have very similar members:

```
ImmutableDictionary<int, string> dictionary =
    ImmutableDictionary<int, string>.Empty;
dictionary = dictionary.Add(10, "Ten");
dictionary = dictionary.Add(21, "Twenty-One");
dictionary = dictionary.SetItem(10, "Diez");

// Displays "10Diez" and "21Twenty-One" in an unpredictable order.
foreach (KeyValuePair<int, string> item in dictionary)
  Trace.WriteLine(item.Key + item.Value);

string ten = dictionary[10];
// ten == "Diez"

dictionary = dictionary.Remove(21);
```

Note the use of `SetItem`. In a mutable dictionary, you could try doing something like `dictionary[key] = item`, but immutable dictionaries must return the updated immutable dictionary, so they use the `SetItem` method instead:

```
ImmutableSortedDictionary<int, string> sortedDictionary =
    ImmutableSortedDictionary<int, string>.Empty;
sortedDictionary = sortedDictionary.Add(10, "Ten");
sortedDictionary = sortedDictionary.Add(21, "Twenty-One");
sortedDictionary = sortedDictionary.SetItem(10, "Diez");

// Displays "10Diez" followed by "21Twenty-One".
foreach (KeyValuePair<int, string> item in sortedDictionary)
  Trace.WriteLine(item.Key + item.Value);

string ten = sortedDictionary[10];
// ten == "Diez"
```

```
sortedDictionary = sortedDictionary.Remove(21);
```

Unsorted dictionaries and sorted dictionaries have similar performance, but I recommend you use an unordered dictionary unless you need your elements to be sorted (see Table 9-4). Unsorted dictionaries can be a little faster overall. Furthermore, unsorted dictionaries can be used with any key types, whereas sorted dictionaries require their key types to be fully comparable.

Table 9-4. Performance of immutable dictionaries

Operation	ImmutableDictionary<TK,TV>	ImmutableSortedDictionary<TK,TV>
Add	O(log N)	O(log N)
SetItem	O(log N)	O(log N)
Item[key]	O(log N)	O(log N)
Remove	O(log N)	O(log N)

Discussion

In my experience, dictionaries are a common and useful tool when dealing with application state. They can be used in any kind of key/value or lookup scenario.

Like other immutable collections, immutable dictionaries have a builder mechanism for efficient construction if the dictionary contains many elements. For example, if you load your initial reference data at startup, you should use the builder mechanism to construct the initial immutable dictionary. On the other hand, if your reference data is gradually built up during your application's execution, then using the regular immutable dictionary Add method is likely acceptable.

> ImmutableDictionary<TK, TV> and ImmutableSortedDiction
> ary<TK, TV> are in the System.Collections.Immutable (*http://
> bit.ly/sys-coll-imm*) NuGet package.

See Also

Recipe 9.5 covers threadsafe mutable dictionaries.

The MSDN documentation on ImmutableDictionary<TK,TV>.Builder (*http://bit.ly/msdn-imd*) covers an efficient way to populate an immutable dictionary.

The MSDN documentation on ImmutableSortedDictionary<TK,TV>.Builder (*http://bit.ly/msdn-isd*) covers an efficient way to populate an immutable sorted dictionary.

9.5 Threadsafe Dictionaries

Problem

You have a key/value collection (e.g., an in-memory cache) that you need to keep in sync, even though multiple threads are both reading from and writing to it.

Solution

The ConcurrentDictionary<TKey, TValue> type in the .NET framework is a true gem of a data structure. It's threadsafe, using a mixture of fine-grained locks and lock-free techniques to ensure fast access in the vast majority of scenarios.

Its API does take a bit of getting used to. It's very different from the standard Dictionary<TKey, TValue> type, since it must deal with concurrent access from multiple threads. But once you have learned the basics in this recipe, you'll find ConcurrentDictionary<TKey, TValue> to be one of the most useful collection types.

First, let's learn how to write a value to the collection. To set the value of a key, you can use AddOrUpdate:

```
var dictionary = new ConcurrentDictionary<int, string>();
string newValue = dictionary.AddOrUpdate(0,
    key => "Zero",
    (key, oldValue) => "Zero");
```

AddOrUpdate is a bit complex because it must do several things, depending on the current contents of the concurrent dictionary. The first method argument is the key. The second argument is a delegate that transforms the key (in this case, 0) into a value to be added to the dictionary (in this case, "Zero"). This delegate is only invoked if the key doesn't exist in the dictionary. The third argument is another delegate that transforms the key (0) and the old value into an updated value to be stored in the dictionary ("Zero"). This delegate is only invoked if the key does exist in the dictionary. AddOrUpdate returns the new value for that key (the same value that was returned by one of the delegates).

Now for the part that really bends your brain: in order for the concurrent dictionary to work properly, AddOrUpdate *might* have to invoke either (or both) delegates multiple times. This is very rare, but it *can* happen. So your delegates should be simple and fast and not cause side effects. This means that your delegate should only create the value; it shouldn't change any other variables in your application. The same principle holds for all delegates you pass to methods on ConcurrentDictionary<TKey, TValue>.

There are several other ways to add values to a dictionary. One shortcut is to just use indexing syntax:

```
// Using the same "dictionary" as above.
// Adds (or updates) key 0 to have the value "Zero".
dictionary[0] = "Zero";
```

Indexing syntax is less powerful; it doesn't give you the ability to update a value based on the existing value. The syntax is simpler and works fine, however, if you already have the value you want to store in the dictionary.

Let's look at how to read a value. This can be easily done via TryGetValue:

```
// Using the same "dictionary" as above.
bool keyExists = dictionary.TryGetValue(0, out string currentValue);
```

TryGetValue will return true and set the out value if the key was found in the dictionary. If the key wasn't found, TryGetValue will return false. You can also use indexing syntax to read values, but I find that much less useful because it'll throw an exception if a key isn't found. Keep in mind that a concurrent dictionary has multiple threads reading, updating, adding, and removing values; in many situations, it's difficult to know whether a key exists or not until you attempt to read it.

Removing values is just as easy as reading them:

```
// Using the same "dictionary" as above.
bool keyExisted = dictionary.TryRemove(0, out string removedValue);
```

TryRemove is almost identical to TryGetValue, except (of course) it removes the key/value pair if the key was found in the dictionary.

Discussion

Although ConcurrentDictionary<TKey, TValue> is threadsafe, that doesn't mean its operations are atomic. If multiple threads call AddOrUpdate concurrently, it's possible for both of them to detect that the key isn't present, and both of them concurrently execute their delegate that creates a new value.

I think ConcurrentDictionary<TKey, TValue> is awesome, mainly because of the incredibly powerful AddOrUpdate method. However, it doesn't fit the bill in every situation. ConcurrentDictionary<TKey, TValue> is best when you have multiple threads reading and writing to a shared collection. If the updates are not constant (if they're more rare), then ImmutableDictionary<TKey, TValue> may be a better choice.

ConcurrentDictionary<TKey, TValue> is best in a shared-data situation, where multiple threads share the same collection. If some threads only add elements and other threads only remove elements, you'd be better served by a producer/consumer collection.

ConcurrentDictionary<TKey, TValue> isn't the only threadsafe collection. The BCL also provides ConcurrentStack<T>, ConcurrentQueue<T>, and ConcurrentBag<T>.

Threadsafe collections are commonly used as producer/consumer collections, which will be covered in the rest of this chapter.

See Also

Recipe 9.4 covers immutable dictionaries, which are ideal if the contents of the dictionary change very rarely.

9.6 Blocking Queues

Problem

You need a conduit to pass messages or data from one thread to another. For example, one thread could be loading data, which it pushes down the conduit as it loads; meanwhile, there are other threads on the receiving end of the conduit that receive the data and process it.

Solution

The .NET type `BlockingCollection<T>` was designed to be this kind of conduit. By default, `BlockingCollection<T>` is a blocking queue, providing first-in, first-out behavior.

A blocking queue needs to be shared by multiple threads, and it's usually defined as a private, read-only field:

```
private readonly BlockingCollection<int> _blockingQueue =
    new BlockingCollection<int>();
```

Usually, a thread will *either* add items to the collection *or* remove items from the collection, but not both. Threads that add items are called *producer threads*, and threads that remove items are called *consumer threads*.

Producer threads can add items by calling `Add`, and when the producer thread is finished (when all items have been added), it can then finish the collection by calling `CompleteAdding`. This notifies the collection that no more items will be added to it, and the collection can then inform its consumers that there are no more items.

Here's a simple example of a producer that adds two items and then marks the collection complete:

```
_blockingQueue.Add(7);
_blockingQueue.Add(13);
_blockingQueue.CompleteAdding();
```

Consumer threads usually run in a loop, waiting for the next item and then process-ing it. If you take the producer code and put it in a separate thread (e.g., via Task.Run), then you can consume those items like this:

```
// Displays "7" followed by "13".
foreach (int item in _blockingQueue.GetConsumingEnumerable())
  Trace.WriteLine(item);
```

If you want to have multiple consumers, GetConsumingEnumerable can be called from multiple threads at the same time. However, each item is only passed to one of those threads. When the collection is completed, the enumerable completes.

Discussion

The preceding examples all use GetConsumingEnumerable for the consumer threads; this is the most common scenario. However, there's also a Take member that enables a consumer to just consume a single item rather than run a loop consuming all the items.

When you use conduits like this, you do need to consider what happens if your pro-ducers run faster than your consumers. If you're producing items faster than you can consume them, then you may need to throttle your queue.

Blocking queues are great when you have a separate thread (such as a threadpool thread) acting as a producer or consumer. They're not as great when you want to access the conduit asynchronously—for example, if a UI thread wants to act as a con-sumer. Recipe 9.8 covers asynchronous queues.

Whenever you introduce a conduit like this into your application, consider switching to the TPL Dataflow library. A lot of the time, using TPL Dataflow is simpler than building your own conduits and background threads.

BufferBlock<T> from TPL Dataflow can act like a blocking queue, and TPL Dataflow allows building a pipeline or mesh for processing. In many simpler cases, though, ordinary blocking queues like BlockingCollection<T> are the appropriate design choice.

You could also use AsyncEx library's AsyncProducerConsumerQueue<T>, which can act like a blocking queue.

See Also

Recipe 9.7 covers blocking stacks and bags, if you want a similar conduit without first-in, first-out semantics.

Recipe 9.8 covers queues that have asynchronous rather than blocking APIs.

Recipe 9.12 covers queues that have both asynchronous and blocking APIs.

Recipe 9.9 covers queues that throttle their number of items.

9.7 Blocking Stacks and Bags

Problem

You need a conduit to pass messages or data from one thread to another, but you don't want (or need) the conduit to have first-in, first-out semantics.

Solution

The .NET type `BlockingCollection<T>` acts as a blocking queue by default, but it can also act like any kind of producer/consumer collection. It's actually a wrapper around a threadsafe collection that implements `IProducerConsumerCollection<T>`.

So, you can create a `BlockingCollection<T>` with last-in, first-out (stack) semantics or unordered (bag) semantics:

```
BlockingCollection<int> _blockingStack = new BlockingCollection<int>(
    new ConcurrentStack<int>());
BlockingCollection<int> _blockingBag = new BlockingCollection<int>(
    new ConcurrentBag<int>());
```

It's important to keep in mind that there are now race conditions around the ordering of the items. If you let the same producer code execute before any consumer code, and then execute the consumer code after the producer code, then the order of the items will be exactly like a stack:

```
// Producer code
_blockingStack.Add(7);
_blockingStack.Add(13);
_blockingStack.CompleteAdding();

// Consumer code
// Displays "13" followed by "7".
foreach (int item in _blockingStack.GetConsumingEnumerable())
  Trace.WriteLine(item);
```

When the producer code and consumer code are on different threads (which is the usual case), the consumer always gets the most recently added item next. For example, the producer could add 7, the consumer could take 7, the producer could add 13, and the consumer could take 13. The consumer does *not* wait for `CompleteAdding` to be called before it returns the first item.

Discussion

The same considerations around throttling that apply to blocking queues also apply to blocking stacks and bags. If your producers run faster than your consumers and you need to limit the memory usage of your blocking stack/bag, you can use throttling as shown in Recipe 9.9.

This recipe uses `GetConsumingEnumerable` for the consumer code; this is the most common scenario. There is also a `Take` member that enables a consumer to just consume a single item rather than run a loop consuming all the items.

If you want to access shared stacks or bags asynchronously rather than by blocking (for example, having your UI thread act as a consumer), see Recipe 9.11.

See Also

Recipe 9.6 covers blocking queues, which are much more commonly used than blocking stacks or bags.

Recipe 9.11 covers asynchronous stacks and bags.

9.8 Asynchronous Queues

Problem

You need a conduit to pass messages or data from one part of code to another in a first-in, first-out manner, without blocking threads.

For example, one piece of code could be loading data, which it pushes down the conduit as it loads; meanwhile, the UI thread is receiving the data and displaying it.

Solution

What you need is a queue with an asynchronous API. There is no type like this in the core .NET framework, but there are a couple of options available from NuGet.

The first option is to use Channels. Channels are a modern library for asynchronous producer/consumer collections, with a nice emphasis on high performance for high-volume scenarios. Producers generally write items to a channel using `WriteAsync`, and when they are all done producing, one of them calls `Complete` to notify the channel that there won't be any more items in the future, like this:

```
Channel<int> queue = Channel.CreateUnbounded<int>();

// Producer code
ChannelWriter<int> writer = queue.Writer;
await writer.WriteAsync(7);
```

```
await writer.WriteAsync(13);
writer.Complete();

// Consumer code
// Displays "7" followed by "13".
ChannelReader<int> reader = queue.Reader;
await foreach (int value in reader.ReadAllAsync())
  Trace.WriteLine(value);
```

This more natural consumer code uses asynchronous streams; see Chapter 3 for more information. As of this writing, asynchronous streams are only available on the newest .NET platforms; older platforms can use the following pattern:

```
// Consumer code (older platforms)
// Displays "7" followed by "13".
ChannelReader<int> reader = queue.Reader;
while (await reader.WaitToReadAsync())
  while (reader.TryRead(out int value))
    Trace.WriteLine(value);
```

Note the double while loop in the consumer code for older platforms; this is normal. WaitToReadAsync will asynchronously wait until an item is available or the channel has been marked complete; it returns true when there is an item available to be read. TryRead will attempt to read an item (immediately and synchronously), returning true if an item was read. If TryRead returns false, this could be because there's no item available *right now*, or it could be because the channel has been marked complete and there will never be any more items. So, when TryRead returns false, the inner while loop exits and the consumer again calls WaitToReadAsync, which will return false if the channel has been marked complete.

Another producer/consumer queue option is to use BufferBlock<T> from the TPL Dataflow library. BufferBlock<T> is quite similar to a channel. The following example shows how to declare a BufferBlock<T>, what the producer code looks like, and what the consumer code looks like:

```
var _asyncQueue = new BufferBlock<int>();

// Producer code
await _asyncQueue.SendAsync(7);
await _asyncQueue.SendAsync(13);
_asyncQueue.Complete();

// Consumer code
// Displays "7" followed by "13".
while (await _asyncQueue.OutputAvailableAsync())
  Trace.WriteLine(await _asyncQueue.ReceiveAsync());
```

The example consumer code uses OutputAvailableAsync, which is really only useful if you have just a single consumer. If you have multiple consumers, it is possible that OutputAvailableAsync will return true for more than one consumer even though

there is only one item. If the queue is completed, then ReceiveAsync will throw Inva
lidOperationException. So if you have multiple consumers, the consumer code usually looks more like the following:

```
while (true)
{
  int item;
  try
  {
    item = await _asyncQueue.ReceiveAsync();
  }
  catch (InvalidOperationException)
  {
    break;
  }
  Trace.WriteLine(item);
}
```

You can also use the AsyncProducerConsumerQueue<T> type from the Nito.AsyncEx
NuGet library. The API is similar to but not exactly the same as BufferBlock<T>:

```
var _asyncQueue = new AsyncProducerConsumerQueue<int>();

// Producer code
await _asyncQueue.EnqueueAsync(7);
await _asyncQueue.EnqueueAsync(13);
_asyncQueue.CompleteAdding();

// Consumer code
// Displays "7" followed by "13".
while (await _asyncQueue.OutputAvailableAsync())
  Trace.WriteLine(await _asyncQueue.DequeueAsync());
```

This consumer code also uses OutputAvailableAsync and has the same problems as
BufferBlock<T>. If you have multiple consumers, the consumer code usually looks
more like the following:

```
while (true)
{
  int item;
  try
  {
    item = await _asyncQueue.DequeueAsync();
  }
  catch (InvalidOperationException)
  {
    break;
  }
  Trace.WriteLine(item);
}
```

Discussion

I recommend using Channels for asynchronous producer/consumer queues whenever possible. They have multiple sampling options in addition to throttling, and they are highly optimized. However, if your application logic can be expressed as a "pipeline" through which data flows, then TPL Dataflow may be a more natural fit. The final option is `AsyncProducerConsumerQueue<T>`, which may make sense if your application is already using other types from `AsyncEx`.

 Channels can be found in the `System.Threading.Channels` (*http://bit.ly/sys-thrd-chanls*) NuGet package. The `BufferBlock<T>` type is in the `System.Threading.Tasks.Dataflow` (*http://bit.ly/nuget-df*) NuGet package. The `AsyncProducerConsumerQueue<T>` type is in the `Nito.AsyncEx` (*http://bit.ly/nito-async*) NuGet package.

See Also

Recipe 9.6 covers producer/consumer queues with blocking semantics rather than asynchronous semantics.

Recipe 9.12 covers producer/consumer queues that have *both* blocking and asynchronous semantics.

Recipe 9.7 covers asynchronous stacks and bags if you want a similar conduit without first-in, first-out semantics.

9.9 Throttling Queues

Problem

You have a producer/consumer queue, and your producers might run faster than your consumers, which would cause undesired memory usage. You also want to keep all the queue items, so you need a way to throttle the producers.

Solution

When you use producer/consumer queues, you do need to consider what happens if your producers run faster than your consumers, unless you're sure that your consumers will *always* run faster. If you're producing items faster than you can consume them, then you may need to throttle your queue. You can throttle a queue by designating a maximum number of elements. When a queue is "full," it applies backpressure to the producers, blocking them until there is more room in the queue.

Channels can be throttled by creating a bounded channel rather than an unbounded channel. Since channels are asynchronous, producers will be asynchronously throttled:

```
Channel<int> queue = Channel.CreateBounded<int>(1);
ChannelWriter<int> writer = queue.Writer;

// This Write completes immediately.
await writer.WriteAsync(7);

// This Write (asynchronously) waits for the 7 to be removed
// before it enqueues the 13.
await writer.WriteAsync(13);

writer.Complete();
```

BufferBlock<T> has built-in support for throttling, explored in more detail in Recipe 5.4. With dataflow blocks, you set the BoundedCapacity option:

```
var queue = new BufferBlock<int>(
    new DataflowBlockOptions { BoundedCapacity = 1 });

// This Send completes immediately.
await queue.SendAsync(7);

// This Send (asynchronously) waits for the 7 to be removed
// before it enqueues the 13.
await queue.SendAsync(13);

queue.Complete();
```

The producer in the preceding code snippet uses the asynchronous SendAsync API; the same approach works for the synchronous Post API.

The AsyncEx type AsyncProducerConsumerQueue<T> has support for throttling. Just construct the queue with the appropriate value:

```
var queue = new AsyncProducerConsumerQueue<int>(maxCount: 1);

// This Enqueue completes immediately.
await queue.EnqueueAsync(7);

// This Enqueue (asynchronously) waits for the 7 to be removed
// before it enqueues the 13.
await queue.EnqueueAsync(13);

queue.CompleteAdding();
```

Blocking producer/consumer queues also support throttling. You can use Blocking Collection<T> to throttle the number of items by passing the appropriate value when you create it:

```
var queue = new BlockingCollection<int>(boundedCapacity: 1);

// This Add completes immediately.
queue.Add(7);

// This Add waits for the 7 to be removed before it adds the 13.
queue.Add(13);

queue.CompleteAdding();
```

Discussion

Throttling is necessary whenever producers can run faster than consumers. One scenario you must consider is whether it's possible for producers to run faster than consumers if your application is running on different hardware than yours. Some throttling is usually necessary to ensure your application will run on future hardware and/or cloud instances, which are generally more constrained than developer machines.

Throttling will cause backpressure on the producers, slowing them down to ensure that consumers are able to process all items, without causing undue memory pressure. If you don't need to process *every* item, you can choose to sample instead of throttle. See Recipe 9.10 for sampling producer/consumer queues.

 Channels are in the System.Threading.Channels (*http://bit.ly/sys-thrd-chanls*) NuGet package. The BufferBlock<T> type is in the System.Threading.Tasks.Dataflow (*http://bit.ly/nuget-df*) NuGet package. The AsyncProducerConsumerQueue<T> type is in the Nito.AsyncEx (*http://bit.ly/nito-async*) NuGet package.

See Also

Recipe 9.8 covers basic asynchronous producer/consumer queue usage.

Recipe 9.6 covers basic synchronous producer/consumer queue usage.

Recipe 9.10 covers sampling producer/consumer queues, an alternative to throttling.

9.10 Sampling Queues

Problem

You have a producer/consumer queue, but your producers may run faster than your consumers, which is causing undesired memory usage. You don't need to keep all the queue items; you need a way to filter the queue items so that the slower producers only need to process the important ones.

Solution

Channels are the easiest way to apply sampling to input items. One common example is to always take the latest *n* items, discarding the oldest items once the queue is full:

```
Channel<int> queue = Channel.CreateBounded<int>(
    new BoundedChannelOptions(1)
    {
        FullMode = BoundedChannelFullMode.DropOldest,
    });
ChannelWriter<int> writer = queue.Writer;

// This Write completes immediately.
await writer.WriteAsync(7);

// This Write also completes immediately.
// The 7 is discarded unless a consumer has already retrieved it.
await writer.WriteAsync(13);
```

This is an easy way to tame input streams, keeping them from flooding your consumers.

There are other `BoundedChannelFullMode` options as well. For example, if you wanted the *oldest* items to be preserved, you could discard any new items once the channel is full:

```
Channel<int> queue = Channel.CreateBounded<int>(
    new BoundedChannelOptions(1)
    {
        FullMode = BoundedChannelFullMode.DropWrite,
    });
ChannelWriter<int> writer = queue.Writer;

// This Write completes immediately.
await writer.WriteAsync(7);

// This Write also completes immediately.
// The 13 is discarded unless a consumer has already retrieved the 7.
await writer.WriteAsync(13);
```

Discussion

Channels are great for doing simple sampling like this. A particularly useful option in many situations is `BoundedChannelFullMode.DropOldest`. More complex sampling would need to be done by the consumers themselves.

If you need to do time-based sampling, such as "only 10 items per second," use System.Reactive. System.Reactive has natural operators for working with time.

Channels are located in the System.Threading.Channels (*http://bit.ly/sys-thrd-chanls*) NuGet package.

See Also

Recipe 9.9 covers throttling channels, which limits the number of items in the channel by blocking producers rather than dropping items.

Recipe 9.8 covers basic channel usage, including producer and consumer code.

Recipe 6.4 covers throttling and sampling using System.Reactive, which supports time-based sampling.

9.11 Asynchronous Stacks and Bags

Problem

You need a conduit to pass messages or data from one part of code to another, but you don't want (or need) the conduit to have first-in, first-out semantics.

Solution

The Nito.AsyncEx library provides a type AsyncCollection<T>, which acts like an asynchronous queue by default, but it can also act like any kind of producer/consumer collection. The wrapper around an IProducerConsumerCollection<T>, AsyncCollection<T> is also the async equivalent of the .NET BlockingCollection<T>, which is covered in Recipe 9.7.

AsyncCollection<T> supports last-in, first-out (stack) or unordered (bag) semantics, based on whatever collection you pass to its constructor:

```
var _asyncStack = new AsyncCollection<int>(
    new ConcurrentStack<int>());
var _asyncBag = new AsyncCollection<int>(
    new ConcurrentBag<int>());
```

Note that there's a race condition around the ordering of items in the stack. If all producers complete before consumers start, then the order of items is like a regular stack:

```
// Producer code
await _asyncStack.AddAsync(7);
await _asyncStack.AddAsync(13);
_asyncStack.CompleteAdding();

// Consumer code
```

```
// Displays "13" followed by "7".
while (await _asyncStack.OutputAvailableAsync())
  Trace.WriteLine(await _asyncStack.TakeAsync());
```

When both producers and consumers are executing concurrently (which is the usual case), the consumer will always get the most recently added item next. This will cause the collection as a whole to act not quite like a stack. Of course, the bag collection has no ordering at all.

AsyncCollection<T> has support for throttling, which is necessary if producers may add to the collection faster than the consumers can remove from it. Just construct the collection with the appropriate value:

```
var _asyncStack = new AsyncCollection<int>(
    new ConcurrentStack<int>(), maxCount: 1);
```

Now the same producer code will asynchronously wait as needed:

```
// This Add completes immediately.
await _asyncStack.AddAsync(7);

// This Add (asynchronously) waits for the 7 to be removed
// before it enqueues the 13.
await _asyncStack.AddAsync(13);

_asyncStack.CompleteAdding();
```

The example consumer code uses OutputAvailableAsync, which has the same limitation described in Recipe 9.8. If you have multiple consumers, the consumer code usually looks more like the following:

```
while (true)
{
  int item;
  try
  {
    item = await _asyncStack.TakeAsync();
  }
  catch (InvalidOperationException)
  {
    break;
  }
  Trace.WriteLine(item);
}
```

Discussion

AsyncCollection<T> is just the asynchronous equivalent of BlockingCollection<T> with a slightly different API.

The `AsyncCollection<T>` type is in the `Nito.AsyncEx` (*http://bit.ly/nito-async*) NuGet package.

See Also

Recipe 9.8 covers asynchronous queues, which are much more common than asynchronous stacks or bags.

Recipe 9.7 covers synchronous (blocking) stacks and bags.

9.12 Blocking/Asynchronous Queues

Problem

You need a conduit to pass messages or data from one part of code to another in a first-in, first-out manner, and you need the flexibility to treat either the producer end or the consumer end as synchronous or asynchronous.

For example, a background thread may be loading data and pushing it into the conduit, and you want the background thread to synchronously block if the conduit is too full. At the same time, the UI thread is receiving data from the conduit, and you want the UI thread to asynchronously pull data from the conduit so the UI remains responsive.

Solution

After looking at blocking queues in Recipe 9.6 and asynchronous queues in Recipe 9.8, now we'll learn about a few queue types that support both blocking and asynchronous APIs.

The first is `BufferBlock<T>` and `ActionBlock<T>` from the TPL Dataflow NuGet library. `BufferBlock<T>` can be easily used as an asynchronous producer/consumer queue (see Recipe 9.8 for more details):

```
var queue = new BufferBlock<int>();

// Producer code
await queue.SendAsync(7);
await queue.SendAsync(13);
queue.Complete();

// Consumer code for a single consumer
while (await queue.OutputAvailableAsync())
  Trace.WriteLine(await queue.ReceiveAsync());
```

```
// Consumer code for multiple consumers
while (true)
{
  int item;
  try
  {
    item = await queue.ReceiveAsync();
  }
  catch (InvalidOperationException)
  {
    break;
  }

  Trace.WriteLine(item);
}
```

As you can see in the following example, `BufferBlock<T>` also supports a synchronous API for both producers and consumers:

```
var queue = new BufferBlock<int>();

// Producer code
queue.Post(7);
queue.Post(13);
queue.Complete();

// Consumer code
while (true)
{
  int item;
  try
  {
    item = queue.Receive();
  }
  catch (InvalidOperationException)
  {
    break;
  }

  Trace.WriteLine(item);
}
```

The consumer code using `BufferBlock<T>` is rather awkward, since it isn't the "dataflow way" of writing code. The TPL Dataflow library includes a number of blocks that can be linked together, enabling you to define a reactive mesh. In this case, a producer/consumer queue completing with a particular action can be defined using `ActionBlock<T>`:

```
// Consumer code is passed to queue constructor.
ActionBlock<int> queue = new ActionBlock<int>(item => Trace.WriteLine(item));

// Asynchronous producer code
```

```
await queue.SendAsync(7);
await queue.SendAsync(13);

// Synchronous producer code
queue.Post(7);
queue.Post(13);
queue.Complete();
```

If the TPL Dataflow library isn't available on your desired platform(s), then there is an AsyncProducerConsumerQueue<T> type in Nito.AsyncEx that also supports both synchronous and asynchronous methods:

```
var queue = new AsyncProducerConsumerQueue<int>();

// Asynchronous producer code
await queue.EnqueueAsync(7);
await queue.EnqueueAsync(13);

// Synchronous producer code
queue.Enqueue(7);
queue.Enqueue(13);

queue.CompleteAdding();

// Asynchronous single consumer code
while (await queue.OutputAvailableAsync())
  Trace.WriteLine(await queue.DequeueAsync());

// Asynchronous multi-consumer code
while (true)
{
  int item;
  try
  {
    item = await queue.DequeueAsync();
  }
  catch (InvalidOperationException)
  {
    break;
  }
  Trace.WriteLine(item);
}

// Synchronous consumer code
foreach (int item in queue.GetConsumingEnumerable())
  Trace.WriteLine(item);
```

Discussion

I recommend using BufferBlock<T> or ActionBlock<T> if possible because the TPL Dataflow library has been more extensively tested than the Nito.AsyncEx library.

However, `AsyncProducerConsumerQueue<T>` may be useful if your application is already using other types from the `AsyncEx` library.

It is also possible to use `System.Threading.Channels` synchronously, but only indirectly. Their natural API is asynchronous, but since they are threadsafe collections, you can force them to work synchronously by wrapping your production or consumption code inside a `Task.Run` and then blocking on the task returned from `Task.Run`, like this:

```
Channel<int> queue = Channel.CreateBounded<int>(10);

// Producer code
ChannelWriter<int> writer = queue.Writer;
Task.Run(async () =>
{
  await writer.WriteAsync(7);
  await writer.WriteAsync(13);
  writer.Complete();
}).GetAwaiter().GetResult();

// Consumer code
ChannelReader<int> reader = queue.Reader;
Task.Run(async () =>
{
  while (await reader.WaitToReadAsync())
    while (reader.TryRead(out int value))
      Trace.WriteLine(value);
}).GetAwaiter().GetResult();
```

TPL Dataflow blocks, `AsyncProducerConsumerQueue<T>`, and Channels all support throttling by passing options during construction. Throttling is necessary when you have producers that push items faster than your consumers can consume them, which could cause your application to take up large amounts of memory.

The `BufferBlock<T>` and `ActionBlock<T>` types are in the `System.Threading.Tasks.Dataflow` (*http://bit.ly/nuget-df*) NuGet package. The `AsyncProducerConsumerQueue<T>` type is in the `Nito.AsyncEx` (*http://bit.ly/nito-async*) NuGet package. Channels are in the `System.Threading.Channels` (*http://bit.ly/sys-thrd-chanls*) NuGet package.

See Also

Recipe 9.6 covers blocking producer/consumer queues.

Recipe 9.8 covers asynchronous producer/consumer queues.

Recipe 5.4 covers throttling dataflow blocks.

CHAPTER 10

Cancellation

The .NET 4.0 framework introduced exhaustive and well-designed cancellation support. This support is cooperative, which means that cancellation can be requested but not enforced on code. Since cancellation is cooperative, it isn't possible to cancel code unless it is written to support cancellation. For this reason, I recommend supporting cancellation in as much of your own code as possible.

Cancellation is a type of signal, with two different sides: a source that triggers the cancellation and a receiver that then responds to the cancellation. In .NET, the source is `CancellationTokenSource` and the receiver is `CancellationToken`. The recipes in this chapter cover both sources and receivers of cancellation in normal usage and describe how to use the cancellation support to interoperate with nonstandard forms of cancellation.

Cancellation is treated as a special kind of error. The convention is that canceled code will throw an exception of type `OperationCanceledException` (or a derived type, such as `TaskCanceledException`). This way the calling code knows that the cancellation was observed.

To indicate to calling code that your method supports cancellation, you should take a `CancellationToken` as a parameter. This parameter is usually the last parameter, unless your method also reports progress (Recipe 2.3). You can also consider providing an overload or default parameter value for consumers that do not require cancellation:

```
public void CancelableMethodWithOverload(CancellationToken cancellationToken)
{
  // Code goes here.
}

public void CancelableMethodWithOverload()
{
```

```
    CancelableMethodWithOverload(CancellationToken.None);
}

public void CancelableMethodWithDefault(
    CancellationToken cancellationToken = default)
{
    // Code goes here.
}
```

CancellationToken.None represents a cancellation token that will never be canceled, and is a special value that is equivalent to default(CancellationToken). Consumers pass this value when they don't ever want the operation to be canceled.

Asynchronous streams have a similar but more complex way of handling cancellation. Canceling asynchronous streams is covered in detail in Recipe 3.4.

10.1 Issuing Cancellation Requests

Problem

Your code calls cancelable code (that takes a CancellationToken) and you need to cancel it.

Solution

The CancellationTokenSource type is the source for a CancellationToken. It only enables code to respond to cancellation requests; the CancellationTokenSource members enable code to request cancellation.

Each CancellationTokenSource is independent from every other one (unless you link them, as considered in Recipe 10.8). The Token property returns a Cancella tionToken for that source, and the Cancel method issues the actual cancellation request.

The following code illustrates creating a CancellationTokenSource and using Token and Cancel. The code uses an async method because it's easier to illustrate in a short code sample; the same Token/Cancel pair is used to cancel all kinds of code:

```
void IssueCancelRequest()
{
    using var cts = new CancellationTokenSource();
    var task = CancelableMethodAsync(cts.Token);

    // At this point, the operation has been started.

    // Issue the cancellation request.
    cts.Cancel();
}
```

In the preceding example code, the task variable is ignored after it has started running; in real-world code, that task would probably be stored somewhere and awaited so that the end user is aware of the final result.

When you cancel code, there is almost always a race condition. The cancelable code may have been *just about to finish* when the cancel request is made, and if it doesn't happen to check its cancellation token before finishing, it will actually complete successfully. In fact, when you cancel code, there are three possibilities: it may respond to the cancellation request (throwing OperationCanceledException), it may finish successfully, or it may finish with an error unrelated to the cancellation (throwing a different exception).

The following code is just like the last, except that it awaits the task, illustrating all three possible results:

```
async Task IssueCancelRequestAsync()
{
  using var cts = new CancellationTokenSource();
  var task = CancelableMethodAsync(cts.Token);

  // At this point, the operation is happily running.

  // Issue the cancellation request.
  cts.Cancel();

  // (Asynchronously) wait for the operation to finish.
  try
  {
    await task;
    // If we get here, the operation completed successfully
    //  before the cancellation took effect.
  }
  catch (OperationCanceledException)
  {
    // If we get here, the operation was canceled before it completed.
  }
  catch (Exception)
  {
    // If we get here, the operation completed with an error
    //  before the cancellation took effect.
    throw;
  }
}
```

Normally, setting up the CancellationTokenSource and issuing the cancellation are in separate methods. Once you cancel a CancellationTokenSource instance, it is permanently canceled. If you need another source, you must create another instance. The following code is a more realistic GUI-based example that uses one button to start an asynchronous operation and another button to cancel it. It also disables and enables `StartButton` and `CancelButton` so that there can only be one operation at a time:

```
private CancellationTokenSource _cts;

private async void StartButton_Click(object sender, RoutedEventArgs e)
{
  StartButton.IsEnabled = false;
  CancelButton.IsEnabled = true;
  try
  {
    _cts = new CancellationTokenSource();
    CancellationToken token = _cts.Token;
    await Task.Delay(TimeSpan.FromSeconds(5), token);
    MessageBox.Show("Delay completed successfully.");
  }
  catch (OperationCanceledException)
  {
    MessageBox.Show("Delay was canceled.");
  }
  catch (Exception)
  {
    MessageBox.Show("Delay completed with error.");
    throw;
  }
  finally
  {
    StartButton.IsEnabled = true;
    CancelButton.IsEnabled = false;
  }
}

private void CancelButton_Click(object sender, RoutedEventArgs e)
{
  _cts.Cancel();
  CancelButton.IsEnabled = false;
}
```

Discussion

The most realistic example in this recipe used a GUI application, but don't get the impression that cancellation is just for user interfaces. Cancellation has its place on the server as well; for example, ASP.NET provides a cancellation token representing the request timeout or client disconnect. It's true that cancellation token sources are rarer on the server side, but there's no reason you can't use them; they're useful if you need to cancel for some reason not covered by ASP.NET cancellation, such as an additional timeout for a portion of the request processing.

See Also

Recipe 10.4 covers passing tokens to `async` code.

Recipe 10.5 covers passing tokens to parallel code.

Recipe 10.6 covers using tokens with reactive code.

Recipe 10.7 covers passing tokens to dataflow meshes.

10.2 Responding to Cancellation Requests by Polling

Problem

You have a loop in your code that needs to support cancellation.

Solution

When you have a processing loop in your code, then there isn't a lower-level API to which you can pass the `CancellationToken`. In this case, you should periodically check whether the token has been canceled. The following code observes the token periodically while executing a CPU-bound loop:

```
public int CancelableMethod(CancellationToken cancellationToken)
{
  for (int i = 0; i != 100; ++i)
  {
    Thread.Sleep(1000); // Some calculation goes here.
    cancellationToken.ThrowIfCancellationRequested();
  }
  return 42;
}
```

If your loop is very tight (i.e., if the body of your loop executes very quickly), then you may want to limit how often you check your cancellation token. As always, measure your performance before and after a change like this before deciding which way is best. The following code is similar to the previous example, but it has more iterations of a faster loop, so I added a limit to how often the token is checked:

```
public int CancelableMethod(CancellationToken cancellationToken)
{
  for (int i = 0; i != 100000; ++i)
  {
    Thread.Sleep(1); // Some calculation goes here.
    if (i % 1000 == 0)
      cancellationToken.ThrowIfCancellationRequested();
  }
  return 42;
}
```

The proper limit to use depends entirely on how much work you're doing and how responsive the cancellation needs to be.

Discussion

The majority of the time, your code should just pass through the CancellationToken to the next layer. There are examples of this in Recipes 10.4, 10.5, 10.6, and 10.7. The polling technique in this recipe should only be used if you have a processing loop that needs to support cancellation.

There's another member on CancellationToken called IsCancellationRequested, which starts returning true when the token is canceled. Some people use this member to respond to cancellation, usually by returning a default or null value. I do not recommend this approach for most code. The standard cancellation pattern is to raise an OperationCanceledException, which is taken care of by ThrowIfCancellationRequested. If code further up the stack wants to catch the exception and act like the result is null, then that's fine, but any code taking a CancellationToken should follow the standard cancellation pattern. If you do decide not to follow the cancellation pattern, at least document it clearly.

ThrowIfCancellationRequested works by *polling* the cancellation token; your code has to call it at regular intervals. There's also a way to register a callback that is invoked when cancellation is requested. The callback approach is more about interoperating with other cancellation systems; Recipe 10.9 covers using callbacks with cancellation.

See Also

Recipe 10.4 covers passing tokens to async code.

Recipe 10.5 covers passing tokens to parallel code.

Recipe 10.6 covers using tokens with reactive code.

Recipe 10.7 covers passing tokens to dataflow meshes.

Recipe 10.9 covers using callbacks instead of polling to respond to cancellation requests.

Recipe 10.1 covers issuing a cancellation request.

10.3 Canceling Due to Timeouts

Problem

You have some code that needs to stop running after a timeout.

Solution

Cancellation is a natural solution for timeout situations. A timeout is just one type of cancellation request. The code that needs to be canceled merely observes the cancellation token just like any other cancellation; it should neither know nor care that the cancellation source is a timer.

There are some convenience methods for cancellation token sources that automatically issue a cancel request based on a timer. You can pass the timeout into the constructor:

```
async Task IssueTimeoutAsync()
{
  using var cts = new CancellationTokenSource(TimeSpan.FromSeconds(5));
  CancellationToken token = cts.Token;
  await Task.Delay(TimeSpan.FromSeconds(10), token);
}
```

Alternatively, if you already have a CancellationTokenSource instance, you can start a timeout for that instance:

```
async Task IssueTimeoutAsync()
{
  using var cts = new CancellationTokenSource();
  CancellationToken token = cts.Token;
  cts.CancelAfter(TimeSpan.FromSeconds(5));
  await Task.Delay(TimeSpan.FromSeconds(10), token);
}
```

Discussion

To execute code with a timeout, use CancellationTokenSource and CancelAfter (or the constructor). There are other ways to do the same thing, but using the existing cancellation system is the easiest and most efficient option.

Remember that the code to be canceled needs to observe the cancellation token; it isn't possible to easily cancel un-cancelable code.

See Also

Recipe 10.4 covers passing tokens to async code.

Recipe 10.5 covers passing tokens to parallel code.

Recipe 10.6 covers using tokens with reactive code.

Recipe 10.7 covers passing tokens to dataflow meshes.

10.4 Canceling async Code

Problem

You are using `async` code and need to support cancellation.

Solution

The simplest way to support cancellation in asynchronous code is to just pass the `CancellationToken` through to the next layer. The following example code performs an asynchronous delay and then returns a value; it supports cancellation by passing the token to `Task.Delay`:

```
public async Task<int> CancelableMethodAsync(CancellationToken cancellationToken)
{
  await Task.Delay(TimeSpan.FromSeconds(2), cancellationToken);
  return 42;
}
```

Many asynchronous APIs support `CancellationToken`, so enabling cancellation yourself is usually a simple matter of taking a token and passing it along. As a general rule, if your method calls APIs that take `CancellationToken`, then your method should also take a `CancellationToken` and pass it to every API that supports it.

Discussion

Unfortunately, some methods don't support cancellation. When you're in this situation, there's no easy solution. It's not possible to safely stop arbitrary code unless it's wrapped in a separate executable. If your code calls code that doesn't support cancellation, and if you don't want to wrap that code in a separate executable, you do always have the option of *pretending* to cancel the operation by ignoring the result.

Cancellation should be provided as an option whenever possible. This is because proper cancellation at a higher level depends on proper cancellation at the lower level. So, when you're writing your own `async` methods, try your best to include support for cancellation; you never know what higher-level method will want to call yours, and it might need cancellation.

See Also

Recipe 10.1 covers issuing a cancellation request.

Recipe 10.3 covers using cancellation as a timeout.

10.5 Canceling Parallel Code

Problem

You are using parallel code and need to support cancellation.

Solution

The easiest way to support cancellation is to pass the `CancellationToken` through to the parallel code. `Parallel` methods support this by taking a `ParallelOptions` instance. You can set the `CancellationToken` on a `ParallelOptions` instance in the following manner:

```
void RotateMatrices(IEnumerable<Matrix> matrices, float degrees,
    CancellationToken token)
{
  Parallel.ForEach(matrices,
      new ParallelOptions { CancellationToken = token },
      matrix => matrix.Rotate(degrees));
}
```

Alternatively, it's possible to observe the `CancellationToken` directly in your loop body:

```
void RotateMatrices2(IEnumerable<Matrix> matrices, float degrees,
    CancellationToken token)
{
  // Warning: not recommended; see below.
  Parallel.ForEach(matrices, matrix =>
  {
    matrix.Rotate(degrees);
    token.ThrowIfCancellationRequested();
  });
}
```

The alternative method is more work and doesn't compose as well because the parallel loop will wrap the `OperationCanceledException` within an `AggregateException`. Also, if you pass the `CancellationToken` as part of a `ParallelOptions` instance, the `Parallel` class may make more intelligent decisions about how often to check the token. For these reasons, it's best to pass the token as an option. If you pass the token as an option, you could *also* pass the token to the loop body, but you don't want to *only* pass the token to the loop body.

Parallel LINQ (PLINQ) also has built-in support for cancellation, using the `WithCan cellation` operator:

```
IEnumerable<int> MultiplyBy2(IEnumerable<int> values,
    CancellationToken cancellationToken)
{
```

```
    return values.AsParallel()
        .WithCancellation(cancellationToken)
        .Select(item => item * 2);
}
```

Discussion

Supporting cancellation for parallel work is important for a good user experience. If your application is doing parallel work, it'll use a large amount of CPU at least for a short time. High CPU usage is something that users notice, even if it doesn't interfere with other applications on the same machine. So, I recommend supporting cancellation whenever you do parallel computation (or any other CPU-intensive work), even if the total time spent with high CPU usage isn't extremely long.

See Also

Recipe 10.1 covers issuing a cancellation request.

10.6 Canceling System.Reactive Code

Problem

You have some reactive code, and you need it to be cancelable.

Solution

The System.Reactive library has a notion of a *subscription* to an observable stream. Your code can dispose of the subscription to unsubscribe from the stream. In many cases, this is sufficient to logically cancel the stream. For example, the following code subscribes to mouse clicks when one button is pressed and unsubscribes (cancels the subscription) when another button is pressed:

```
private IDisposable _mouseMovesSubscription;

private void StartButton_Click(object sender, RoutedEventArgs e)
{
  IObservable<Point> mouseMoves = Observable
      .FromEventPattern<MouseEventHandler, MouseEventArgs>(
          handler => (s, a) => handler(s, a),
          handler => MouseMove += handler,
          handler => MouseMove -= handler)
      .Select(x => x.EventArgs.GetPosition(this));
  _mouseMovesSubscription = mouseMoves.Subscribe(value =>
  {
    MousePositionLabel.Content = "(" + value.X + ", " + value.Y + ")";
  });
}
```

```
private void CancelButton_Click(object sender, RoutedEventArgs e)
{
  if (_mouseMovesSubscription != null)
    _mouseMovesSubscription.Dispose();
}
```

It's quite convenient to make System.Reactive work with the `CancellationToken Source`/`CancellationToken` system that everything else uses for cancellation. The rest of this recipe covers ways that System.Reactive observables interact with `CancellationToken`.

The first major use case is when the observable code is wrapped in asynchronous code. The basic approach was covered in Recipe 8.5, and now you want to add `CancellationToken` support. In general, the easiest way to do this is to perform all operations using reactive operators and then call `ToTask` to convert the last resulting element to an awaitable task. The following code shows how to asynchronously take the last element in a sequence:

```
CancellationToken cancellationToken = ...
IObservable<int> observable = ...
int lastElement = await observable.TakeLast(1).ToTask(cancellationToken);
// or: int lastElement = await observable.ToTask(cancellationToken);
```

Taking the first element is very similar; just modify the observable before calling `ToTask`:

```
CancellationToken cancellationToken = ...
IObservable<int> observable = ...
int firstElement = await observable.Take(1).ToTask(cancellationToken);
```

Asynchronously converting the entire observable sequence to a task is likewise similar:

```
CancellationToken cancellationToken = ...
IObservable<int> observable = ...
IList<int> allElements = await observable.ToList().ToTask(cancellationToken);
```

Finally, let's consider the reverse situation. We've looked at several ways to handle situations where System.Reactive code responds to `CancellationToken`—that is, where a `CancellationTokenSource` cancel request is translated into a disposal of that subscription. It's also possible to go the other way: issuing a cancellation request as a response to disposal.

The `FromAsync`, `StartAsync`, and `SelectMany` operators all support cancellation, as seen in Recipe 8.6. These operators cover the vast majority of use cases. Rx also provides a `CancellationDisposable` type that cancels a `CancellationToken` when disposed. You can use `CancellationDisposable` directly, like this:

```
using (var cancellation = new CancellationDisposable())
{
```

```
      CancellationToken token = cancellation.Token;
      // Pass the token to methods that respond to it.
    }
    // At this point, the token is canceled.
```

Discussion

System.Reactive (Rx) has its own notion of cancellation: disposing subscriptions. This recipe looked at several ways to make Rx play nicely with the universal cancellation framework introduced in .NET 4.0. As long as you are in the Rx world portion of your code, use the Rx subscription/disposal system; it's cleanest if you only introduce `CancellationToken` support at the boundaries.

See Also

Recipe 8.5 covers asynchronous wrappers around Rx code (without cancellation support).

Recipe 8.6 covers Rx wrappers around asynchronous code (with cancellation support).

Recipe 10.1 covers issuing a cancellation request.

10.7 Canceling Dataflow Meshes

Problem

You are using dataflow meshes and need to support cancellation.

Solution

The best way to support cancellation in your code is to pass the `CancellationToken` through to a cancelable API. Each block in a dataflow mesh supports cancellation as a part of its `DataflowBlockOptions`. If you want to extend your custom dataflow block with cancellation support, set the `CancellationToken` property on the block options:

```
IPropagatorBlock<int, int> CreateMyCustomBlock(
    CancellationToken cancellationToken)
{
  var blockOptions = new ExecutionDataflowBlockOptions
  {
    CancellationToken = cancellationToken
  };
  var multiplyBlock = new TransformBlock<int, int>(item => item * 2,
      blockOptions);
  var addBlock = new TransformBlock<int, int>(item => item + 2,
      blockOptions);
  var divideBlock = new TransformBlock<int, int>(item => item / 2,
```

```
    blockOptions);

  var flowCompletion = new DataflowLinkOptions
  {
    PropagateCompletion = true
  };
  multiplyBlock.LinkTo(addBlock, flowCompletion);
  addBlock.LinkTo(divideBlock, flowCompletion);

  return DataflowBlock.Encapsulate(multiplyBlock, divideBlock);
}
```

In this example, I applied the `CancellationToken` to every block in the mesh, which isn't strictly necessary. Since I'm also propagating completion along the links, I could apply it to the first block and allow it to propagate through. Cancellations are considered a special form of error, so the blocks further down the pipeline would be completed with an error as that error propagates through. That said, if I'm canceling a mesh, I may as well cancel every block simultaneously, so in this case I usually set the `CancellationToken` option on every block.

Discussion

In dataflow meshes, cancellation is *not* a form of flush. When a block is canceled, it drops all its input and refuses to take any new items. So if you cancel a block while it's running, you *will* lose data.

See Also

Recipe 10.1 covers issuing a cancellation request.

10.8 Injecting Cancellation Requests

Problem

You have a layer of your code that needs to respond to cancellation requests and also issue its own cancellation requests to the next layer.

Solution

The .NET 4.0 cancellation system has built-in support for this scenario, known as *linked cancellation tokens*. A cancellation token source can be created linked to one (or many) existing tokens. When you create a linked cancellation token source, the resulting token is canceled when any of the existing tokens is canceled or when the linked source is explicitly canceled.

The following code performs an asynchronous HTTP request. The token passed into the `GetWithTimeoutAsync` method represents cancellation requested by the end user, and the `GetWithTimeoutAsync` method also applies a timeout to the request:

```
async Task<HttpResponseMessage> GetWithTimeoutAsync(HttpClient client,
    string url, CancellationToken cancellationToken)
{
  using CancellationTokenSource cts = CancellationTokenSource
      .CreateLinkedTokenSource(cancellationToken);
  cts.CancelAfter(TimeSpan.FromSeconds(2));
  CancellationToken combinedToken = cts.Token;

  return await client.GetAsync(url, combinedToken);
}
```

The resulting `combinedToken` is canceled when either the user cancels the existing `cancellationToken` or when the linked source is canceled by `CancelAfter`.

Discussion

Although the preceding example only used a single `CancellationToken` source, the `CreateLinkedTokenSource` method can take any number of cancellation tokens as parameters. This enables you to create a single combined token from which you can implement your logical cancellation. For example, ASP.NET provides a cancellation token that represents the user disconnecting (`HttpContext.RequestAborted`); handler code may create a linked token that responds to either a user disconnecting or its own cancellation reason, such as a timeout.

Keep in mind the lifetime of the linked cancellation token source. The previous example is the usual use case, where one or more cancellation tokens are passed into the method, which then links them together and passes them on as a combined token. Note also that the example code uses the `using` statement, which ensures that the linked cancellation token source is disposed of when the operation is complete (and the combined token is no longer being used). Consider what would happen if the code didn't dispose of the linked cancellation token source: it's possible that the `GetWithTimeoutAsync` method may be called multiple times with the same (long-lived) existing token, in which case the code would link a new token source each time the method is invoked. Even after the HTTP requests complete (and nothing is using the combined token), that linked source is still attached to the existing token. To prevent memory leaks like this, dispose of the linked cancellation token source when you no longer need the combined token.

See Also

Recipe 10.1 covers issuing cancellation requests in general.

Recipe 10.3 covers using cancellation as a timeout.

10.9 Interop with Other Cancellation Systems

Problem

You have some external or legacy code with its own notion of cancellation, and you want to control it using a standard CancellationToken.

Solution

The CancellationToken has two primary ways to respond to a cancellation request: polling (covered in Recipe 10.2) and callbacks (the subject of this recipe). Polling is normally used for CPU-bound code, such as data processing loops; callbacks are normally used in all other scenarios. You can register a callback for a token using the CancellationToken.Register method.

For example, let's say you're wrapping the System.Net.NetworkInformation.Ping type and you want to be able to cancel a ping. The Ping class already has a Task-based API but does not support CancellationToken. Instead, the Ping type has its own SendAsyncCancel method that you can use to cancel a ping. To do this, register a callback that invokes that method:

```
async Task<PingReply> PingAsync(string hostNameOrAddress,
    CancellationToken cancellationToken)
{
  using var ping = new Ping();
  Task<PingReply> task = ping.SendPingAsync(hostNameOrAddress);
  using CancellationTokenRegistration _ = cancellationToken
      .Register(() => ping.SendAsyncCancel());
  return await task;
}
```

Now, when a cancellation is requested, the CancellationToken will invoke the SendAsyncCancel method for you, canceling the SendPingAsync method.

Discussion

The CancellationToken.Register method can be used to interoperate with any kind of alternative cancellation system. But do bear in mind that when a method takes a CancellationToken, a cancellation request should only cancel that one operation. Some alternative cancellation systems implement a cancel by closing some resource, which can cancel multiple operations; this kind of cancellation system doesn't map well to a CancellationToken. If you do decide to wrap that kind of cancellation in a CancellationToken, you should document its unusual cancellation semantics.

Keep in mind the lifetime of the callback registration. The Register method returns a disposable that should be disposed of when that callback is no longer needed. The preceding example code uses a `using` statement to clean up when the asynchronous operation completes. If the code didn't have that `using` statement, then each time the code is called with the same (long-lived) `CancellationToken`, it would add another callback (which in turn keeps the `Ping` object alive). To avoid memory and resource leaks, dispose of the callback registration when you no longer need the callback.

See Also

Recipe 10.2 covers responding to a cancellation token by polling rather than callbacks.

Recipe 10.1 covers issuing cancellation requests in general.

CHAPTER 11

Functional-Friendly OOP

Modern programs require asynchronous programming; these days servers must scale better than ever, and end-user applications must be more responsive than ever. Developers are finding that they must learn asynchronous programming, and as they explore this world, they find that it often clashes with the traditional object-oriented programming that they're accustomed to.

The core reason for this is because asynchronous programming is functional. By "functional," I don't mean "it works"; I mean it's a functional style of programming instead of a procedural style of programming. A lot of developers learned basic functional programming in college and have hardly touched it since. If code like (car (cdr '(3 5 7))) gives you a chill as repressed memories come flooding back, then you may be in that category. But don't fear; modern asynchronous programming isn't that hard once you get used to it.

The major breakthrough with async is that you can still think procedurally while programming asynchronously. This makes asynchronous methods easier to write and understand. However, under the covers, asynchronous code is still functional in nature, and this causes some problems when people try to force async methods into classical object-oriented designs. The recipes in this chapter deal with those friction points where asynchronous code clashes with object-oriented programming.

These friction points are especially noticeable when translating an existing OOP code base into an async-friendly code base.

11.1 Async Interfaces and Inheritance

Problem

You have a method in your interface or base class that you want to make asynchronous.

Solution

The key to understanding this problem and its solution is to realize that `async` is an implementation detail. The `async` keyword can only be applied to methods with implementations; it isn't possible to apply it to abstract methods or interface methods (unless they have default implementations). However, you can define a method with the same signature as an `async` method, just without the `async` keyword.

Remember that *types* are awaitable, not *methods*. You can `await` a `Task` returned by a method, whether or not that method is implemented using `async`. So, an interface or abstract method can just return a `Task` (or `Task<T>`), and the return value of that method is awaitable.

The following code defines an interface with an asynchronous method (without the `async` keyword), an implementation of that interface (with `async`), and an independent method that consumes a method of the interface (via `await`):

```
interface IMyAsyncInterface
{
  Task<int> CountBytesAsync(HttpClient client, string url);
}

class MyAsyncClass : IMyAsyncInterface
{
  public async Task<int> CountBytesAsync(HttpClient client, string url)
  {
    var bytes = await client.GetByteArrayAsync(url);
    return bytes.Length;
  }
}

async Task UseMyInterfaceAsync(HttpClient client, IMyAsyncInterface service)
{
  var result = await service.CountBytesAsync(client, "http://www.example.com");
  Trace.WriteLine(result);
}
```

This same pattern works for abstract methods in base classes.

An asynchronous method signature only means that the implementation *may* be asynchronous. It is possible for the actual implementation to be synchronous if it has no real asynchronous work to do. For example, a test stub may implement the same interface (without `async`) by using something like `FromResult`:

```
class MyAsyncClassStub : IMyAsyncInterface
{
  public Task<int> CountBytesAsync(HttpClient client, string url)
  {
    return Task.FromResult(13);
  }
}
```

Discussion

At the time of this writing, `async` and `await` are still gaining traction. As asynchronous methods become more common, asynchronous methods on interfaces and base classes will become more common as well. They're not that hard to work with if you keep in mind that it is the return type that is awaitable (not the method), and that an asynchronous method definition may be implemented either asynchronously or synchronously.

See Also

Recipe 2.2 covers returning a completed task, implementing an asynchronous method signature with synchronous code.

11.2 Async Construction: Factories

Problem

You are coding a type that requires some asynchronous work to be done in its constructor.

Solution

Constructors cannot be `async`, nor can they use the `await` keyword. It would certainly be useful to `await` in a constructor, but this would change the C# language considerably.

One possibility is to have a constructor paired with an `async` initialization method, so the type could be used like this:

```
var instance = new MyAsyncClass();
await instance.InitializeAsync();
```

This approach has some disadvantages. It can be easy to forget to call the `Initiali zeAsync` method, and the instance isn't usable immediately after it's constructed.

A better solution is to make the type its own factory. The following type illustrates the asynchronous factory method pattern:

```
class MyAsyncClass
{
  private MyAsyncClass()
  {
  }

  private async Task<MyAsyncClass> InitializeAsync()
  {
    await Task.Delay(TimeSpan.FromSeconds(1));
    return this;
  }

  public static Task<MyAsyncClass> CreateAsync()
  {
    var result = new MyAsyncClass();
    return result.InitializeAsync();
  }
}
```

The constructor and InitializeAsync method are private so that other code cannot possibly misuse them; so the only way of creating an instance is via the static CreateAsync factory method. Calling code cannot access the instance until after the initialization is complete.

Other code can create an instance like this:

```
MyAsyncClass instance = await MyAsyncClass.CreateAsync();
```

Discussion

The primary advantage of this pattern is that there's no way that other code can get an uninitialized instance of MyAsyncClass. That's why I prefer this pattern over other approaches whenever I can use it.

Unfortunately, this approach does not work in some scenarios—in particular, when your code is using a dependency injection provider. No major dependency injection or inversion of control library works with async code. If you find yourself in one of these scenarios, there are a couple of alternatives that you can consider.

If the instance you're creating is actually a shared resource, then you can use the asynchronous lazy type discussed in Recipe 14.1. Otherwise, you can use the asynchronous initialization pattern discussed in Recipe 11.3.

Here's an example of what *not* to do:

```
class MyAsyncClass
{
  public MyAsyncClass()
```

```
  {
    InitializeAsync();
  }

  // BAD CODE!!
  private async void InitializeAsync()
  {
    await Task.Delay(TimeSpan.FromSeconds(1));
  }
}
```

At first glance, this seems like a reasonable approach: you get a regular constructor that kicks off an asynchronous operation; however, there are several drawbacks that are due to the use of `async void`. The first problem is that when the constructor completes, the instance is still being asynchronously initialized, and there isn't an obvious way to determine when the asynchronous initialization has completed. The second problem is with error handling: any exceptions raised from `InitializeAsync` can't be caught by any `catch` clauses surrounding the object construction.

See Also

Recipe 11.3 covers the asynchronous initialization pattern, a way of doing asynchronous construction that works with dependency injection/inversion of control containers.

Recipe 14.1 covers asynchronous lazy initialization, which is a viable solution if the instance is conceptually a shared resource or service.

11.3 Async Construction: The Asynchronous Initialization Pattern

Problem

You are coding a type that requires some asynchronous work to be done in its constructor, but you cannot use the asynchronous factory pattern (Recipe 11.2) because the instance is created via reflection (e.g., a dependency injection/inversion of control library, data binding, `Activator.CreateInstance`, and so on).

Solution

When you encounter this scenario, you *have* to return an uninitialized instance, though you can mitigate this situation by applying a common pattern: the asynchronous initialization pattern. Every type that requires asynchronous initialization should define a property, like this:

```
Task Initialization { get; }
```

I usually like to define this in a marker interface for types that require asynchronous initialization:

```
/// <summary>
/// Marks a type as requiring asynchronous initialization
/// and provides the result of that initialization.
/// </summary>
public interface IAsyncInitialization
{
  /// <summary>
  /// The result of the asynchronous initialization of this instance.
  /// </summary>
  Task Initialization { get; }
}
```

When you implement this pattern, you should start the initialization (and assign the Initialization property) in the constructor. The results of the asynchronous initialization (including any exceptions) are exposed via that Initialization property. Here's an example implementation of a simple type using asynchronous initialization:

```
class MyFundamentalType : IMyFundamentalType, IAsyncInitialization
{
  public MyFundamentalType()
  {
    Initialization = InitializeAsync();
  }

  public Task Initialization { get; private set; }

  private async Task InitializeAsync()
  {
    // Asynchronously initialize this instance.
    await Task.Delay(TimeSpan.FromSeconds(1));
  }
}
```

If you're using a dependency injection/inversion of control library, you can create and initialize an instance of this type using code like the following:

```
IMyFundamentalType instance = UltimateDIFactory.Create<IMyFundamentalType>();
var instanceAsyncInit = instance as IAsyncInitialization;
if (instanceAsyncInit != null)
  await instanceAsyncInit.Initialization;
```

You can extend this pattern to allow composition of types with asynchronous initialization. In the following example another type that depends on an IMyFundamental Type is defined:

```
class MyComposedType : IMyComposedType, IAsyncInitialization
{
  private readonly IMyFundamentalType _fundamental;
```

```
public MyComposedType(IMyFundamentalType fundamental)
{
  _fundamental = fundamental;
  Initialization = InitializeAsync();
}

public Task Initialization { get; private set; }

private async Task InitializeAsync()
{
  // Asynchronously wait for the fundamental instance to initialize,
  //  if necessary.
  var fundamentalAsyncInit = _fundamental as IAsyncInitialization;
  if (fundamentalAsyncInit != null)
    await fundamentalAsyncInit.Initialization;

  // Do our own initialization (synchronous or asynchronous).
  ...
}
}
```

The composed type waits for all of its components to initialize before it proceeds with its initialization. The rule to follow is that every component should be initialized by the end of InitializeAsync. This ensures that all dependent types are initialized as part of the composed initialization. Any exceptions from a component initialization are propagated to the composed type's initialization.

Discussion

If you can, I recommend using asynchronous factories (Recipe 11.2) or asynchronous lazy initialization (Recipe 14.1) instead of this solution. Those are the best approaches because you never expose an uninitialized instance. However, if your instances are created by dependency injection/inversion of control, data binding, and so on, then you're forced to expose an uninitialized instance, and in that case I recommend using the asynchronous initialization pattern in this recipe.

Remember from the recipe on asynchronous interfaces (Recipe 11.1) that an asynchronous method signature only means that the method *may* be asynchronous. The MyComposedType.InitializeAsync code is a good example of this: if the IMyFundamentalType instance does not also implement IAsyncInitialization and MyComposedType has no asynchronous initialization of its own, then its InitializeAsync method completes synchronously.

The code for checking whether an instance implements IAsyncInitialization and initializing it is a bit awkward, and it becomes more so when you have a composed type that depends on a larger number of components. It's easy enough to create a helper method that can be used to simplify the code:

```
public static class AsyncInitialization
{
  public static Task WhenAllInitializedAsync(params object[] instances)
  {
    return Task.WhenAll(instances
        .OfType<IAsyncInitialization>()
        .Select(x => x.Initialization));
  }
}
```

You can call InitializeAllAsync and pass in whatever instances you want initialized; the method will ignore instances that don't implement IAsyncInitialization. The initialization code for a composed type that depends on three injected instances can then look like the following:

```
private async Task InitializeAsync()
{
 // Asynchronously wait for all 3 instances to initialize, if necessary.
 await AsyncInitialization.WhenAllInitializedAsync(_fundamental,
     _anotherType, _yetAnother);

 // Do our own initialization (synchronous or asynchronous).
 ...
}
```

See Also

Recipe 11.2 covers asynchronous factories, which are a way to do asynchronous construction without exposing uninitialized instances.

Recipe 14.1 covers asynchronous lazy initialization, which can be used if the instance is a shared resource or service.

Recipe 11.1 covers asynchronous interfaces.

11.4 Async Properties

Problem

You have a property that you want to make async. The property is not used in data binding.

Solution

This is a problem that often comes up when converting existing code to use async; in this situation, you have a property whose getter invokes a method that is now asynchronous. However, there's no such thing as an "asynchronous property." It's not possible to use the async keyword with a property, and that's a good thing. Property getters should return current values; they shouldn't be kicking off background operations:

```
// What we think we want (does not compile).
public int Data
{
  async get
  {
    await Task.Delay(TimeSpan.FromSeconds(1));
    return 13;
  }
}
```

When you find that your code wants an "asynchronous property," what your code really *needs* is something a little different. The solution depends on whether your property value needs to be evaluated once or multiple times; you have a choice between these semantics:

- A value that is asynchronously evaluated each time it is read
- A value that is asynchronously evaluated once and is cached for future access

If your "asynchronous property" needs to kick off a new (asynchronous) evaluation each time it's read, then it's not a *property*; it's a *method* in disguise. If you encountered this situation when converting synchronous code to asynchronous, then it's time to admit that the original design was actually incorrect; the property should have been a method all along:

```
// As an asynchronous method.
public async Task<int> GetDataAsync()
{
  await Task.Delay(TimeSpan.FromSeconds(1));
  return 13;
}
```

It is *possible* to return a Task<int> directly from a property, as the following code shows:

```
// This "async property" is an asynchronous method.
// This "async property" is a Task-returning property.
public Task<int> Data
{
  get { return GetDataAsync(); }
}

private async Task<int> GetDataAsync()
{
  await Task.Delay(TimeSpan.FromSeconds(1));
  return 13;
}
```

I do not recommend this approach, however. If every access to a property is going to kick off a new asynchronous operation, then that "property" should really be a method. The fact that it's an asynchronous method makes it clearer that a new asynchronous operation is initiated every time, so the API isn't misleading. Recipes 11.3 and 11.6 do use task-returning properties, but those properties apply to the instance as a whole; they don't start a new asynchronous operation every time they are read.

Sometimes you want the property value evaluated every time it's retrieved. Other times you want the property to only kick off a single (asynchronous) evaluation and cache that resulting value for future use. In this case, you can use asynchronous lazy initialization. That solution is covered in detail in Recipe 14.1, but in the meantime, here's an example of what the code would look like:

```
// As a cached value
public AsyncLazy<int> Data
{
  get { return _data; }
}

private readonly AsyncLazy<int> _data =
    new AsyncLazy<int>(async () =>
    {
      await Task.Delay(TimeSpan.FromSeconds(1));
      return 13;
    });
```

The code will only execute the asynchronous evaluation once and then return that same value to all callers. Calling code looks like the following:

```
int value = await instance.Data;
```

In this case, the property syntax is appropriate since there's only one evaluation happening.

Discussion

One of the important questions to ask yourself is whether reading the property should start a new asynchronous operation; if the answer is yes, then use an asynchronous *method* instead of a property. If the property should act as a lazy-evaluated cache, then use asynchronous initialization (see Recipe 14.1). In this recipe I didn't cover properties that are used in data binding; I cover those in Recipe 14.3.

When you're converting a synchronous property to an "asynchronous property," here's an example of what *not* to do:

```
private async Task<int> GetDataAsync()
{
  await Task.Delay(TimeSpan.FromSeconds(1));
  return 13;
}
```

```
public int Data
{
  // BAD CODE!!
  get { return GetDataAsync().Result; }
}
```

While we're on the subject of properties in `async` code, it's worth thinking about how state relates to asynchronous code. This is especially true if you're converting a synchronous code base to asynchronous. Consider any state that you expose in your API (e.g., via properties); for each piece of state, ask yourself, what is the current state of an object that has an asynchronous operation in progress? There's no right answer, but it's important to think about the semantics you want and to document them.

For example, consider `Stream.Position`, which represents the current offset of the stream pointer. With the synchronous API, when you call `Stream.Read` or `Stream.Write`, the reading/writing is done and `Stream.Position` is updated to reflect the new position before the `Read` or `Write` method returns. The semantics are clear for synchronous code.

Now, consider `Stream.ReadAsync` and `Stream.WriteAsync`: when should `Stream.Position` be updated? When the read/write operation is complete, or before it actually happens? If it's updated before the operation completes, is it updated synchronously by the time `ReadAsync`/`WriteAsync` returns, or could it happen shortly after that?

This is a great example of how a property that exposes state has perfectly clear semantics for synchronous code but no obviously correct semantics for asynchronous code. It's not the end of the world—you just need to think about your entire API when async-enabling your types and document the semantics you choose.

See Also

Recipe 14.1 covers asynchronous lazy initialization in detail.

Recipe 14.3 covers "asynchronous properties" that need to support data binding.

11.5 Async Events

Problem

You have an event that you need to use with handlers that might be `async`, and you need to detect whether the event handlers have completed. Note that this is a rare situation when raising an event; usually, when you raise an event, you don't care when the handlers complete.

Solution

It's not feasible to detect when `async void` handlers have returned, so you need some alternative way to detect when the asynchronous handlers have completed. The Universal Windows platform introduced a concept called *deferrals* that you can use to track asynchronous handlers. An asynchronous handler allocates a deferral before its first `await` and later notifies the deferral when it completes. Synchronous handlers don't need to use deferrals.

The `Nito.AsyncEx` library includes a type called a `DeferralManager`, which is used by the component raising the event. This deferral manager then permits event handlers to allocate deferrals and keeps track of when all the deferrals have completed.

For each of your events where you need to wait for the handlers to complete, you first extend your event arguments type:

```
public class MyEventArgs : EventArgs, IDeferralSource
{
  private readonly DeferralManager _deferrals = new DeferralManager();

  ... // Your own constructors and properties

  public IDisposable GetDeferral()
  {
    return _deferrals.DeferralSource.GetDeferral();
  }

  internal Task WaitForDeferralsAsync()
  {
    return _deferrals.WaitForDeferralsAsync();
  }
}
```

When you're dealing with asynchronous event handlers, it's best to make your event arguments type threadsafe. The easiest way to do this is to make it immutable (i.e., have all its properties be read-only).

Then, each time you raise the event, you can (asynchronously) wait for all asynchronous event handlers to complete. The following code will return a completed task if there are no handlers; otherwise, it'll create a new instance of your event arguments type, pass it to the handlers, and wait for any asynchronous handlers to complete:

```
public event EventHandler<MyEventArgs> MyEvent;

private async Task RaiseMyEventAsync()
{
  EventHandler<MyEventArgs> handler = MyEvent;
  if (handler == null)
    return;
```

```
    var args = new MyEventArgs(...);
    handler(this, args);
    await args.WaitForDeferralsAsync();
}
```

Asynchronous event handlers can then use the deferral within a using block; the
deferral notifies the deferral manager when it is disposed:

```
async void AsyncHandler(object sender, MyEventArgs args)
{
  using IDisposable deferral = args.GetDeferral();
  await Task.Delay(TimeSpan.FromSeconds(2));
}
```

This is slightly different than how Universal Windows deferrals work. In the Universal Windows API, each event that needs deferrals defines its own deferral type, and
that deferral type has an explicit Complete method rather than being IDisposable.

Discussion

There are logically two different kinds of events used in .NET, with very different
semantics. I call these *notification events* and *command events*; this isn't official terminology, just some terms that I chose for clarity. A notification event is an event that is
raised to notify other components of some situation. A notification is purely one-
way; the sender of the event doesn't care whether there are any receivers of the event.
With notifications, the sender and receiver can be entirely disconnected. Most events
are notification events; one example is a button click.

In contrast, a command event is an event that is raised to implement some functionality on behalf of the sending component. Command events aren't "events" in the true
sense of the term, though they are often implemented as .NET events. The sender of a
command must wait until the receiver handles it before moving on. If you use events
to implement the Visitor pattern, then those are command events. Lifecycle events
are also command events, so ASP.NET page lifecycle events and many UI framework
events, such as Xamarin's Application.PageAppearing, fall into this category. Any
UI framework event that is actually an implementation is also a command event (e.g.,
BackgroundWorker.DoWork).

Notification events don't require any special code to enable asynchronous handlers;
the event handlers can be async void and work just fine. When the event sender
raises the event, the asynchronous event handlers aren't completed immediately, but
that doesn't matter because they're just notification events. So, if your event is a notification event, the grand total amount of work you need to do to support asynchronous
handlers is: nothing.

Command events are a different story. When you have a command event, you need a way to detect when the handlers have completed. The preceding solution with deferrals should only be used for command events.

 The DeferralManager type is in the Nito.AsyncEx (*http://bit.ly/nito-async*) NuGet package.

See Also

Chapter 2 covers the basics of asynchronous programming.

11.6 Async Disposal

Problem

You have a type that has asynchronous operations but also needs to enable disposal of its resources.

Solution

There are a couple of common options for dealing with existing operations when disposing of an instance: you can either treat the disposal as a cancellation request that is applied to all existing operations, or you can implement an actual *asynchronous disposal*.

Treating disposal as a cancellation has a historic precedence on Windows; types such as file streams and sockets cancel any existing reads or writes when they are closed. By defining your own private CancellationTokenSource and passing that token to your internal operations, you can do something very similar in .NET. With the following code, Dispose will cancel the operations but won't wait for those operations to complete:

```
class MyClass : IDisposable
{
  private readonly CancellationTokenSource _disposeCts =
      new CancellationTokenSource();

  public async Task<int> CalculateValueAsync()
  {
    await Task.Delay(TimeSpan.FromSeconds(2), _disposeCts.Token);
    return 13;
  }

  public void Dispose()
```

```
    {
      _disposeCts.Cancel();
    }
  }
}
```

The code shows the basic pattern around Dispose. In a real-world app, you should put in checks that the object is not already disposed of and also enable the user to supply her own CancellationToken (using the technique from Recipe 10.8):

```
public async Task<int> CalculateValueAsync(CancellationToken cancellationToken)
{
  using CancellationTokenSource combinedCts = CancellationTokenSource
      .CreateLinkedTokenSource(cancellationToken, _disposeCts.Token);
  await Task.Delay(TimeSpan.FromSeconds(2), combinedCts.Token);
  return 13;
}
```

Calling code will have any existing operations canceled when Dispose is called:

```
async Task UseMyClassAsync()
{
  Task<int> task;
  using (var resource = new MyClass())
  {
    task = resource.CalculateValueAsync(default);
  }

  // Throws OperationCanceledException.
  var result = await task;
}
```

For some types, implementing Dispose as a cancellation request works just fine (e.g., HttpClient has these semantics). However, other types need to know when all the operations have completed. For these types, you need some kind of asynchronous disposal.

Asynchronous disposal is a technique introduced with C# 8.0 and .NET Core 3.0. The BCL introduced a new IAsyncDisposable interface that is an asynchronous equivalent of IDisposable. The language simultaneously introduced an await using statement that is the asynchronous equivalent of using. So types that would like to do asynchronous work during disposal now have that capability:

```
class MyClass : IAsyncDisposable
{
  public async ValueTask DisposeAsync()
  {
    await Task.Delay(TimeSpan.FromSeconds(2));
  }
}
```

The return type of DisposeAsync is ValueTask and not Task, but the standard async and await keywords work just as well with ValueTask as they do with Task.

Types implementing `IAsyncDisposable` are usually consumed by `await using`:

```
await using (var myClass = new MyClass())
{
  ...
} // DisposeAsync is invoked (and awaited) here.
```

If you need to avoid context using `ConfigureAwait(false)`, that is possible, but it's a bit more awkward because you have to declare your variable outside the `await using` statement:

```
var myClass = new MyClass();
await using (myClass.ConfigureAwait(false))
{
  ...
} // DisposeAsync is invoked (and awaited) here with ConfigureAwait(false).
```

Discussion

Asynchronous disposal is definitely easier than implementing `Dispose` as a cancellation request, and the more complex approach should only be used when you really need it. In fact, most of the time you can get away with not disposing anything at all, which is certainly the easiest approach because you don't have to do anything.

This recipe has two patterns for handling disposal; it's also possible to use *both* of them if you want. Using both would give your type the semantics of a clean shutdown if the client code uses `await using`, and a "cancel" if the client code uses `Dispose`. I wouldn't recommend this in general, but it is an option.

See Also

Recipe 10.8 covers linked cancellation tokens.

Recipe 11.1 covers asynchronous interfaces.

Recipe 2.10 discusses implementing methods returning `ValueTask`.

Recipe 2.7 covers avoiding context using `ConfigureAwait(false)`.

CHAPTER 12

Synchronization

When your application makes use of concurrency (as practically all .NET applications do), then you need to watch out for situations in which one piece of code needs to update data while other code needs to access the same data. Whenever this happens, you need to *synchronize* access to the data. The recipes in this chapter cover the most common types used to synchronize access. However, if you use the other recipes in this book appropriately, you'll find that a lot of the more common synchronization is already done for you by the respective libraries. Before diving into the synchronization recipes, let's take a closer look at some common situations where synchronization may or may not be required.

 The synchronization explanations in this section are slightly simplified, but the conclusions are all correct.

There are two major types of synchronization: *communication* and *data protection*. Communication is used when one piece of code needs to notify another piece of code of some condition (e.g., a new message has arrived). I'll cover communication more thoroughly in this chapter's recipes; the remainder of this introduction discusses data protection.

You need to use synchronization to protect shared data when *all three* of these conditions are true:

- Multiple pieces of code are running concurrently.
- These pieces are accessing (reading or writing) the same data.

- At least one piece of code is updating (writing) the data.

The reason for the first condition should be obvious; if your entire code runs from top to bottom and nothing ever happens concurrently, then you never have to worry about synchronization. This is the case for some simple Console applications, but the vast majority of .NET applications do use *some* kind of concurrency. The second condition means that if each piece of code has its own local data that it doesn't *share*, then there's no need for synchronization; the local data is never accessed from any other pieces of code. There's also no need for synchronization if there is shared data but the data never changes, such as if the data is defined using immutable types. The third condition covers scenarios like configuration values and the like that are set at the beginning of the application and then never change. If the shared data is only read, then it doesn't need synchronization; only data that is both *shared* and *updated* needs synchronization.

The purpose of data protection is to provide each piece of code with a consistent view of the data. If one piece of code is updating the data, then you can use synchronization to make those updates appear atomic to the rest of the system.

It takes some practice to learn when synchronization is necessary, so we'll walk through a few examples before starting the recipes in this chapter. As our first example, consider the following code:

```
async Task MyMethodAsync()
{
  int value = 10;
  await Task.Delay(TimeSpan.FromSeconds(1));
  value = value + 1;
  await Task.Delay(TimeSpan.FromSeconds(1));
  value = value - 1;
  await Task.Delay(TimeSpan.FromSeconds(1));
  Trace.WriteLine(value);
}
```

If the `MyMethodAsync` method is called from a threadpool thread (e.g., from within `Task.Run`), then the lines of code accessing `value` may run on separate threadpool threads. But does it need synchronization? No, because none of them can be running at the same time. The method is asynchronous, but it's also sequential (meaning it progresses one part at a time).

OK, let's complicate the example a bit. This time we'll run concurrent asynchronous code:

```
private int value;

async Task ModifyValueAsync()
{
  await Task.Delay(TimeSpan.FromSeconds(1));
  value = value + 1;
```

```
    }

    // WARNING: may require synchronization; see discussion below.
    async Task<int> ModifyValueConcurrentlyAsync()
    {
      // Start three concurrent modifications.
      Task task1 = ModifyValueAsync();
      Task task2 = ModifyValueAsync();
      Task task3 = ModifyValueAsync();

      await Task.WhenAll(task1, task2, task3);

      return value;
    }
```

This code above is starting three modifications that run concurrently. Does it need synchronization? It depends. If you know that the method is called from a GUI or ASP.NET context (or any context that only allows one piece of code to run at a time), synchronization won't be necessary because when the actual data modification code runs, it runs at a different time than the other two data modifications. For example, if the preceding code is run in a GUI context, there's only one UI thread that will execute each of the data modifications, so it *must* do them one at a time. So, if you know the context is a one-at-a-time context, then there's no synchronization needed. However, if that same method is called from a threadpool thread (e.g., from Task.Run), then synchronization *would* be necessary. In that case, the three data modifications could run on separate threadpool threads and update data.Value simultaneously, so you would need to synchronize access to data.Value.

Now let's consider one more wrinkle:

```
    private int value;

    async Task ModifyValueAsync()
    {
      int originalValue = value;
      await Task.Delay(TimeSpan.FromSeconds(1));
      value = originalValue + 1;
    }
```

Consider what happens if ModifyValueAsync is called multiple times concurrently. Even if it is called from a one-at-a-time context, the data member is shared between each invocation of ModifyValueAsync, and the value may change any time that method does an await. You may want to apply synchronization even in a one-at-a-time context if you want to avoid that kind of sharing. Put another way, to make it so that each call to ModifyValueAsync waits until all previous calls have completed, you'll need to add synchronization. This is true even if the context ensures that only one thread is used for all the code (i.e., the UI thread). Synchronization in this scenario is a kind of *throttling* for asynchronous methods (see Recipe 12.2).

Let's look at one more `async` example. You can use `Task.Run` to do what I call "simple parallelism"—a basic kind of parallel processing that doesn't provide the efficiency and configurability that the true parallelism of `Parallel`/PLINQ does. The following code updates a shared value using simple parallelism:

```
// BAD CODE!!
async Task<int> SimpleParallelismAsync()
{
  int value = 0;
  Task task1 = Task.Run(() => { value = value + 1; });
  Task task2 = Task.Run(() => { value = value + 1; });
  Task task3 = Task.Run(() => { value = value + 1; });
  await Task.WhenAll(task1, task2, task3);
  return value;
}
```

This code has three separate tasks running on the thread pool (via `Task.Run`), all modifying the same `value`. So, our synchronization conditions apply, and we certainly do need synchronization here. Note that we do need synchronization even though `value` is a local variable; it's still *shared* between threads even though it's local to the one method.

Moving on to true parallel code, let's consider an example that uses the `Parallel` type:

```
void IndependentParallelism(IEnumerable<int> values)
{
  Parallel.ForEach(values, item => Trace.WriteLine(item));
}
```

Since this code uses `Parallel`, we must assume the body of the parallel loop (`item => Trace.WriteLine(item)`) can be running on multiple threads. However, the body of the loop only reads from its own data; there's no data sharing between threads here. The `Parallel` class divides the data among threads so that none of them has to share its data. Each thread running its loop body is independent from all the other threads running the same loop body. So, no synchronization of the preceding code is necessary.

Let's look at an aggregation example similar to the one covered in Recipe 4.2:

```
// BAD CODE!!
int ParallelSum(IEnumerable<int> values)
{
  int result = 0;
  Parallel.ForEach(source: values,
      localInit: () => 0,
      body: (item, state, localValue) => localValue + item,
      localFinally: localValue => { result += localValue; });
  return result;
}
```

In this example, the code is again using multiple threads; this time, each thread starts with its local value initialized to 0 (`() => 0`), and for each input value processed by that thread, it adds the input value to its local value (`(item, state, localValue) => localValue + item`). Finally, all the local values are added to the return value (`local Value => { result += localValue; }`). The first two steps aren't problematic because there's nothing shared between threads; each thread's local and input values are independent from all other threads' local and input values. The final step is problematic, however; when each thread's local value is added to the return value, this is a situation where there's a shared variable (`result`) that is accessed by multiple threads and updated by all of them. So, you'd need to use synchronization in that final step (see Recipe 12.1).

The PLINQ, dataflow, and reactive libraries are very similar to the `Parallel` examples: as long as your code is just dealing with its own input, it doesn't have to worry about synchronization. I find that if I use these libraries appropriately, there's very little need for me to add synchronization to most of my code.

Lastly, let's discuss collections. Remember that the three conditions requiring synchronization are *multiple pieces of code*, *shared data*, and *data updates*.

Immutable types are naturally threadsafe because they *cannot* change; it's not possible to update an immutable collection, so no synchronization is necessary. For example, the following code doesn't require synchronization because when each separate threadpool thread pushes a value onto the stack, it's creating a new immutable stack with that value, leaving the original `stack` unchanged:

```
async Task<bool> PlayWithStackAsync()
{
    ImmutableStack<int> stack = ImmutableStack<int>.Empty;

    Task task1 = Task.Run(() => Trace.WriteLine(stack.Push(3).Peek()));
    Task task2 = Task.Run(() => Trace.WriteLine(stack.Push(5).Peek()));
    Task task3 = Task.Run(() => Trace.WriteLine(stack.Push(7).Peek()));
    await Task.WhenAll(task1, task2, task3);

    return stack.IsEmpty; // Always returns true.
}
```

When your code uses immutable collections, it's common to have a shared "root" variable that is not itself immutable. In that case, you *do* have to use synchronization. In the following code, each thread pushes a value onto the stack (creating a new immutable stack) and then updates the shared root variable; the code *does* need synchronization to update the `stack` variable:

```
// BAD CODE!!
async Task<bool> PlayWithStackAsync()
{
    ImmutableStack<int> stack = ImmutableStack<int>.Empty;
```

```
    Task task1 = Task.Run(() => { stack = stack.Push(3); });
    Task task2 = Task.Run(() => { stack = stack.Push(5); });
    Task task3 = Task.Run(() => { stack = stack.Push(7); });
    await Task.WhenAll(task1, task2, task3);

    return stack.IsEmpty;
}
```

Threadsafe collections (e.g., ConcurrentDictionary) are quite different. Unlike immutable collections, threadsafe collections can be updated. But they have all the synchronization they need built in, so you don't have to worry about synchronizing collection changes. If the following code updated a Dictionary instead of a Concur rentDictionary, it would need synchronization; but since it's updating a Concurrent Dictionary, it doesn't need synchronization:

```
async Task<int> ThreadsafeCollectionsAsync()
{
  var dictionary = new ConcurrentDictionary<int, int>();

  Task task1 = Task.Run(() => { dictionary.TryAdd(2, 3); });
  Task task2 = Task.Run(() => { dictionary.TryAdd(3, 5); });
  Task task3 = Task.Run(() => { dictionary.TryAdd(5, 7); });
  await Task.WhenAll(task1, task2, task3);

  return dictionary.Count; // Always returns 3.
}
```

12.1 Blocking Locks

Problem

You have some shared data and need to safely read and write it from multiple threads.

Solution

The best solution for this situation is to use the lock statement. When a thread enters a lock, it'll prevent any other threads from entering that lock until the lock is released:

```
class MyClass
{
  // This lock protects the _value field.
  private readonly object _mutex = new object();

  private int _value;

  public void Increment()
  {
    lock (_mutex)
    {
```

```
        _value = _value + 1;
      }
    }
}
```

Discussion

There are many other kinds of locks in the .NET framework, such as `Monitor`, `Spin Lock`, and `ReaderWriterLockSlim`. In most applications, these lock types should almost never be used directly. In particular, it's natural for developers to jump to `Read erWriterLockSlim` when there is no need for that level of complexity. The basic `lock` statement handles 99% of cases quite well.

There are four important guidelines when using locks:

- Restrict lock visibility.
- Document what the lock protects.
- Minimize code under lock.
- Never execute arbitrary code while holding a lock.

First, you should strive to restrict lock visibility. The object used in the `lock` statement should be a private field and never should be exposed to any method outside the class. There's usually at most one lock member per type; if you have more than one, consider refactoring that type into separate types. You *can* lock on any reference type, but I prefer to have a field specifically for use with the `lock` statement, as in the last example. If you do lock on another instance, be sure that it is private to your class; it should not have been passed in to the constructor or returned from a property getter. You should never `lock(this)` or lock on any instance of `Type` or `string`; these locks can cause deadlocks because they are accessible from other code.

Second, document what the lock protects. This step is easy to overlook when initially writing the code but becomes more important as the code grows in complexity.

Third, do your best to minimize the code that is executed while holding a lock. One thing to watch for is blocking calls; ideally, your code should never block while holding a lock.

Finally, do not ever call arbitrary code under lock. Arbitrary code can include raising events, invoking virtual methods, or invoking delegates. If you must execute arbitrary code, do so after the lock is released.

See Also

Recipe 12.2 covers `async`-compatible locks. The `lock` statement is not compatible with `await`.

Recipe 12.3 covers signaling between threads. The `lock` statement is intended to protect shared data, not to send signals between threads.

Recipe 12.5 covers throttling, which is a generalization of locking. A lock can be thought of as throttling to one at a time.

12.2 Async Locks

Problem

You have some shared data and need to safely read and write it from multiple code blocks, which may be using `await`.

Solution

The .NET framework `SemaphoreSlim` type has been updated in .NET 4.5 to be compatible with `async`. Here's how you can use it:

```
class MyClass
{
  // This lock protects the _value field.
  private readonly SemaphoreSlim _mutex = new SemaphoreSlim(1);

  private int _value;

  public async Task DelayAndIncrementAsync()
  {
    await _mutex.WaitAsync();
    try
    {
      int oldValue = _value;
      await Task.Delay(TimeSpan.FromSeconds(oldValue));
      _value = oldValue + 1;
    }
    finally
    {
      _mutex.Release();
    }
  }
}
```

You can also use the `AsyncLock` type from the `Nito.AsyncEx` library, which has a slightly more elegant API:

```
class MyClass
{
  // This lock protects the _value field.
  private readonly AsyncLock _mutex = new AsyncLock();

  private int _value;
```

```
public async Task DelayAndIncrementAsync()
{
  using (await _mutex.LockAsync())
  {
    int oldValue = _value;
    await Task.Delay(TimeSpan.FromSeconds(oldValue));
    _value = oldValue + 1;
  }
}
}
```

Discussion

The same guidelines from Recipe 12.1 also apply here, specifically:

- Restrict lock visibility.
- Document what the lock protects.
- Minimize code under lock.
- Never execute arbitrary code while holding a lock.

Keep your lock instances private; do not expose them outside the class. Be sure to clearly document (and carefully think through) exactly what a lock instance protects. Minimize code that is executed while holding a lock. In particular, do not call arbitrary code; this includes raising events, invoking virtual methods, and invoking delegates.

The AsyncLock type is in the Nito.AsyncEx (*http://bit.ly/nito-async*) NuGet package.

See Also

Recipe 12.4 covers async-compatible signaling. Locks are intended to protect shared data, not act as signals.

Recipe 12.5 covers throttling, which is a generalization of locking. A lock can be thought of as throttling to one at a time.

12.3 Blocking Signals

Problem

You have to send a notification from one thread to another.

Solution

The most common and general-purpose cross-thread signal is `ManualResetEvent` `Slim`. A manual-reset event can be in one of two states: signaled or unsignaled. Any thread may set the event to a signaled state or reset the event to an unsignaled state. A thread may also wait for the event to be signaled.

The following two methods are invoked by separate threads; one thread waits for a signal from the other:

```
class MyClass
{
  private readonly ManualResetEventSlim _initialized =
      new ManualResetEventSlim();

  private int _value;

  public int WaitForInitialization()
  {
    _initialized.Wait();
    return _value;
  }

  public void InitializeFromAnotherThread()
  {
    _value = 13;
    _initialized.Set();
  }
}
```

Discussion

`ManualResetEventSlim` is a great general-purpose signal from one thread to another, but you should only use it when appropriate. If the "signal" is actually a *message* sending some piece of data across threads, then consider using a producer/consumer queue. On the other hand, if the signals are just used to coordinate access to shared data, then you should use a lock instead.

There are other thread synchronization signal types in the .NET framework that are less commonly used. If `ManualResetEventSlim` doesn't suit your needs, consider `AutoResetEvent`, `CountdownEvent`, or `Barrier`.

`ManualResetEventSlim` is a synchronous signal, so `WaitForInitialization` will block the calling thread until the signal is sent. If you want to wait for a signal without blocking a thread, then you want an asynchronous signal, as described in Recipe 12.4.

See Also

Recipe 9.6 covers blocking producer/consumer queues.

Recipe 12.1 covers blocking locks.

Recipe 12.4 covers async-compatible signals.

12.4 Async Signals

Problem

You need to send a notification from one part of the code to another, and the receiver of the notification must wait for it asynchronously.

Solution

Use TaskCompletionSource<T> to send the notification asynchronously, if the notification only needs to be sent once. The sending code calls TrySetResult, and the receiving code awaits its Task property:

```
class MyClass
{
  private readonly TaskCompletionSource<object> _initialized =
      new TaskCompletionSource<object>();

  private int _value1;
  private int _value2;

  public async Task<int> WaitForInitializationAsync()
  {
    await _initialized.Task;
    return _value1 + _value2;
  }

  public void Initialize()
  {
    _value1 = 13;
    _value2 = 17;
    _initialized.TrySetResult(null);
  }
}
```

The TaskCompletionSource<T> type can be used to asynchronously wait for any kind of situation—in this case, a notification from another part of the code. This works well if the signal is only sent once, but doesn't work as well if you need to turn the signal off as well as on.

The Nito.AsyncEx library contains a type AsyncManualResetEvent, which is an approximate equivalent of ManualResetEvent for asynchronous code. The following example is fabricated, but it shows how to use the AsyncManualResetEvent type:

```
class MyClass
{
  private readonly AsyncManualResetEvent _connected =
      new AsyncManualResetEvent();

  public async Task WaitForConnectedAsync()
  {
    await _connected.WaitAsync();
  }

  public void ConnectedChanged(bool connected)
  {
    if (connected)
      _connected.Set();
    else
      _connected.Reset();
  }
}
```

Discussion

Signals are a general-purpose notification mechanism. But if that "signal" is a *message*, used to send data from one piece of code to another, then consider using a producer/consumer queue. Similarly, do not use general-purpose signals just to coordinate access to shared data; in that situation, use an asynchronous lock.

 The AsyncManualResetEvent type is in the Nito.AsyncEx (*http://bit.ly/nito-async*) NuGet package.

See Also

Recipe 9.8 covers asynchronous producer/consumer queues.

Recipe 12.2 covers asynchronous locks.

Recipe 12.3 covers blocking signals, which can be used for notifications across threads.

12.5 Throttling

Problem

You have highly concurrent code that is actually *too* concurrent, and you need some way to throttle the concurrency.

Code is too concurrent when parts of the application are unable to keep up with other parts, causing data items to build up and consume memory. In this scenario, throttling parts of the code can prevent memory issues.

Solution

The solution varies based on the type of concurrency your code is doing. These solutions all restrict concurrency to a specific value. Reactive Extensions has more powerful options, such as sliding time windows; throttling for System.Reactive observables is covered more thoroughly in Recipe 6.4.

Dataflow and parallel code all have built-in options for throttling concurrency:

```
IPropagatorBlock<int, int> DataflowMultiplyBy2()
{
  var options = new ExecutionDataflowBlockOptions
  {
    MaxDegreeOfParallelism = 10
  };

  return new TransformBlock<int, int>(data => data * 2, options);
}

// Using Parallel LINQ (PLINQ)
IEnumerable<int> ParallelMultiplyBy2(IEnumerable<int> values)
{
  return values.AsParallel()
      .WithDegreeOfParallelism(10)
      .Select(item => item * 2);
}

// Using the Parallel class
void ParallelRotateMatrices(IEnumerable<Matrix> matrices, float degrees)
{
  var options = new ParallelOptions
  {
    MaxDegreeOfParallelism = 10
  };
  Parallel.ForEach(matrices, options, matrix => matrix.Rotate(degrees));
}
```

Concurrent asynchronous code can be throttled by using SemaphoreSlim:

```
async Task<string[]> DownloadUrlsAsync(HttpClient client,
    IEnumerable<string> urls)
{
  using var semaphore = new SemaphoreSlim(10);
  Task<string>[] tasks = urls.Select(async url =>
  {
    await semaphore.WaitAsync();
    try
    {
```

```
      return await client.GetStringAsync(url);
    }
    finally
    {
      semaphore.Release();
    }
  }).ToArray();
  return await Task.WhenAll(tasks);
}
```

Discussion

Throttling may be necessary when you find your code is using too many resources (for example, CPU or network connections). Bear in mind that end users usually have less powerful machines than developers, so it's better to throttle by a little too much than not enough.

See Also

Recipe 6.4 covers throttling for reactive code.

CHAPTER 13

Scheduling

When a piece of code executes, it has to run on some thread somewhere. A *scheduler* is an object that decides where a certain piece of code runs. There are a few different scheduler types in the .NET framework, and they're used with slight differences by parallel and dataflow code.

I recommend that you *not* specify a scheduler whenever possible; the defaults are usually correct. For example, the `await` operator in asynchronous code will automatically resume the method within the same context unless you override this default, as described in Recipe 2.7. Similarly, reactive code has reasonable default contexts for raising its events, which you can override with `ObserveOn`, as described in Recipe 6.2.

If you need other code to execute in a specific context (e.g., a UI thread context or an ASP.NET request context), then you can use the scheduling recipes in this chapter to control the scheduling of your code.

13.1 Scheduling Work to the Thread Pool

Problem

You have a piece of code that you explicitly want to execute on a threadpool thread.

Solution

The vast majority of the time, you'll want to use `Task.Run`, which is quite simple. The following code blocks a threadpool thread for 2 seconds:

```
Task task = Task.Run(() =>
{
  Thread.Sleep(TimeSpan.FromSeconds(2));
});
```

Task.Run also understands return values and asynchronous lambdas just fine. The task returned by Task.Run in the following code will complete after 2 seconds with a result of 13:

```
Task<int> task = Task.Run(async () =>
{
  await Task.Delay(TimeSpan.FromSeconds(2));
  return 13;
});
```

Task.Run returns a Task (or Task<T>), which can be naturally consumed by asynchronous or reactive code.

Discussion

Task.Run is ideal for UI applications, when you have time-consuming work to do that cannot be done on the UI thread. For example, Recipe 8.4 uses Task.Run to push parallel processing to a threadpool thread. However, do not use Task.Run on ASP.NET unless you're *absolutely* sure you know what you're doing. On ASP.NET, request handling code is already running on a threadpool thread, so pushing it onto *another* threadpool thread is usually counterproductive.

Task.Run is an effective replacement for BackgroundWorker, Delegate.BeginInvoke, and ThreadPool.QueueUserWorkItem. None of those older APIs should be used in new code; code using Task.Run is much easier to write correctly and maintain over time. Furthermore, Task.Run handles the vast majority of use cases for Thread, so most uses of Thread can also be replaced with Task.Run (with the rare exception of single-thread apartment threads).

Parallel and dataflow code executes on the thread pool by default, so there's usually no need to use Task.Run with code executed by the Parallel, Parallel LINQ, or TPL Dataflow libraries.

If you're doing dynamic parallelism, then use Task.Factory.StartNew instead of Task.Run. This is necessary because the Task returned by Task.Run has its default options configured for asynchronous use (i.e., to be consumed by asynchronous or reactive code). It also doesn't support advanced concepts, such as parent/child tasks, which are more common in dynamic parallel code.

See Also

Recipe 8.6 covers consuming asynchronous code (such as the task returned from Task.Run) with reactive code.

Recipe 8.4 covers asynchronously waiting for parallel code, which is most easily done via Task.Run.

Recipe 4.4 covers dynamic parallelism, a scenario where you should use `Task.Factory.StartNew` instead of `Task.Run`.

13.2 Executing Code with a Task Scheduler

Problem

You have multiple pieces of code that you need to execute in a certain way. For example, you may need all the pieces of code to execute on the UI thread, or you may need to execute only a certain number at a time.

This recipe deals with how to define and construct a scheduler for those pieces of code. Actually applying that scheduler is the subject of the next two recipes.

Solution

There are quite a few different types in .NET that can handle scheduling; this recipe focuses on `TaskScheduler` because it's portable and relatively easy to use.

The simplest `TaskScheduler` is `TaskScheduler.Default`, which queues work to the thread pool. You will seldomly specify `TaskScheduler.Default` in your own code, but it's important to be aware of it, since it's the default for many scheduling scenarios. `Task.Run`, parallel, and dataflow code all use `TaskScheduler.Default`.

You can capture a specific *context* and later schedule work back to it by using `TaskScheduler.FromCurrentSynchronizationContext`:

```
TaskScheduler scheduler = TaskScheduler.FromCurrentSynchronizationContext();
```

This code creates a `TaskScheduler` to capture the current `SynchronizationContext` and schedule code onto that context. `SynchronizationContext` is a type that represents a general-purpose scheduling context. There are several different contexts in the .NET framework; most UI frameworks provide a `SynchronizationContext` that represents the UI thread, and ASP.NET before Core provided a `SynchronizationContext` that represented the HTTP request context.

`ConcurrentExclusiveSchedulerPair` is another powerful type introduced in .NET 4.5; this is actually *two* schedulers that are related to each other. The `ConcurrentScheduler` member is a scheduler that allows multiple tasks to execute at the same time, as long as no task is executing on the `ExclusiveScheduler`. The `ExclusiveScheduler` only executes code one task at a time, and only when there's no task already executing on the `ConcurrentScheduler`:

```
var schedulerPair = new ConcurrentExclusiveSchedulerPair();
TaskScheduler concurrent = schedulerPair.ConcurrentScheduler;
TaskScheduler exclusive = schedulerPair.ExclusiveScheduler;
```

One common utilization for `ConcurrentExclusiveSchedulerPair` is to just use the `ExclusiveScheduler` to ensure only one task is executed at a time. Code that executes on the `ExclusiveScheduler` will run on the thread pool but will be restricted to executing exclusive of all other code using the same `ExclusiveScheduler` instance.

Another use for `ConcurrentExclusiveSchedulerPair` is as a throttling scheduler. You can create a `ConcurrentExclusiveSchedulerPair` that will limit its own concurrency. In this scenario, the `ExclusiveScheduler` is usually not used:

```
var schedulerPair = new ConcurrentExclusiveSchedulerPair(
    TaskScheduler.Default, maxConcurrencyLevel: 8);
TaskScheduler scheduler = schedulerPair.ConcurrentScheduler;
```

Note that this kind of throttling only throttles code while it is *executing*; it's quite different than the kind of logical throttling covered in Recipe 12.5. In particular, asynchronous code is not considered to be executing while it is awaiting an operation. The `ConcurrentScheduler` throttles executing code; other throttling, such as `SemaphoreSlim`, throttles at a higher level (i.e., an entire `async` method).

Discussion

You may have noticed that the last code example passed `TaskScheduler.Default` into the constructor for `ConcurrentExclusiveSchedulerPair`. This is because `ConcurrentExclusiveSchedulerPair` applies its concurrent/exclusive logic around an existing `TaskScheduler`.

This recipe introduces `TaskScheduler.FromCurrentSynchronizationContext`, which is useful for executing code on a captured context. It is also possible to use `SynchronizationContext` directly to execute code on that context; however, I don't recommend this approach. Whenever possible, use the `await` operator to resume on an implicitly captured context, or use a `TaskScheduler` wrapper.

Don't ever use platform-specific types to execute code on a UI thread. WPF, Silverlight, iOS, and Android all provide the `Dispatcher` type, Universal Windows uses the `CoreDispatcher`, and Windows Forms has the `ISynchronizeInvoke` interface (i.e., `Control.Invoke`). Do not use any of these types in new code; just pretend they don't exist. Using them ties your code to a specific platform unnecessarily. `SynchronizationContext` is a general-purpose abstraction around these types.

System.Reactive (Rx) introduces a more general scheduler abstraction: `IScheduler`. An Rx scheduler is capable of wrapping any other kind of scheduler; the `TaskPoolScheduler` will wrap any `TaskFactory` (which contains a `TaskScheduler`). The Rx team also defined an `IScheduler` implementation that can be manually controlled for testing. If you do need to use a scheduler abstraction, I'd recommend the `IScheduler` from Rx; it's well designed, well defined, and test friendly. However, most of the time you don't need a scheduler abstraction, and earlier libraries, such as the Task Parallel Library (TPL) and TPL Dataflow, only understand the `TaskScheduler` type.

See Also

Recipe 13.3 covers applying a `TaskScheduler` to parallel code.

Recipe 13.4 covers applying a `TaskScheduler` to dataflow code.

Recipe 12.5 covers higher-level logical throttling.

Recipe 6.2 covers System.Reactive schedulers for event streams.

Recipe 7.6 covers the System.Reactive test scheduler.

13.3 Scheduling Parallel Code

Problem

You need to control how the individual pieces of code are executed in parallel code.

Solution

Once you create an appropriate `TaskScheduler` instance (see Recipe 13.2), you can include it in the options that you pass to a `Parallel` method. The following code takes a sequence of sequences of matrices. It starts a bunch of parallel loops and wants to limit the *total* parallelism of all loops simultaneously, regardless of how many matrices are in each sequence:

```
void RotateMatrices(IEnumerable<IEnumerable<Matrix>> collections, float degrees)
{
  var schedulerPair = new ConcurrentExclusiveSchedulerPair(
      TaskScheduler.Default, maxConcurrencyLevel: 8);
  TaskScheduler scheduler = schedulerPair.ConcurrentScheduler;
  ParallelOptions options = new ParallelOptions { TaskScheduler = scheduler };
  Parallel.ForEach(collections, options,
      matrices => Parallel.ForEach(matrices, options,
          matrix => matrix.Rotate(degrees)));
}
```

Discussion

`Parallel.Invoke` also takes an instance of `ParallelOptions`, so you can pass a `Task Scheduler` to `Parallel.Invoke` the same way as `Parallel.ForEach`. If you're doing dynamic parallel code, you can pass `TaskScheduler` directly to `TaskFactory.Start New` or `Task.ContinueWith`.

There is no way to pass a `TaskScheduler` to Parallel LINQ (PLINQ) code.

See Also

Recipe 13.2 covers common task schedulers and how to choose between them.

13.4 Dataflow Synchronization Using Schedulers

Problem

You need to control how the individual pieces of code are executed in dataflow code.

Solution

Once you create an appropriate `TaskScheduler` instance (see Recipe 13.2), you can include it in the options that you pass to a dataflow block. When called from the UI thread, the following code creates a dataflow mesh that multiplies all of its input values by two (using the thread pool) and then appends the resulting values to the items of a list box (on the UI thread):

```
var options = new ExecutionDataflowBlockOptions
{
  TaskScheduler = TaskScheduler.FromCurrentSynchronizationContext(),
};
var multiplyBlock = new TransformBlock<int, int>(item => item * 2);
var displayBlock = new ActionBlock<int>(
    result => ListBox.Items.Add(result), options);
multiplyBlock.LinkTo(displayBlock);
```

Discussion

Specifying a `TaskScheduler` is especially useful in coordinating the actions of blocks in different parts of your dataflow mesh. For example, you can utilize the `Concurren tExclusiveSchedulerPair.ExclusiveScheduler` to ensure that blocks A and C never execute code at the same time, while allowing block B to execute whenever it wants.

Keep in mind that synchronization by `TaskScheduler` only applies while the code is *executing*. For example, if you have an action block that runs asynchronous code and apply an exclusive scheduler, the code isn't considered running when it is awaiting.

You can specify a `TaskScheduler` for any kind of dataflow block. Even though a block may not execute your code (e.g., `BufferBlock<T>`), it still has housekeeping tasks that it needs to do, and it'll use the provided `TaskScheduler` for all of its internal work.

See Also

Recipe 13.2 covers common task schedulers and how to choose between them.

CHAPTER 14

Scenarios

In this chapter, we'll take a look at a variety of types and techniques to address some common scenarios when writing concurrent programs. These kinds of scenarios could fill up another entire book, so I've selected just a few that I've found the most useful.

14.1 Initializing Shared Resources

Problem

You have a resource that is shared between multiple parts of your code. This resource needs to be initialized the first time it is accessed.

Solution

The .NET framework includes a type specifically for this purpose: Lazy<T>. You construct an instance of the Lazy<T> type with a factory delegate that is used to initialize the instance. The instance is then made available via the Value property. The following code illustrates the Lazy<T> type:

```
static int _simpleValue;
static readonly Lazy<int> MySharedInteger = new Lazy<int>(() => _simpleValue++);

void UseSharedInteger()
{
  int sharedValue = MySharedInteger.Value;
}
```

No matter how many threads call UseSharedInteger simultaneously, the factory delegate is only executed once, and all threads wait for the same instance. Once it's created, the instance is cached and all future access to the Value property returns the same instance (in the preceding example, MySharedInteger.Value will always be 0).

A very similar approach can be used if the initialization requires asynchronous work; in this case, you can use a Lazy<Task<T>>:

```
static int _simpleValue;
static readonly Lazy<Task<int>> MySharedAsyncInteger =
    new Lazy<Task<int>>(async () =>
    {
      await Task.Delay(TimeSpan.FromSeconds(2)).ConfigureAwait(false);
      return _simpleValue++;
    });

async Task GetSharedIntegerAsync()
{
  int sharedValue = await MySharedAsyncInteger.Value;
}
```

In this example, the delegate returns a Task<int>, that is, an integer value determined asynchronously. No matter how many parts of the code call Value simultaneously, the Task<int> is only created once and returned to all callers. Each caller then has the option of (asynchronously) waiting until the task completes by passing the task to await.

The preceding code is an acceptable pattern, but there are some additional considerations. For one, the asynchronous delegate may be executed on any thread that calls Value, and that delegate will execute within that context. If there are different thread types that may call Value (e.g., a UI thread and a threadpool thread, or two different ASP.NET request threads), then it may be better to always execute the asynchronous delegate on a threadpool thread. This is easy enough to do by wrapping the factory delegate in a call to Task.Run:

```
static int _simpleValue;
static readonly Lazy<Task<int>> MySharedAsyncInteger =
  new Lazy<Task<int>>(() => Task.Run(async () =>
  {
    await Task.Delay(TimeSpan.FromSeconds(2));
    return _simpleValue++;
  }));

async Task GetSharedIntegerAsync()
{
  int sharedValue = await MySharedAsyncInteger.Value;
}
```

Another consideration is that the Task<T> instance is only created once. If the asynchronous delegate throws an exception, then the Lazy<Task<T>> will cache that faulted task. This is seldom desirable; usually it's better to re-execute the delegate the next time the lazy value is requested rather than to cache the exception. There isn't a way to "reset" the Lazy<T>, but you can create a new class that handles re-creating the Lazy<T> instance:

```
public sealed class AsyncLazy<T>
{
  private readonly object _mutex;
  private readonly Func<Task<T>> _factory;
  private Lazy<Task<T>> _instance;

  public AsyncLazy(Func<Task<T>> factory)
  {
    _mutex = new object();
    _factory = RetryOnFailure(factory);
    _instance = new Lazy<Task<T>>(_factory);
  }

  private Func<Task<T>> RetryOnFailure(Func<Task<T>> factory)
  {
    return async () =>
    {
      try
      {
        return await factory().ConfigureAwait(false);
      }
      catch
      {
        lock (_mutex)
        {
          _instance = new Lazy<Task<T>>(_factory);
        }
        throw;
      }
    };
  }

  public Task<T> Task
  {
    get
    {
      lock (_mutex)
        return _instance.Value;
    }
  }
}

static int _simpleValue;
static readonly AsyncLazy<int> MySharedAsyncInteger =
  new AsyncLazy<int>(() => Task.Run(async () =>
  {
    await Task.Delay(TimeSpan.FromSeconds(2));
    return _simpleValue++;
```

```
    }));

    async Task GetSharedIntegerAsync()
    {
      int sharedValue = await MySharedAsyncInteger.Task;
    }
```

Discussion

The final code sample in this recipe is a general code pattern for asynchronous lazy initialization, and it's a bit awkward. The `AsyncEx` library includes an `AsyncLazy<T>` type that acts just like a `Lazy<Task<T>>` that executes its factory delegate on the thread pool and has an option for retrying on failure. It can also be awaited directly, so the declaration and usage look like the following:

```
static int _simpleValue;
private static readonly AsyncLazy<int> MySharedAsyncInteger =
  new AsyncLazy<int>(async () =>
  {
    await Task.Delay(TimeSpan.FromSeconds(2));
    return _simpleValue++;
  },
  AsyncLazyFlags.RetryOnFailure);

public async Task UseSharedIntegerAsync()
{
  int sharedValue = await MySharedAsyncInteger;
}
```

The `AsyncLazy<T>` type is in the `Nito.AsyncEx` (*http://bit.ly/nito-async*) NuGet package.

See Also

Chapter 1 covers basic `async`/`await` programming.

Recipe 13.1 covers scheduling work to the thread pool.

14.2 System.Reactive Deferred Evaluation

Problem

You want to create a new source observable whenever someone subscribes to it. For example, you want each subscription to represent a different request to a web service.

Solution

The System.Reactive library has an operator `Observable.Defer`, which will execute a delegate each time the observable is subscribed to. This delegate acts as a factory that creates an observable. The following code uses `Defer` to call an asynchronous method every time someone subscribes to the observable:

```
void SubscribeWithDefer()
{
  var invokeServerObservable = Observable.Defer(
      () => GetValueAsync().ToObservable());
  invokeServerObservable.Subscribe(_ => { });
  invokeServerObservable.Subscribe(_ => { });

  Console.ReadKey();
}

async Task<int> GetValueAsync()
{
  Console.WriteLine("Calling server...");
  await Task.Delay(TimeSpan.FromSeconds(2));
  Console.WriteLine("Returning result...");
  return 13;
}
```

If you execute this code, you should see this output:

```
Calling server...
Calling server...
Returning result...
Returning result...
```

Discussion

Your own code usually does not subscribe to an observable more than once, but some System.Reactive operators do in their implementation. For example, the `Observable.While` operator will resubscribe to a source sequence as long as its condition is true. `Defer` enables you to define an observable that is reevaluated every time a new subscription comes in. This is useful if you need to refresh or update the data for that observable.

See Also

Recipe 8.6 covers wrapping asynchronous methods in observables.

14.3 Asynchronous Data Binding

Problem

You are retrieving data asynchronously and need to data-bind the results (e.g., in the ViewModel of a Model-View-ViewModel design).

Solution

When a property is used in data binding, it must immediately and synchronously return some kind of result. If the actual value needs to be determined asynchronously, you can return a default result and later update the property with the correct value.

Keep in mind that asynchronous operations may fail as well as succeed. Since you're writing a ViewModel, you could use data binding to update the UI for an error condition as well.

The `Nito.Mvvm.Async library` has a type `NotifyTask` that can be used for this:

```
class MyViewModel
{
  public MyViewModel()
  {
    MyValue = NotifyTask.Create(CalculateMyValueAsync());
  }

  public NotifyTask<int> MyValue { get; private set; }

  private async Task<int> CalculateMyValueAsync()
  {
    await Task.Delay(TimeSpan.FromSeconds(10));
    return 13;
  }
}
```

It's possible to data-bind to various properties on the `NotifyTask<T>` property, as this example shows:

```
<Grid>
  <Label Content="Loading..."
      Visibility="{Binding MyValue.IsNotCompleted,
         Converter={StaticResource BooleanToVisibilityConverter}}"/>
  <Label Content="{Binding MyValue.Result}"
      Visibility="{Binding MyValue.IsSuccessfullyCompleted,
         Converter={StaticResource BooleanToVisibilityConverter}}"/>
  <Label Content="An error occurred" Foreground="Red"
      Visibility="{Binding MyValue.IsFaulted,
         Converter={StaticResource BooleanToVisibilityConverter}}"/>
</Grid>
```

The MvvmCross library has a `MvxNotifyTask` that is much the same as `Notify Task<T>`.

Discussion

It's also possible to write your own data-binding wrapper instead of using the one from the libraries. The following code gives the basic idea:

```
class BindableTask<T> : INotifyPropertyChanged
{
  private readonly Task<T> _task;

  public BindableTask(Task<T> task)
  {
    _task = task;
    var _ = WatchTaskAsync();
  }

  private async Task WatchTaskAsync()
  {
    try
    {
      await _task;
    }
    catch
    {
    }

    OnPropertyChanged("IsNotCompleted");
    OnPropertyChanged("IsSuccessfullyCompleted");
    OnPropertyChanged("IsFaulted");
    OnPropertyChanged("Result");
  }

  public bool IsNotCompleted { get { return !_task.IsCompleted; } }
  public bool IsSuccessfullyCompleted
  {
    get { return _task.Status == TaskStatus.RanToCompletion; }
  }
  public bool IsFaulted { get { return _task.IsFaulted; } }
  public T Result
  {
    get { return IsSuccessfullyCompleted ? _task.Result : default; }
  }

  public event PropertyChangedEventHandler PropertyChanged;

  protected virtual void OnPropertyChanged(string propertyName)
  {
    PropertyChanged?.Invoke(this, new PropertyChangedEventArgs(propertyName));
```

```
    }
  }
```

Note that this has an empty `catch` clause on purpose: that code specifically does want to catch all exceptions and handle those conditions via data binding. Also, the code explicitly does not want to use `ConfigureAwait(false)` because the `Property Changed` event should be raised on the UI thread.

 The `NotifyTask` type is in the `Nito.Mvvm.Async` (*http://bit.ly/nito-m-async*) NuGet package. The `MvxNotifyTask` type is in the MvvmCross (*http://bit.ly/m-cross*) NuGet package.

See Also

Chapter 1 covers basic `async`/`await` programming.

Recipe 2.7 covers using `ConfigureAwait`.

14.4 Implicit State

Problem

You have some state variables that need to be accessible at different points in your call stack. For example, you have a current operation identifier that you want to use for logging but that you don't want to add as a parameter to every method.

Solution

The best solution is to add parameters to your methods, store data as members of a class, or use dependency injection to provide data to the different parts of your code. In some situations, however, that would overcomplicate the code.

The `AsyncLocal<T>` type enables you to give your state an object where it can live on a logical "context." The following code shows how to use `AsyncLocal<T>` to set an operation identifier that is later read by a logging method:

```
private static AsyncLocal<Guid> _operationId = new AsyncLocal<Guid>();

async Task DoLongOperationAsync()
{
  _operationId.Value = Guid.NewGuid();

  await DoSomeStepOfOperationAsync();
}

async Task DoSomeStepOfOperationAsync()
```

```
{
  await Task.Delay(100); // Some async work

  // Do some logging here.
  Trace.WriteLine("In operation: " + _operationId.Value);
}
```

Many times, it's useful to have a more complex data structure (such as a stack of values) in a single AsyncLocal<T> instance. This is possible, with one caveat: you should only store immutable data in the AsyncLocal<T>. Whenever you need to update the data, then you should overwrite the existing value. It is often helpful to hide the AsyncLocal<T> inside a helper type that ensures the stored data is immutable and updated correctly:

```
internal sealed class AsyncLocalGuidStack
{
  private readonly AsyncLocal<ImmutableStack<Guid>> _operationIds =
      new AsyncLocal<ImmutableStack<Guid>>();

  private ImmutableStack<Guid> Current =>
      _operationIds.Value ?? ImmutableStack<Guid>.Empty;

  public IDisposable Push(Guid value)
  {
    _operationIds.Value = Current.Push(value);
    return new PopWhenDisposed(this);
  }

  private void Pop()
  {
    ImmutableStack<Guid> newValue = Current.Pop();
    if (newValue.IsEmpty)
      newValue = null;
    _operationIds.Value = newValue;
  }

  public IEnumerable<Guid> Values => Current;

  private sealed class PopWhenDisposed : IDisposable
  {
    private AsyncLocalGuidStack _stack;

    public PopWhenDisposed(AsyncLocalGuidStack stack) =>
        _stack = stack;

    public void Dispose()
    {
      _stack?.Pop();
      _stack = null;
    }
  }
}
```

```
private static AsyncLocalGuidStack _operationIds = new AsyncLocalGuidStack();

async Task DoLongOperationAsync()
{
  using (_operationIds.Push(Guid.NewGuid()))
    await DoSomeStepOfOperationAsync();
}

async Task DoSomeStepOfOperationAsync()
{
  await Task.Delay(100); // some async work

  // Do some logging here.
  Trace.WriteLine("In operation: " +
      string.Join(":", _operationIds.Values));
}
```

The wrapper type ensures that the underlying data is immutable and that new values are pushed onto the stack. It also provides a convenient IDisposable way of popping values off the stack.

Discussion

Older code may use the ThreadStatic attribute for contextual state used by synchronous code. When converting older code to be asynchronous, AsyncLocal<T> is a prime candidate for replacing ThreadStaticAttribute. AsyncLocal<T> works for both synchronous and asynchronous code, and should be the default choice for implicit state in modern applications.

See Also

Chapter 1 covers basic async/await programming.

Chapter 9 covers several immutable collections, for when you need to store complex data as implicit state.

14.5 Identical Synchronous and Asynchronous Code

Problem

You have some code that needs to be exposed through both synchronous and asynchronous APIs, but you don't want to duplicate the logic. You'll often encounter this situation when updating code to be asynchronous, but existing synchronous consumers cannot (yet) be changed.

Solution

If you can, try to organize your code along modern design guidelines, like Ports and Adapters (Hexagonal Architecture), which separate your business logic from side effects such as I/O. If you can get into that situation, then there's no need to expose both synchronous and asynchronous APIs for anything; your business logic would always be synchronous, and the I/O would always be asynchronous.

However, that's a very lofty goal, and in The Real World, brownfield code can be messy, and there's rarely time to make it perfect before adopting asynchronous code. Existing APIs often need to be maintained for backwards compatibility, even if they were poorly designed.

There is no perfect solution in this scenario. Many developers attempt to have the synchronous code call the asynchronous code, or have the asynchronous code call the synchronous code, but both of those approaches are anti-patterns. The Boolean Argument Hack is the one that I tend to prefer in this situation. It's a way to keep all the logic in a single method while exposing both synchronous and asynchronous APIs.

The primary idea of the Boolean Argument Hack is that there's a private core method containing the logic. That core method has an asynchronous signature and takes a boolean argument determining whether the core method should be asynchronous or not. If the boolean argument specifies that the core method should be synchronous, then it *must* return an already-completed task. Then you can write both asynchronous and synchronous API methods that forward to the core method:

```
private async Task<int> DelayAndReturnCore(bool sync)
{
  int value = 100;

  // Do some work.
  if (sync)
    Thread.Sleep(value); // Call synchronous API.
  else
    await Task.Delay(value); // Call asynchronous API.

  return value;
}

// Asynchronous API
public Task<int> DelayAndReturnAsync() =>
    DelayAndReturnCore(sync: false);

// Synchronous API
public int DelayAndReturn() =>
    DelayAndReturnCore(sync: true).GetAwaiter().GetResult();
```

The asynchronous API `DelayAndReturnAsync` invokes `DelayAndReturnCore` with the boolean `sync` parameter set to `false`; this means that `DelayAndReturnCore` may behave asynchronously, and it uses `await` on the underlying asynchronous "delay" API `Task.Delay`. The task returned from `DelayAndReturnCore` is returned directly to the caller of `DelayAndReturnAsync`.

The synchronous API `DelayAndReturn` invokes `DelayAndReturnCore` with the boolean `sync` parameter set to `true`; this means that `DelayAndReturnCore` *must* behave synchronously, and it uses the underlying synchronous "delay" API `Thread.Sleep`. The task returned by `DelayAndReturnCore` must already be complete, so it's safe to extract the result. `DelayAndReturn` uses `GetAwaiter().GetResult()` to retrieve the result from the task; this avoids an `AggregateException` wrapper that can happen if it were to use the `Task<T>.Result` property.

Discussion

This isn't an ideal solution, but it's one that can help with real-world applications.

Now, a few caveats for this solution. The most disastrous problems will arise if the `Core` method doesn't properly honor its `sync` parameter. If the `Core` method ever returns an incomplete task when `sync` is `true`, then the synchronous API can easily deadlock; the only reason the synchronous API can block on its task is that it knows that the task is already complete. Similarly, if the `Core` method blocks a thread when `sync` is `false`, then the application isn't as efficient as it should be.

One improvement that could be made to this solution is to add a check in the synchronous API, validating that the returned task is in fact completed. If it's ever not completed, then there is a serious coding bug.

See Also

Chapter 1 covers basic `async`/`await` programming, including a discussion of deadlocks that can happen when blocking on asynchronous code in general.

14.6 Railway Programming with Dataflow Meshes

Problem

You have a dataflow mesh set up, but some data items fail to process. You want to respond to these errors in a way that keeps your dataflow mesh operational.

Solution

By default, if a block encounters an exception when processing a data item, that block will fault, preventing it from processing any more data items. The core idea of this solution is to treat exceptions as just another kind of data. If the dataflow mesh operates on types that can be *either* an exception *or* data, then the mesh can remain operational even when exceptions occur and continue to process other data items.

This is sometimes called "railway" programming because the items in the mesh can be viewed as traveling on one of two separate tracks. There's the normal "data" track: if everything goes perfectly, the item stays on the "data" track and travels through the mesh, being transformed and operated on, until it reaches the end of the mesh. The second track is the "error" track; in any block, if an exception is raised when processing an item, that exception transfers to the "error" track and travels through the mesh. Exception items aren't processed; they are just passed on from block to block, so they also reach the end of the mesh. The terminal blocks in the mesh end up receiving a sequence of items, each of which is either a data item or exception item; a data item represents data that has completed the entire mesh successfully, and an exception item represents a processing error at some point in the mesh.

In order to set up this kind of "railway" programming, you first need to define a type that represents either a data item or an exception. If you want to use a pre-built one, there are a few available. This kind of type is common in the functional programming community, where it's commonly called `Try` or `Error` or `Exceptional`, and is a special case of the `Either` monad. I've defined my own `Try<T>` type that you can use as an example; it's in the `Nito.Try` NuGet package (*https://www.nuget.org/packages/Nito.Try/*) and the source code is on GitHub (*https://github.com/StephenCleary/Try*).

Once you have some kind of `Try<T>` type, setting up the mesh is a bit tedious but not terrible. The type of each dataflow block should be changed from `T` to `Try<T>`, and any processing in that block should be done by mapping one `Try<T>` value to another. With my `Try<T>` type, this is done by calling `Try<T>.Map`. I find it helpful to define small factory methods for railway-oriented dataflow blocks instead of having that extra code inline. The following code is an example of a helper method that constructs a `TransformBlock` that operates on `Try<T>` values by calling `Try<T>.Map`:

```
private static TransformBlock<Try<TInput>, Try<TOutput>>
    RailwayTransform<TInput, TOutput>(Func<TInput, TOutput> func)
{
  return new TransformBlock<Try<TInput>, Try<TOutput>>(t => t.Map(func));
}
```

With helpers like these in place, the dataflow mesh creation code is more straightforward:

```
var subtractBlock = RailwayTransform<int, int>(value => value - 2);
var divideBlock = RailwayTransform<int, int>(value => 60 / value);
```

```
var multiplyBlock = RailwayTransform<int, int>(value => value * 2);

var options = new DataflowLinkOptions { PropagateCompletion = true };
subtractBlock.LinkTo(divideBlock, options);
divideBlock.LinkTo(multiplyBlock, options);

// Insert data items into the first block.
subtractBlock.Post(Try.FromValue(5));
subtractBlock.Post(Try.FromValue(2));
subtractBlock.Post(Try.FromValue(4));
subtractBlock.Complete();

// Receive data/exception items from the last block.
while (await multiplyBlock.OutputAvailableAsync())
{
  Try<int> item = await multiplyBlock.ReceiveAsync();
  if (item.IsValue)
    Console.WriteLine(item.Value);
  else
    Console.WriteLine(item.Exception.Message);
}
```

Discussion

Railway programming is a great way to avoid faulting dataflow blocks. Since railway programming is a functional programming construct based on monads, it's a bit awkward when translated to .NET, but it is usable. If you have a dataflow mesh that needs to be fault-tolerant, then railway programming is certainly worth it.

See Also

Recipe 5.2 covers the normal way exceptions fault blocks and can propagate through a mesh if railway programming is not used.

14.7 Throttling Progress Updates

Problem

You have a long-running operation that reports progress, and you display progress updates in the UI. But the progress updates arrive too rapidly, causing your UI to be unresponsive.

Solution

Consider the following code, which reports progress very quickly:

```
private string Solve(IProgress<int> progress)
{
  // Count as quickly as possible for 3 seconds.
```

```
  var endTime = DateTime.UtcNow.AddSeconds(3);
  int value = 0;
  while (DateTime.UtcNow < endTime)
  {
    value++;
    progress?.Report(value);
  }
  return value.ToString();
}
```

You can execute this code from a GUI application by wrapping it in `Task.Run` and passing in an `IProgress<T>`. The following example code is for WPF, but the same concepts apply regardless of GUI platform (WPF, Xamarin, or Windows Forms):

```
// For simplicity, this code updates a label directly.
// In a real-world MVVM application, those assignments
//   would instead be updating a ViewModel property
//   which is data-bound to the actual UI.
private async void StartButton_Click(object sender, RoutedEventArgs e)
{
  MyLabel.Content = "Starting...";
  var progress = new Progress<int>(value => MyLabel.Content = value);
  var result = await Task.Run(() => Solve(progress));
  MyLabel.Content = $"Done! Result: {result}";
}
```

This code will cause the UI to become unresponsive for quite some time, about 20 seconds on my machine, and then suddenly the UI is responsive again and only displays the `"Done! Result:"` message. The intermediate progress reports were never seen. What is happening is that the background code is sending progress reports to the UI thread extremely quickly, so fast that after running for only 3 seconds, it takes the UI thread another 17 seconds or so just to process all those progress reports, updating that label over and over. Lastly, the UI thread updates the label one last time with the `"Done! Result:"` values, and then *finally* has time to repaint the screen, displaying the updated label value to the user.

The first thing to realize is that we need to throttle the progress reports. It's the only way to ensure the UI has enough time to repaint itself between progress updates. The next thing to realize is that we want to throttle based on *time*, not the *number* of reports. While you may be tempted to throttle the progress reports by only sending one out of every hundred or so, this isn't ideal for reasons discussed in the "Discussion" section.

The fact that we want to deal with *time* indicates that we should consider System.Reactive. And, in fact, System.Reactive has operators specifically designed to throttle on time. So, it sounds like System.Reactive will play a role in this solution.

To get started, you can define an `IProgress<T>` implementation that raises an event for each progress report, and then create an observable that receives those progress reports by wrapping that event:

```
public static class ObservableProgress
{
  private sealed class EventProgress<T> : IProgress<T>
  {
    void IProgress<T>.Report(T value) => OnReport?.Invoke(value);
    public event Action<T> OnReport;
  }

  public static (IObservable<T>, IProgress<T>) Create<T>()
  {
    var progress = new EventProgress<T>();
    var observable = Observable.FromEvent<T>(
        handler => progress.OnReport += handler,
        handler => progress.OnReport -= handler);
    return (observable, progress);
  }
}
```

The method `ObservableProgress.Create<T>` will create a pair: one `IObservable<T>` and one `IProgress<T>`, where all progress reports sent to the `IProgress<T>` will be sent to the subscribers of the `IObservable<T>`. We now have an observable stream for our progress reports; the next step is to throttle it.

We want to update the UI slowly enough that it can remain responsive, and we want to update the UI quickly enough that users can see the updates. Human perception is considerably slower than computer displays, so there's a large window of possible values. If you prefer true readability, throttling to one update every second or so may be sufficient. If you prefer more real-time feedback, I find that one update every 100 or 200 milliseconds (ms) is fast enough that the user sees that something is happening fast and gets a general sense of the progress details, while still being slow enough for the UI to remain responsive.

Another point to keep in mind is that progress reports can be raised from other threads—in this case, they are raised from a background thread. The throttling should be done as close to the source as possible, so we want to keep the throttling on the background thread. However, the code that updates the UI needs to be run on the UI thread. With this in mind, you can define a `CreateForUi` method that handles both the throttling and the transition to the UI thread:

```
public static class ObservableProgress
{
  // Note: this must be called from the UI thread.
  public static (IObservable<T>, IProgress<T>) CreateForUi<T>(
      TimeSpan? sampleInterval = null)
  {
```

```
        var (observable, progress) = Create<T>();
        observable = observable
            .Sample(sampleInterval ?? TimeSpan.FromMilliseconds(100))
            .ObserveOn(SynchronizationContext.Current);
        return (observable, progress);
    }
}
```

Now you have a helper method that will throttle your progress updates before they hit the UI. You can use the helper method in the previous code example in your button click handler:

```
// For simplicity, this code updates a label directly.
// In a real-world MVVM application, those assignments
//    would instead be updating a ViewModel property
//    which is data-bound to the actual UI.
private async void StartButton_Click(object sender, RoutedEventArgs e)
{
  MyLabel.Content = "Starting...";
  var (observable, progress) = ObservableProgress.CreateForUi<int>();
  string result;
  using (observable.Subscribe(value => MyLabel.Content = value))
    result = await Task.Run(() => Solve(progress));
  MyLabel.Content = $"Done! Result: {result}";
}
```

The new code calls our helper method `ObservableProgress.CreateForUi`, which creates the `IObservable<T>` and `IProgress<T>` pair. The code subscribes to the progress updates and keeps that going until `Solve` is done. Finally, it passes the `IProgress<T>` to the long-running `Solve` method. As `Solve` calls `IProgress<T>.Report`, those reports are first sampled within a 100 ms time window, with one update every 100-ms being forwarded to the UI thread and used to update the label text. The UI is now fully responsive!

Discussion

This recipe is a fun combination of other recipes in this book! No new techniques were introduced; we just walked through which recipes to combine to come up with this solution.

An alternative solution to this problem that you may see a lot in the wild is the "modulus solution." The idea behind this solution is that `Solve` itself has to throttle its own progress updates; for example, if the code only wanted to process one update for every 100 actual updates, then the code may use some modulus technique like `if (value % 100 == 0) progress?.Report(value);`.

There are a couple of problems with the modulus approach. The first is that there's no "correct" modulus value; usually, the developer tries various values until it works well on their own laptop. The same code, however, may not behave well when running on a client's massive server or inside an underpowered virtual machine. In addition, different platforms and environments cache very differently, which can make code run much faster (or slower) than expected. And, of course, the capabilities of the "latest" computer hardware do change over time. So the modulus value only ends up being a guess; it's not going to be correct everywhere and throughout all time.

The other problem with the modulus approach is that it's trying to fix the problem in the wrong part of the code. This problem is purely a UI issue; it's the UI that has a problem, and it's the UI layer that should provide the fix for it. In the example code for this recipe, `Solve` represents some background business processing logic; it shouldn't be concerned with UI-specific issues. A Console app may want to use a very different modulus than a WPF app.

The one thing that the modulus approach is correct on is that it's best to throttle the updates *before* sending the updates to the UI thread. The solution in this recipe also does this: it throttles the updates immediately and synchronously on the background thread before sending them to the UI thread. By injecting its own `IProgress<T>` implementation, the UI is able to do its own throttling without requiring any changes to the `Solve` method itself.

See Also

Recipe 2.3 covers using `IProgress<T>` to report progress from long-running operations.

Recipe 13.1 covers using `Task.Run` to run synchronous code on a threadpool thread.

Recipe 6.1 covers using `FromEvent` to wrap .NET events into observables.

Recipe 6.4 covers using `Sample` to throttle observables by time.

Recipe 6.2 covers using `ObserveOn` to move observable notifications to another context.

Legacy Platform Support

Many of the technologies discussed in this book have some support for older platforms as well. If you're in the unfortunate situation where you need to support these
platforms, the information in this appendix may help you determine which technologies are available. Using these technologies on older platforms isn't ideal; and even if
you get it working, bear in mind that the only long-term solution is to update the
platform target for your code. This appendix is intended mainly as a historical reference and not as a recommendation; that said, maintainers of old code may find it useful.

Table A-1 summarizes the support of legacy platforms for different techniques.

Table A-1. Legacy platform support

Platform	async	Parallel	Reactive	Dataflow	Concurrent collections	Immutable collections
.NET 4.5	✓	✓	NuGet	NuGet	✓	NuGet
.NET 4.0	NuGet	✓	NuGet	✗	✓	✗
Windows Phone Apps 8.1	✓	✓	NuGet	NuGet	✓	NuGet
Windows Phone SL 8.0	✓	✗	NuGet	NuGet	✗	NuGet
Windows Phone SL 7.1	NuGet	✗	NuGet	✗	✗	✗
Silverlight 5	NuGet	✗	NuGet	✗	✗	✗

Legacy Platform Support for Async

If you need `async` support on older legacy platforms, install the NuGet package for
`Microsoft.Bcl.Async` (*http://bit.ly/micro-async*).

Do not use `Microsoft.Bcl.Async` to enable async code on ASP.NET running on .NET 4.0! The ASP.NET pipeline was updated in .NET 4.5 to be async-aware, and you must use .NET 4.5 or newer for async ASP.NET projects. `Microsoft.Bcl.Async` is only for non-ASP.NET applications.

Table A-2. Legacy platform support for async

Platform	Async support
.NET 4.5	✓
.NET 4.0	NuGet: `Microsoft.Bcl.Async`
Windows Phone Apps 8.1	✓
Windows Phone SL 8.0	✓
Windows Phone 7.1	NuGet: `Microsoft.Bcl.Async`
Silverlight 5	NuGet: `Microsoft.Bcl.Async`

When using `Microsoft.Bcl.Async`, many of the members on the modern `Task` type are on the `TaskEx` type, including `Delay`, `FromResult`, `WhenAll`, and `WhenAny`.

Legacy Platform Support for Dataflow

To use TPL Dataflow, install the NuGet package `System.Threading.Tasks.Dataflow` (*http://bit.ly/nuget-df*) into your application. The TPL Dataflow library has limited platform support for older platforms (Table A-3).

Do not use the old `Microsoft.Tpl.Dataflow` package. It is no longer maintained.

Table A-3. Legacy platform support for TPL Dataflow

Platform	Dataflow support
.NET 4.5	NuGet: `System.Threading.Tasks.Dataflow`
.NET 4.0	✗
Windows Phone Apps 8.1	NuGet: `System.Threading.Tasks.Dataflow`
Windows Phone SL 8.0	NuGet: `System.Threading.Tasks.Dataflow`
Windows Phone SL 7.1	✗
Silverlight 5	✗

Legacy Platform Support for System.Reactive

To use System.Reactive, install the NuGet package System.Reactive (*http://bit.ly/sys-reactive*) into your application. System.Reactive historically has had wide platform support (Table A-4); however, most of the legacy platforms are no longer supported:

Table A-4. Legacy platform support for System.Reactive

Platform	Reactive support
.NET 4.7.2	NuGet: System.Reactive
.NET 4.5	NuGet: System.Reactive v3.x
.NET 4.0	NuGet: Rx.Main
Windows Phone Apps 8.1	NuGet: System.Reactive v3.x
Windows Phone SL 8.0	NuGet: System.Reactive v3.x
Windows Phone SL 7.1	NuGet: Rx.Main
Silverlight 5	NuGet: Rx.Main

 The old Rx.Main package is no longer maintained.

Recognizing and Interpreting Asynchronous Patterns

The benefits of asynchronous code have been well understood for decades before .NET was invented. In the early days of .NET, several different styles of asynchronous code were developed, used here and there, and eventually discarded. These were not all bad ideas; many of them paved the way for the modern async/await approach. However, there's a lot of legacy code out there that uses older asynchronous patterns. This appendix will discuss the more common patterns, explaining how they work and how to integrate them with modern code.

Sometimes, the same type is updated over the years, acquiring more and more members as it supports multiple asynchronous patterns. Perhaps the best example of this is the Socket class. Here are some of the members of the Socket class for the core Send operation:

```
class Socket
{
  // Synchronous
  public int Send(byte[] buffer, int offset, int size, SocketFlags flags);

  // APM
  public IAsyncResult BeginSend(byte[] buffer, int offset, int size,
      SocketFlags flags, AsyncCallback callback, object state);
  public int EndSend(IAsyncResult result);

  // Custom, very close to APM
  public IAsyncResult BeginSend(byte[] buffer, int offset, int size,
      SocketFlags flags, out SocketError error,
      AsyncCallback callback, object state);
  public int EndSend(IAsyncResult result, out SocketError error);

  // Custom
```

```
    public bool SendAsync(SocketAsyncEventArgs e);

    // TAP (as an extension method)
    public Task<int> SendAsync(ArraySegment<byte> buffer,
        SocketFlags socketFlags);

    // TAP (as an extension method) using more efficient types
    public ValueTask<int> SendAsync(ReadOnlyMemory<byte> buffer,
        SocketFlags socketFlags, CancellationToken cancellationToken = default);
}
```

Sadly, with most documentation being alphabetical and with tons of overloads in an attempt to simplify usage, types like Socket become difficult to understand. Hopefully the guidelines in this section will help.

Task-Based Asynchronous Pattern (TAP)

The Task-Based Asynchronous Pattern (TAP) is the modern asynchronous API pattern that is ready for use with await. Each asynchronous operation is represented by a single method that returns an awaitable. An "awaitable" is any type that can be consumed by await; this is usually Task or Task<T> but may also be ValueTask, Value Task<T>, a type defined by a framework (e.g., IAsyncAction or IAsyncOperation<T>, used by Universal Windows applications), or even a custom type defined by a library.

It is common for TAP methods to have an Async suffix. However, this is just a convention; not all TAP methods have an Async suffix. It can be skipped if the API developer believes the asynchronous context is sufficiently implied; e.g., Task.WhenAll and Task.WhenAny do not have an Async suffix. Furthermore, keep in mind that the Async suffix may be present on *non*-TAP methods (e.g., WebClient.DownloadStringAsync is not a TAP method). The usual pattern in this case is for the TAP method to have a TaskAsync suffix (e.g., WebClient.DownloadStringTaskAsync is a TAP method).

Methods that return asynchronous streams also follow a TAP-like pattern, with Async used as a suffix. Even though they don't return awaitables, they do return awaitable streams—types that can be consumed using await foreach.

The Task-Based Asynchronous Pattern can be recognized by these characteristics:

1. The operation is represented by a single method.

2. The method returns an awaitable or an awaitable stream.

3. The method usually ends with Async.

Here's an example of a type with a TAP API:

```
class ExampleHttpClient
{
  public Task<string> GetStringAsync(Uri requestUri);
```

```
    // Synchronous equivalent, for comparison
    public string GetString(Uri requestUri);
}
```

Consuming the Task-Based Asynchronous Pattern is done using `await` and is covered by large portions of this book. If you somehow got to this appendix without knowing how to use `await`, then I'm not sure I can help you at this point, but you can try reading Chapters 1 and 2 anyway to see if they jog your memory.

Asynchronous Programming Model (APM)

After TAP, the Asynchronous Programming Model (APM) pattern is probably the next most-common pattern you'll encounter. It was the first pattern where asynchronous operations had first-class object representations. The telltale sign of this pattern is the `IAsyncResult` objects in conjunction with a pair of methods that manage the operation, one starting with `Begin` and the other starting with `End`.

`IAsyncResult` was strongly influenced by native overlapped I/O (*http://bit.ly/sync-ipop*). The APM pattern allows consuming code to behave either synchronously or asynchronously. The consuming code can choose from these options:

- Block for the operation to complete. This is done by calling the `End` method.
- Poll for the operation to complete while doing something else.
- Supply a callback delegate to invoke when the operation completes.

In all cases, the consuming code must eventually call the `End` method to retrieve the results of the asynchronous operation. If the operation is not completed when `End` is called, it'll block the calling thread until the operation completes.

The `Begin` method takes an `AsyncCallback` parameter and an `object` parameter (usually called `state`) as its last two parameters. These are used by consuming code to provide a callback delegate to invoke when the operation completes. The `object` parameter can be whatever you want; this is a holdover from the very early days of .NET, before lambda methods or even anonymous methods existed. It is just used to provide context to the `AsyncCallback` parameter.

The APM is fairly widespread among Microsoft libraries, but is not as common in the wider .NET ecosystem. This is because there were never any `IAsyncResult` implementations made available for reuse, and implementing that interface correctly is fairly complex. In addition, it is difficult to compose APM-based systems. I've seen only a few custom `IAsyncResult` implementations in the wild; all of these were some version of Jeffrey Richter's general-purpose `IAsyncResult` implementation, as published in his article, "Concurrent Affairs: Implementing the CLR Asynchronous Programming Model," from the March 2007 edition of *MSDN Magazine* (*http://bit.ly/conc-aff*).

The Asynchronous Programming Model pattern can be recognized by these characteristics:

1. The operation is represented by a pair of methods, one starting with `Begin` and the other starting with `End`.

2. The `Begin` method returns an `IAsyncResult`, and takes all normal input parameters, along with an extra `AsyncCallback` parameter and an extra `object` parameter.

3. The `End` method only takes an `IAsyncResult`, and returns the result value, if any.

Here's an example of a type with an APM API:

```
class MyHttpClient
{
  public IAsyncResult BeginGetString(Uri requestUri,
      AsyncCallback callback, object state);
  public string EndGetString(IAsyncResult asyncResult);

  // Synchronous equivalent, for comparison
  public string GetString(Uri requestUri);
}
```

Consume the APM by converting it to TAP using `Task.Factory.FromAsync`; see Recipe 8.2 and the Microsoft docs (*http://bit.ly/interop-async*).

There are some cases in which code *almost* follows the APM pattern, but not quite; e.g.,, the old `Microsoft.TeamFoundation` client libraries did not include the `object` parameter in their `Begin` methods. In these cases, `Task.Factory.FromAsync` will not work, and you then have the choice of two options. The less efficient option is to call the `Begin` method and pass the `IAsyncResult` to `FromAsync`. The less elegant option is to use the more flexible `TaskCompletionSource<T>`; see Recipe 8.3.

Event-Based Asynchronous Programming (EAP)

The Event-Based Asynchronous Programming (EAP) defines a matching method/event pair. The method usually ends in `Async`, and it eventually causes an event to be raised that ends in `Completed`.

There are a few caveats when working with EAP that make it a bit more difficult than it first appears. First, you have to remember to add your handler to the event *before* calling the method; otherwise, you'd have a race condition where the event could happen before you subscribed, and then you'd never see it complete. Second, components written in the EAP pattern usually capture the current `SynchronizationContext` at some point and then raise their event in that context. Some components capture the `SynchronizationContext` in the constructor, and others capture it at the time the method is called and the asynchronous operation begins.

The Event-Based Asynchronous Programming pattern can be recognized by these characteristics:

1. The operation is represented by an event and a method.

2. The event ends in `Completed`.

3. The event args type for the `Completed` event might be descended from `AsyncCompletedEventArgs`.

4. The method usually ends in `Async`.

5. The method returns `void`.

EAP methods ending in `Async` are distinguishable from TAP methods ending in `Async` because the EAP methods return `void`, while the TAP methods return an awaitable type.

Here's an example of a type with an EAP API:

```
class GetStringCompletedEventArgs : AsyncCompletedEventArgs
{
  public string Result { get; }
}

class MyHttpClient
{
  public void GetStringAsync(Uri requestUri);
  public event Action<object, GetStringCompletedEventArgs> GetStringCompleted;

  // Synchronous equivalent, for comparison
  public string GetString(Uri requestUri);
}
```

Consume the EAP by converting it to TAP using `TaskCompletionSource<T>`; see Recipe 8.3 and the Microsoft docs (*http://bit.ly/EAP-MS*).

Continuation Passing Style (CPS)

This is a pattern that is much more common in other languages, particularly JavaScript and TypeScript as used by Node.js developers. In this pattern, each asynchronous operation takes a callback delegate that is invoked when the operation completes, either successfully or with error. A variant of this pattern uses *two* callback delegates, one for success and one for error. This kind of callback is called a "continuation," and the continuation is passed as a parameter, hence the name "continuation passing style." This pattern was never common in the .NET world, but there are a few older open source libraries that used it.

The Continuation Passing Style pattern can be recognized by these characteristics:

1. The operation is represented by a single method.

2. The method takes an extra parameter which is a callback delegate; the callback delegate takes two arguments, one for errors and the other for results.

3. Alternatively, the operation method takes two extra parameters, both callback delegates; one callback delegate is only for errors, and the other callback delegate is only for results.

4. The callback delegates are commonly named done or next.

Here's an example of a type with a continuation-passing style API:

```
class MyHttpClient
{
  public void GetString(Uri requestUri, Action<Exception, string> done);

  // Synchronous equivalent, for comparison
  public string GetString(Uri requestUri);
}
```

Consume CPS by converting it to TAP using TaskCompletionSource<T>, passing callback delegates that just complete the TaskCompletionSource<T>; see Recipe 8.3.

Custom Async Patterns

Very specialized types will sometimes define their own custom asynchronous patterns. The most famous example of this is the Socket type, which defined a pattern that passed around SocketAsyncEventArgs instances representing the operation. The reason this pattern was introduced was that SocketAsyncEventArgs could be reused, thus reducing memory churn for applications that do heavy network activity. Modern applications can use ValueTask<T> with ManualResetValueTaskSourceCore<T> (*http://bit.ly/man-reset-type-doc*) to get similar performance gains.

Custom patterns do not have any common characteristics and are therefore the hardest to recognize. Thankfully, custom asynchronous patterns are rare.

Here's an example of a type with a custom asynchronous API:

```
class MyHttpClient
{
  public void GetString(Uri requestUri,
      MyHttpClientAsynchronousOperation operation);

  // Synchronous equivalent, for comparison
```

```
    public string GetString(Uri requestUri);
}
```

TaskCompletionSource<T> is the only way to consume custom asynchronous patterns; see Recipe 8.3.

ISynchronizeInvoke

All the previous patterns are for asynchronous operations that are started, and once they start, they complete once. Some components follow a subscription model: they represent a push-based stream of events rather than a single operation that starts once and completes once. A good example of a subscription model is the FileSystem Watcher type. To observe file system changes, the consuming code first subscribes to multiple events and then sets the EnableRaisingEvents property to true. Once EnableRaisingEvents is true, multiple file system change events may be raised.

Some components use an ISynchronizeInvoke pattern for their events. They expose a single ISynchronizeInvoke property, and consumers set that property to an implementation that allows the component to schedule work. This is most commonly used to schedule work to a UI thread so that the component's events are raised on the UI thread. By convention, if ISynchronizeInvoke is null, then no synchronizing of the events is done, and they may be raised on background threads.

The ISynchronizeInvoke pattern can be recognized by these characteristics:

1. There is a property of type ISynchronizeInvoke.
2. The property is usually called SynchronizingObject.

Here's an example of a type that uses the ISynchronizeInvoke pattern:

```
class MyHttpClient
{
  public ISynchronizeInvoke SynchronizingObject { get; set; }
  public void StartListening();
  public event Action<string> StringArrived;
}
```

Since ISynchronizeInvoke implies multiple events in a subscription model, the proper way to consume these components is to translate those events to an observable stream, either using FromEvent (see Recipe 6.1) or Observable.Create.

Index

events, in reactive programming, 83
progress updates, 210-214
queues, 135
Throw operator, 96
ThrowIfCancellationRequested method,
149-150
timeouts, 19-21, 19-21, 84-86, 150-151
ToAsyncEnumerable method, 50, 114
ToList method, 107
ToObservable method, 109
ToTask method, 108, 155
TPL (Task Parallel Library), 17, 55
TPL Dataflow library, xii, 17, 65
(see also dataflow)
Try type, 209

U

unbounded queues, 114
unit testing
advantages of, 87-88
async methods, expected to fail, 90-92
async methods, general, 88-90
async void methods, 92-93

dataflow, 93-94
reactive programming, 95-100

V

ValueTask type, 5, 37-40, 46

W

WaitAsync method, 7
Where operator, PLINQ, 63
WhereAwait operator, 49
While operator, 201
Window operator, 81-82
Windows Phone platforms, support for,
215-217
WithCancellation method, 52, 153
WriteToBlockAsync method, 111

X

xUnit framework, 88

Y

yield return statement, 44-46

About the Author

Stephen Cleary is a developer with extensive experience, ranging from ARM Firmware to Azure. He has contributed to open source from the very beginning, starting with the Boost C++ libraries, and has released several libraries and utilities of his own.

Colophon

The animal on the cover of *Concurrency in C# Cookbook*, Second Edition, is a common palm civet (*Paradoxurus hermaphroditus*), also known as the Asian palm civet. Civets are part of the viverrid family, which is comprised of small, cat-like creatures of tropical Africa and Asia. Palm civets are mostly solitary, only seeking the company of other civets during the mating season and while raising young. Though shy and nocturnal, because they sometimes live near and even in human dwellings, some see them as a nuisance animal. Native to Southeast Asia and the Indonesian islands, they were recently introduced into Japan and the Lesser Sunda Islands.

Palm civets grow up to 21 inches long and weigh up to 11 pounds. They have pointed snouts and their fur can be white, grey, and brown, often with darker spots, stripes, or other markings, which sometimes include a facemask that resembles that of a raccoon. Unlike other civet species, their tails lack rings. The palm civet defends itself by ejecting a smelly secretion from its anal scent gland when threatened. Scent also comes into play in mating season, when civets mark trails to locate each other.

Palm civets are mostly frugivorous, playing an important role in maintaining tropical forest biodiversity by dispersing the seeds of the fruit they consume. They also enjoy drinking palm flower sap, which when fermented becomes a sweet liquor known as toddy; this habit has earned them the nickname "toddy cat."

In some parts of its range, palm civets are hunted for food. They are also captured and used to make kopi luwak, a coffee made from beans digested and passed by a civet. Once made using wild animals' droppings, in recent years giant farms have sprung up where captive civets are kept confined in tiny cages and fed only coffee beans. The executive who introduced the kopi luwak fad to the West now opposes it on the grounds of animal cruelty.

Many of the animals on O'Reilly covers are endangered; all of them are important to the world.

The cover image is by Karen Montgomery, based on a black and white engraving from *The Royal Natural History* (1893), by Richard Lydekker. The cover fonts are Gilroy Semibold and Guardian Sans. The text font is Adobe Minion Pro; the heading font is Adobe Myriad Condensed; and the code font is Dalton Maag's Ubuntu Mono.